Praise for *Undivided*

"This powerful and beautiful book exposes deep pain when a devoutly Christian mother must come to terms with her daughter's passionate embrace of Islam. Their struggle toward reconciliation and mutual understanding—through a series of searingly honest conversations—is captivating and potentially helpful to others who face similar challenges. This book highlights the possible cost of living in a radically open, pluralistic society such as ours."

—Samuel E. Karff, rabbi emeritus,
Congregation Beth Israel, Houston

"Patricia and Alana Raybon capture the essence of the national conversation that needs to happen between Christians and Muslims. With intensely personal and deeply spiritual details, *Undivided* challenges us to initiate interfaith dialogue with respectful questions that can lead not just to peaceful coexistence but peaceful partnership."

—The Reverend Mike Cole, General Presbyter, Presbytery
of New Covenant in the Presbyterian Church (U.S.A.)

"*Undivided* left me gutted—in a *good* way. Here is raw honesty regarding valued but strained relationships. Here is vulnerable, personal examination with un-apologetic clinging to the hem of Christ's garment. Here is help for all of us who find ourselves facing the inexplicable differences between us and our loved ones."

—Elisa Morgan, speaker; author, *The Beauty of
Broken*; and cohost, *Discover the Word*

"An exceptionally well-written, honest, and eye-opening account of the attempt by a mother and her daughter to create the relationship that God wants them to have. Valuable insights on their two perspectives, emotions, and values remind us that what we desire to communicate is many times not what is understood by the other party at all—an important lesson for all of us who work in interfaith."

—Shaykh Waleed Basyouni, PhD, Islamic scholar
and vice president, Al Maghrib Institute

"This powerful conversation between a mother and her daughter surrounding issues of faith is riveting and groundbreaking. I believe that this book will inspire and influence many to rely on the power of listening and honest communication as tools for genuine reconciliation."

—Dr. Timothy Tyler, pastor, Shorter
Community A.M.E. Church, Denver

"Patricia and Alana give us the priceless gift of transparency to which most families can relate. They demonstrate how people of different faiths can move beyond mere toleration to an understanding of appreciation. God has used their journey to provide transferable principles that are doable and necessary in all kinds of relationships."

—Dr. Clarence Shuler, president/CEO, BLR: Building Lasting Relationships

"This timely, gorgeous book explores the divide between Christianity and Islam in one family and the intersection of spiritual heritage and independence. Ultimately it's about a mother and a daughter trying to communicate. *Undivided* will leave you wanting to listen well, ask good questions, and work to restore relationship even when core beliefs and life choices are worlds apart."

—Lindsey O'Connor, journalist and author, *The Long Awakening*

"For most of us, the tension between Islam and Christianity plays out only in headlines. In *Undivided* it plays out in the hearts of two very honest, vulnerable people. Patricia and Alana's transparent discussion will surely open the way for many more among us."

—Chris Tiegreen, author, One Year devotionals, including *The One Year Hearing His Voice Devotional*

"To be credible witnesses of the gospel in an ever-changing culture, we need more loving, more honest, and more human stories. We live in a toxic society, where it seems okay to dishonor people simply because they do not agree with us, but in matters of the heart and faith, God calls us to sacrificial love. I thank God for this courageous effort to live faithfully, authentically, and lovingly."

—Natasha Sistrunk Robinson, assistant director, Center for the Development of Evangelical Leadership, Gordon-Conwell Theological Seminary

"I felt the dread and pain of a mother and daughter's courageous endeavor to enter into an interfaith dialogue. Alana's description of her decision to wear hijab was especially poignant. As a grandparent I felt keenly Patricia's struggle to relate to her grandkids while respecting their parents' beliefs. In good stories we look for transformation, and we find it here as the authors move toward mutual understanding. In the end, love wins!"

—Timothy R. Botts, calligraphic artist

"In a world where *debate* seeks to produce winners and losers, *Undivided* is a marvelous and realistic conversation toward *dialogue*, where relationships are built. I loved it!"

—Rev. Stephen D. Quill, interfaith leader and pastor, Houston

"A must-read for all families, *Undivided* is a beautiful story of a Christian mother and a Muslim daughter coming to terms with the existential issues posed by the conversion of her child to a faith that has become increasingly maligned. As the daughter of a woman who was raised a Christian but chose to become Muslim during the 1970s, I wish my mother and grandmother could have read and discussed this book together."

—Zaynab Ansari, scholar-in-residence, Tayseer Foundation

"I needed this book. Discovering how to love across faiths can be a precarious journey, and nothing about this one has been sugarcoated. But on each page I grow in my love and respect, not just for the authors but for the Muslim and Christian neighbors I'm better equipped to know and engage with due to this brave volume. Because of this gift, I will love more like Jesus."

—Margot Starbuck, author, *Small Things With Great Love*

"*Undivided* is a captivating example of faith seeking understanding. Presented as correspondences, it allows the reader to peek in on a rich theological debate wrapped in the healing of a family. *Undivided* is definitely a worthwhile read for Christians and Muslims alike. It is an exemplary tale of interfaith peace."

—The Reverend Brandee Jasmine Mimitzraiem, MPhil, pastor, Embry Chapel A.M.E. Church, Elizabethtown, KY

"A thought-provoking book about a painful yet liberating journey between a mother and her daughter and their stark religious differences. Through intentional sharing, listening, and reflection, the two of them work toward healing and reconciliation. *Undivided* is a wonderfully written book addressing a difficult topic."

—Dr. Dale Trevino, director, Office of Diversity and Inclusion, Harvard School of Public Health, Boston

"*Undivided* is more than some pithy study of tolerance. After all, who wants to be merely tolerated? *Undivided* is a necessary study of acceptance and raw honesty. The Raybons' deep disclosures challenged me to think and talk about faith in a new way. Something inside of me says I should not have expected less."

—Robin Caldwell

"Without question, this is the most amazing book I have read regarding the trials and triumphs of loved ones navigating the turbulent world of interfaith realities. That a mother and her daughter would share their journey so honestly with equal passion provides hope and inspiration for countless others."

—Brother Jeff S. Fard, Muslim community leader and
founder, Brother Jeff's Cultural Center, Denver

"Our world needs models for authentic conversation across faith lines. Lack of understanding and mistrust run deep. Patricia and Alana provide such a model from within a family. In the end we all are family members needing to have a conversation."

—Rev. Dr. L. James Bankston, retired
United Methodist clergy, Houston

"How can a heartbroken Christian mother and an independent Muslim daughter find peace? They fight for it. With rare honesty and unfiltered emotions, Patricia Raybon and Alana Raybon let readers into their personal, painful, and praise-worthy struggle. *Undivided* will captivate you—heart, mind, and soul."

—Lori Wildenberg, cofounder,
1Corinthians13Parenting.com; and coauthor,
Raising Big Kids with Supernatural Love

"What would it be like to listen in on an intimate, open conversation between a hurting mother and the daughter whose life choices are fueling her pain? In *Undivided* Patricia Raybon and her daughter Alana go to that place of uncomfortable, raw communication with their defenses down and their hearts surrendered to the process of healing years of family heartache. Their story is a beautiful testimony of God's grace in mother-daughter relationships and the joy that can be found when family peace is restored."

—Saundra Dalton-Smith, MD, award-winning author, *Set
Free to Live Free*; and founder, www.IChooseMyBestLife.com

"I loved, loved, loved this book. So open and honest. So full of spiritual truths that go straight to the bone. *Undivided* is a beautifully written, honest, page-turning story of hard-fought peace between mother and daughter. This is no easy journey; there are no trite answers. But the authors share that finding peace with those we love is a journey worth taking. This book might just change the world, one family relationship at a time."

—Becky Johnson, coauthor, *Nourished: A Search
for Health, Happiness and a Full Night's Sleep*

Undivided

A Muslim Daughter,
Her Christian Mother,
Their Path to Peace

Patricia Raybon and Alana Raybon

W Publishing Group

An Imprint of Thomas Nelson

Published in Nashville, Tennessee, by W Publishing Group, an imprint of Thomas Nelson.

Published in association with the literary agency of Ann Spangler and Company.

Thomas Nelson titles may be purchased in bulk for educational, business, fund-raising, or sales promotional use. For information, please e-mail SpecialMarkets@ThomasNelson.com.

Unless otherwise noted, Scripture quotations are taken from the Holy Bible, New International Version®, NIV®. © 1973, 1978, 1984, 2011 by Biblica, Inc.™ Used by permission of Zondervan. All rights reserved worldwide.

Scripture quotations marked CEB are taken from the Common English Bible. © 2011 Common English Bible.

Scripture quotations marked ESV are taken from the ESV® Bible (The Holy Bible, English Standard Version®), © 2001 by Crossway, a publishing ministry of Good News Publishers. Used by permission. All rights reserved.

Scripture quotations marked KJV are taken from the King James Version.

Scripture quotations marked NKJV are taken from the New King James Version®. © 1982 by Thomas Nelson. Used by permission. All rights reserved.

Scripture quotations marked NLT are taken from *Holy Bible*, New Living Translation, © 1996. Used by permission of Tyndale House Publishers, Inc., Wheaton, Illinois 60189. All rights reserved.

Scripture quotations marked ISV are taken from the International Standard Version © 1995–2014 by ISV Foundation. All rights reserved internationally. Used by permission of Davidson Press, LLC.

ISBN 978-0-7180-3579-2 (IE)

Library of Congress Control Number: 2014957693

ISBN 978-0-529-11305-4

Printed in the United States of America

15 16 17 18 19 RRD 5 4 3 2 1

To my agent, Ann Spangler—my mentor, agent, and friend. Thank you for believing I can build bridges.
—Patricia

To Paul, my beloved husband and advocate of peace. Thank you for helping me to see the way.
—Alana

CONTENTS

Acknowledgments

EVERY BOOK NEEDS ALLIES AND FRIENDS. I'M BLESSED BY GOD'S peace and grace to acknowledge this book's strong circle of support, including my upbeat and loving husband, Dan, who believes writing matters and supports me as an author with every word; my amazing agent, Ann Spangler, whose expert advice, wisdom, and friendship never fail to inspire; our brilliant publisher, Matt Baugher of Thomas Nelson's W Publishing Group, who served as leader and champion from start to finish, and his dynamic marketing, editing, and sales team (including Stephanie Newton, Kristi Smith, Emily Sweeney, and Kristen Vasgaard), whose enthusiasm and energy are helping our book find readers worldwide; our stellar senior editor, Paula Major, whose matchless guidance, tireless support, and steady hand led us with assurance and affirmation from opening word to final page; our fantastic publicity team at Choice Media and Communications, including Heather Adams, Beth Gebhard, and Kerry Vance, whose bright, positive, and effective handling turn book publicity into a joy; our talented photographer, Micah Kandros; our book-cover consultant, Brandon Materre; a host of praying friends and phenomenal encouragers, all strong and wonderful, including Sharon Leavitt, Denise Materre, Brenda Quinn, Eliza Cross, the Rev. Dawn Riley Duval, Becky Johnson, Rachel Randolph, Margo Starbuck, Dr. Brenda Salter McNeil, Robin Caldwell, Dr. Timothy E. Tyler, and Dr. Clarence Shuler, among many others; my beautiful family, including my smart and astounding sister, Dr. Lauretta Lyle, my smart and beautiful daughter Joi

Afzal, my smart and amazing son-in-law, Paul "Iesa" Galloway, and the smartest little people in the world—my extraordinary five grandchildren. For all of them, dear heavenly Father, I thank you. Finally, I thank my remarkable daughter Alana Raybon. This is your book, beautiful Alana. Thank you so much for showing me how to write it.

—PATRICIA

WHEN I SAT DOWN AT MY COMPUTER FOR THE FIRST TIME AND BE-gan writing this book, I had many fears and doubts. It was through the love and support of the following people that I owe my sincere appreciation and gratitude for being a part of this incredible journey and for helping me complete this project. All thanks and praise is foremost due to Allah, who has led me this far on a path toward peace; to my husband, Paul, for understanding me so completely, loving me unconditionally, and holding my hand through life; my dad, for making me laugh and helping me keep my eyes on the prize; my sister, Joi, who is always there to listen at the perfect times; my wonderful in-laws, George and Del Galloway, for their constant love, support, and late-night talks; my beautiful sister-in-law, Jessica Deitch, whose counseling sessions helped me heal; our dedicated agent, Ann Spangler, who believed that I could write this book; Sheikh Waleed Basyouni, Imam Isa Parada, and Brother Abdulbari Abdullahi, each for being a source of spiritual guidance and inspiration; Aisha Jalali, for being the most positive person I know; Sakina Gutierrez, whose friendship helped me through so many tough times; Zulayka Lantan and Susan Barrientos, for their generosity, friendship, and help with my babies; my former sixth grade students at ILM Academy, for helping me to see how bright the future can be; our encouraging publisher at Thomas Nelson's W Publishing Group, Matt Baugher, who has helped uplift so many people's lives; the hardworking publicity professionals at Choice Media and Communications, including Heather Adams, Beth Gebhard, and Kerry Vance; the dedicated experts at W, including senior editor Paula Major, Stephanie Newton, Kristen Vasgaard, and Emily Sweeney; our gifted photographer, Micah Kandros; my delightful children, whose laughter reminds me of the meaning of true happiness; my brilliant stepson, whose wisdom far surpasses his age; and my cat, Felix, for keeping me up late at night to write. Lastly, thank you to my mother, for inviting me on this journey. Your faith and strength inspire me. I love you, always.

—ALANA

one

CAN WE TALK?

Patricia

THE ELEPHANT IS IN THE ROOM, AND IT'S BIG. SO IT'S NOT MOVING. Not one turn. Not one inch. Still, my daughter and I talk around it, pretending our ten-ton problem isn't there—insisting it will stay quiet and be okay if we just ignore the obvious and keep on moving. So we're politely jawing about my kitchen cabinets and drawers, nicely talking about my fight to finally clean them out and make some order and find some peace.

"You're decluttering?" Alana says. "Why now? Your kitchen is fine."

But it's not fine. Not really. And neither are we. Not like we used to be. Or maybe never were.

Yet how can I even think such a thing? After all, I know God. I know all my God can do. That's how I boast anyway. Most days I boast, that is.

But it's the day before Mother's Day. Alana has called me on the phone to say hi, tell me she loves me, wish me the best. I'm hanging on to every word, as I always do when my daughters call, ecstatic to hear their living and lovely voices. Yet with Alana, there's always this wish: that things were different—back to the way they once were or the way I wish they'd always been, so long ago now I can't seem to remember.

Like they were? Yes. I wish she was still a Christian. No, that's not the whole of it. I wish on this day before Mother's Day something more. I wish she wasn't a Muslim. So now I've said it. In my heart. And right here on a page. Oh so quiet. But oh so brave. I've said it. Like a prayer. *O my*

1

God. Not boastful. Just a desperate plea. How did my younger baby leave the faith of Christ and stop believing?

On this almost Mother's Day, this mother wants to know: How did we come to this moment in time and, by faith, become divided?

Why, indeed, are we on the phone blah-blahing about my kitchen decluttering project—my countless trips to my neighborhood Bed Bath & Beyond and the Container Store in the fancy neighborhood across town and the Goodwill store down the street and wherever else I can go to chase down plastic shelf organizers and dividers—when the biggest part of our lives, what we believe about God and how we practice that belief, is such a split and holy wreck?

A Christian and a Muslim? In the same family? How, O blessed God, did such a thing happen? Too many times I tried to find an answer. God knows I tried. In prayers. In books. In dreams. In the quiet of silent nights and the roar of jam-packed days. Like mothers of daughters everywhere, I've stood in the silence of a locked room, stared at myself in a mirror, and asked God, why? And how? How in the robust name of Jesus did this happen?

And like those other mothers everywhere, I was angry when I asked. Mad at life. At my daughter. At myself. Maybe angrier at God for not stepping into the messiness of this business we call life and calling a divine stop. But God doesn't work that way.

And look how I say that. As if I do know God. As if I understand God. As if I accept with calm how God moves—and how God doesn't move—and how he lets us wrestle and struggle and grasp and stew and wail and wonder. Then he lets us choose, despite knowing beforehand how we're going to choose—even when he knows we'll choose wrong.

So the psalmist nailed it right? Saying it this way? That God knows "when I sit down or stand up. You know my thoughts even when I'm far away" (Ps. 139:2 NLT)?

So God knew?

He knew. Before this embattled earth was formed, he knew Alana and I would be rumbling over these three defiant words spouted from her beautiful confident mouth: "I'm a Muslim."

My heart didn't stop exactly. It sank straight to the floor.

But not from the announcement. It sank from the struggle that had brought us to this moment. First, those teen years—with their relentless arguments and fussing and door slamming and confusion and yelling. Then the testing years—when, at twenty, Alana joined the Nation of Islam. And I fought that. Arguing against the theology of the Nation. Thundering against the messages that sounded to me like too much hate.

Then at this big, big moment—when my daughter officially renounced Christianity by choosing to leave it for "orthodox Islam," as she called it, I stayed silent.

And neutral.

"Thanks for letting us know," I said. She was twenty-something and a junior in college. So I gripped the phone and asked about school. Her classes. Her teachers. How her car was running.

How her car was running?

Yes, I asked her exactly that.

Then we said a few other neutral things. Have a good afternoon. Thanks for calling. Talk to you later. Then I hung up the phone.

So I didn't fight for Jesus. Not on that day. Not because I didn't care. And not because I didn't love every single thing about Jesus more than life itself—and still love him just as much, if not more now than on that day.

Yet I didn't fight for him because, on that day, I just didn't know how to fight.

My life had changed. My Christian daughter became a Muslim.

And my life and every single thing about life just flat-out flew apart.

So here I sit today, ten years after my daughter made her announcement, staring at my keyboard in my belabored home office—which also is a wreck and needs decluttering and an overhaul. Still, even in this mess, I commit to speak truth about the biggest mountain in my life that has yet to move.

I wish my daughter wasn't a Muslim.

Wrong to say? Probably.

But elephants don't move if they can't see. They are shortsighted and deliberate. If things don't look clear and understandable and logical, they won't budge. Unless they get startled. Then, experts say, they go on a rampage.

And my home and hearth are messy enough already.

I long for logic and order and peace. And I long to talk. To finally look together at the reality of our life—and not end up arguing and slamming doors and yelling and walking away, especially without answers. Surely now—with almost ten years stuck in rubble—we finally can talk. Open and honest. But there's one problem.

My Christian daughter is a Muslim.

So how do we unclutter that? Every little piece of it. All the hard parts. The unexpected pieces. The curious twists and turns of struggling to live across faiths. Can't we clear all that up?

Should we even try?

My mother's heart tells me yes. Getting along but living divided has run its course. It's time to move higher.

Well, that's what my saved, sanctified, filled with the Holy Ghost, Bible-loving soul thinks I should say.

But how will Alana answer?

Will she go with me on this journey? Put her daughter's hand in mine? See where this path to truth and harmony takes us?

Or is she terrified, like me, to try?

Finally, I am ready to hear her answer.

Alana

Why am I a Muslim? It's the big question of my life—and the big conundrum for a mother and a father I love. But my answers aren't simple. And neither is my life. So as I sit in my dark bedroom considering this question, I look over at my husband, who fell asleep watching a UFC fight on the iPad, and hope that I won't have to walk my oldest daughter back to bed for the third time. It's late. I'm exhausted and ready for some peace and quiet.

After a day full of dental appointments for our four-year-old, our two-year old, and me—because I'm pregnant again—plus waiting in the never-ending line at our local post office, I need a moment. But I can't sleep just yet because I'm staring at my computer, trying to figure out a way to explain to my mother why I became a Muslim.

Her question doesn't surprise me. I know that, although we smile and go along with our daily lives as if nothing is wrong, she will probably never be at peace with my decision. Still, I wonder if I will be able to talk to her about such an emotional issue.

My mother and I are really good at talking about easy stuff. Every time she calls, her usual questions are "How're the kids?," "How's the hubby?," and "How's work?" And then I rattle off my own questions about what's going on in her life. She informs me about Dad's choir practice and her recent trip to Saver's, the local thrift store, where she found some "practically new" outfit for a ridiculously low price. We laugh politely and then get off the phone. But we never talk about faith.

I don't think I'm scared to talk to her about it. I just don't know how to begin. I talk about faith all the time to Muslim friends. Even curious coworkers. I occasionally get questioned by parents and students at the elementary school where I teach fourth grade. The shy and reserved looks on their faces make it seem as if they are uncomfortable talking about my faith. I'm so used to the questions that I give automatic responses and make sure to be politically correct since I work in a public school. The kids mostly ask innocent questions based on what they see: "Why do you wear that thing on your head? Aren't you hot?"

I remember one student, a third-grade girl, pulling me aside and whispering, "Are you bald under that scarf?" I grinned and politely replied, "I'm trying to be extra modest." Or I may have said, "I wear loose-fitting clothing because it breathes easily." My student smiled, looking uncomfortable, still staring at me in wonder.

If I can answer questions from someone else, why can't I talk to my mother about my faith?

Most of the conversations with my mom are cut short anyway. I'm either on the way home from work and have to pick up the kids, or I already have the kids, and they're screaming in my ear. We rarely have a decent amount of quiet, uninterrupted time to talk. Even during my visits to Colorado and her visits to Texas, the kids take up so much of our time and attention that there doesn't seem to be the time to just sit down and say, "So, Mom, wanna talk about why I became a Muslim?"

The opportunity just doesn't come up. I don't really mind it. In fact, I think I kind of like avoiding the topic. It all feels so controversial, and I am too tired from work and the kids to deal with controversy.

We've already endured enough drama since my conversion anyway. After I announced it, we didn't *talk*. We shouted, yelled, and debated for hours until I eventually shied away, realizing the downfalls of my naive approach to "convince" her. Embarrassed and ashamed, I allowed our relationship to evolve into one of polite denial. I pretended that there wasn't a divide forming between my mother and me, and I tried to keep in touch.

It was easy because we were apart—she in my native Colorado and me in Texas with my new husband. As a recent college grad, I was busy setting up my fifth-grade classroom. We would chat about my workload and the stress of being a first-year teacher. She would share about her church life and books. It was easy to pretend everything was okay—at least until she and my dad would visit. Then, somehow, the conversation would go in the direction of religion and eventually would erupt into a heated debate. A lot of words were spoken, hardly any of which were productive. We all were left feeling angry, frustrated, and exhausted.

One muggy summer night, in my tiny newlywed apartment, the authenticity of the Bible came up in our post-dinner discussion, and the conversation went downhill fast. Like a scene from an old Western, we all stared intensely across at each other, exhausted from the battle that had just occurred.

"Wait," my husband pleaded, as my parents got up to leave, unable to take any more arguing. "Don't leave like this," he said, holding out his hand to usher them back to the couch.

We sat in silence for a while, allowing our heartbeats to slow. The sounds of Houston's busy streets trailed in from the open patio door. I took a breath and calmed down and then looked back at my parents.

They stared at me with hurt and sadness in their eyes, and I knew that a rift would remain between us.

So, quietly, I decided to leave it alone, realizing that these arguments were destroying my relationship with my parents. The flare-ups arose less and less, and with the birth of my first child, a lovely distraction conveniently appeared.

And now we've actually agreed to talk about it, on paper at least, in a measured back-and-forth discussion. Surprisingly, it was my mother who initiated the idea. Maybe that was the necessary first step—to acknowledge that something has to change. That we can't just go on ignoring the matters that weigh down our hearts. Maybe I'm willing to talk now because, for once, my mother has actually asked the question. I don't recall her ever asking it before. In fact, I rarely remember her ever asking me about how I felt about these issues or my feelings about events in my life. And now she's asked me to discuss one of the most important aspects of my life, and the floodgates are open. So I've agreed to talk in this manner, knowing that it's time to address her concerns and confront our conflict head-on.

The time has flown by. It's been ten years since my conversion, and it's hard for me to understand how so much time could have passed without our sharing our feelings with each other about one of the most significant aspects of our lives.

Something inside me says yes, it needs to be done. Even if it means rehashing the uncomfortable, hurtful, and sometimes embarrassing past that has led up to this moment—when we finally talk.

But are we ready to receive what may come through those gates?

I hope I'm ready, and I hope this journey brings us closer. We have to give it a try.

Patricia

THROUGH THE GATES?

Well, the first thing was Ramadan—the annual Muslim fasting observance that lasts thirty days and thirty nights.

"Thirty?" I said to Alana.

It was July 2012, and we had been making early progress on our project to talk and come clean. We were writing about it all. Me during the day. Alana in the evenings after she put the children to bed. But right away came Ramadan. And our little project came to a screeching halt.

"You're not working?" I pushed Alana. "Not writing?"

"I want to," she said. "But we go to the *masjid* every night."

"You go to the mosque every night?" I said, starting to sound like my old, annoyed self. Thirty days? Every night? My husband, Dan, meantime, had his own questions.

"Ramadan?" He gave me a look. "What's that?"

I sighed. Cast my eyes to heaven. His question, and my frustration about it all, sat smack at the heart of my dismay with interfaith life. We were oddballs while normal, one-faith families share and enjoy their same seasonal holidays—basking in each other's love, laughter, fellowship, gifts, holiday food. That's how I envision it anyway: a Hallmark card of a harmonious family. Gathered together around one unbroken, loving, unified table.

All the things my family and I weren't anymore—if we ever were.

But before I could feel the regret, Alana had said something much bigger. That she never could talk to me. Not about anything. That she, in fact, rarely remembers my ever asking her how she felt about any issues or events in her entire life.

I look over those words, and my eyes want to spin in my head. I want to argue that there was not only talking but also perceiving. That I can't understand how a beautiful daughter can grow up in a house with an on-site mother—a hovering, harnessing, harping, relentlessly involved mother—but say I wasn't there.

That I didn't talk. Implying I must not have cared.

But I read it again, and the realization hits me like a ton of bricks. She's not speaking about talking. She is speaking about asking. She says I never asked.

And hello, Stephen Covey. How did the mentor put it? This Mormon guy? This famous writer speaking across faiths to my Christian heart about misunderstandings? Well, Covey said this: "Most people do not listen with the intent to understand; they listen with the intent to reply." Then he added the fifth of his famous "Seven Habits"—to "seek first to understand, then to be understood."[1] If that's not about asking, what is? So talking is first seeking? About asking? How do you feel? What do you think? What don't you like? Why did you go?

Who do men say that I am?

Jesus.

Stepping in here already? But it's way too soon for the Nazarene. Too soon to seek his intervention in our interfaith dialogue. This is just chapter 1—where we let the petals of the flower that is a book twitch in the breeze and start to open. But just barely. Because a book takes time.

That's what I dare say to Alana. Let it unfold. Don't worry about saying everything in the first chapter. Let it evolve. Slow. Measured. Restrained. Gently. Tender?

But here I am already—in this little personal story about our faith— calling out for the Man. The Savior. The Christ. Pleading for him. Begging him to cut to the chase. To sit smack in the middle of everything. His presence forces me, however, to see what I didn't understand all those years about this faith, this Jesus, this daughter, and this whole how-did-she-turn-into-a-Muslim problem connected with all of it. And here's what I didn't see: the way Jesus healed was first to ask questions.

Who do men say that I am? (Matt. 16:13). He asked it quietly, this perhaps most important question ever asked. Who exactly *is* Jesus? Who is he according to ordinary people anyway? Yet he asked without drama. Without facing down his disciples. Without crossing his arms, twisting his mouth, telling off his rebellious children of God—not even the chief of his rebels, Peter.

So if Jesus could ask without drama, why can't I?

For answers I dive into Google, type the words: *the questions Jesus asked*. And boom! The results number in the tens of millions. That's how many folks long, like me, to expound on Christ's example not to speak but to ask.

I draw in a breath. Click on a site. Scroll down lists. Smile at familiar questions.

Why are you afraid?

Why are you sleeping?

What do you want me to do for you?

As I read, I let my mind turn to my childhood Sunday school years—when "colored" children, like me, in the fifties crowded happily into our kindergarten room at church with our graham crackers and cold milk and warming stories about Jesus. But I've already told that story. Written that story. Spoken about it. Detailed the picture of our little band of tiny Negro disciples—shaped in the crucible of our segregated Jim Crow world—sitting at the knee of our beloved Sunday school teacher, Mildred Hall, while she placed on a felt board the life of Jesus, told so famously in questions.

Don't you want to be healed?

"Wilt thou be made whole?" (John 5:6 KJV)

Then with aging hands Miz Hall placed the cardboard figure of Jesus—pictured as a white man in flowing robes, an irony we never thought to question and she never thought to address. Next she placed a figure of the sick man—also a white man—lying at the pool of Bethesda, waiting for the angels to stir up the healing waters so the ailing man could find his healing. But crowds beat him to it. Beat him for thirty-eight years (John 5:1–7).

Long time. Too long to be confused. In pain. Fearful. Stupid. Dismayed. Crazy? Or like me? Until Jesus steps onto the scene. Walks onto the felt board of my life. Not to preach. But to call me by name. *Patricia.* I can hear his voice, asking, *don't you want to be healed?*

Made whole indeed?

But it's too early in this interfaith journey to tell such a story. To brag he's a miracle-working God. Then to show how he does it. To detail him turning his answer for one sick Bethesda man into the solution for the whole, crazy world. And that was just one of the stories of Jesus asking questions. But for now, all I can say—in my crazy dismay—is that first, Jesus asked.

For him, a question is how talking and healing and loving start.

And Alana says I didn't do that. Or care about that. I indeed have to confess she is right on one score. I *didn't* ask. Not about her life. Her challenges. Her struggles growing up a light-skinned daughter of a light-skinned man and a brown-skinned mother in an all-black church. But I never asked, how does *that* make you feel?

Thus, I didn't ask her any dozens of questions connected to life, family, faith, living, loving. Nor did I ask her about Jesus.

So here we are. I am Christian. She is Muslim. And it's still Ramadan. A holiday of her chosen faith. Yet I don't even know what Ramadan is. Back to Google? No, wait. I should ask Alana about Ramadan. Then I can ask her about so much more.

She reminds me of that. "Shouldn't we be talking about all of this first? Instead of writing about it first?" Now, however, I see what she means: Shouldn't we start with our questions?

But I was too ready then to dive in to this writing again, and she was busy with celebrating her holiday anyway. When I call her, her phone goes to voice mail.

"If you'd like to leave a message . . ."

If I'd like?

I'm desperate to leave a message. But I'm not much of a talker. Never have been. Never knew how. Not like my extroverted friends. My extroverted husband. My extroverted late mother—a master of social small talk, which sounded to me like a foreign language.

That, in fact, was going to be my excuse in this book for our standoff. We haven't talked for a good reason: I'm an introvert. It's my DNA. It's why, at age sixty-something, I rarely show up anymore at the endless schedule of social events that middle-class, black Americans—God bless us—maintain on a relentlessly endless social schedule. They're lovely and beautiful events. Staged in lovely and beautiful venues. Art museums and governors' mansions. Country clubs and rooftop gardens. And hotels. For certain, the hotel chains of the world owe more than a little thanks to extroverted African Americans for busy social lives. But it never stops. For introverts like me, this social calendar was always exhausting. And all about talking. So for a nontalker, it was a kind of torture.

Now I finally see why: I didn't ask questions.

Isn't that the essence of small talk anyway? Not bouncing from topic to topic, trying to find common ground, but asking questions?

All over the world, should Christians and Muslims stop their talking at each other so much—just stop shouting and fighting and killing each other—and just ask questions? What do you think? How do you feel? What do you know?

Do I now have to wonder whether my daughter is a Muslim because, even though I took her to church every single Sunday morning of her life and to all those black social events organized all over Denver, I just didn't understand the verbal golden rule: first ask?

Is that it, Lord?

I pray on this early morning, trying to write down these first steps. Otherwise, I have to bear alone the burden that I created the breach in our family's long faith tradition because I'm not naturally one to sit down and ask a question. To be honest, I'd rather not carry that burden. But I started this journey to learn. To understand how the Bible can say "the tongue is a fire, a world of unrighteousness" as James, the brother of Jesus, put it (3:6 ESV). To remember, indeed, that Jesus healed so often by first opening his mouth. *Do you want to be healed?* Then to know he created the world by speaking it into existence. That's what I believe anyway.

So I plow through my tired desk for a good Bible, believing it will lead me not only to order and a new way of understanding my daughter but also to wisdom.

That is certainly what Alana and I need for this journey.

We need wisdom. Then we need quiet. Without shouting. Or lecturing. Or speechifying or proselytizing. Or showboating. So asking my daughter about faith can't be an evangelizing moment for me.

Not at first.

First, instead, asking Alana a question simply says *you matter*.

How much? More than my desire to see Alana and her family back in the body of Christ? More than my desire to see her sitting at the feet of Jesus? More than my longing to see her walk through the doors of any ordinary church to praise the Lord?

I don't right now have answers to my questions.

But I know, as a mother, that a daughter is worth the effort. So first we have to talk. For certain, we have to ask.

But will you help us, O God?

And, yes, indeed. That is a prayer.

Alana

I'M PRAYING TOO.

But it isn't easy trying to resolve deep issues in your life when life keeps throwing a wrench in the way. It's hard enough talking with two screaming kids in your ear whenever you get on the phone. At the end of a busy day, with the house quiet and calm, I stare at my phone and sigh, thinking maybe Mom and I will talk tomorrow. I know it's too late to call because she goes to sleep so much earlier than we do.

Ramadan came, and a month passed by with no progress in written conversation. After that was a two-week Mediterranean cruise that my parents had been saving for and planning for years. "I'm not even bringing my laptop," Mom said happily. *Project put on hold again*, I thought.

Meanwhile, my due date keeps approaching, and the doctor says I'm dilating. That means I go into immediate nesting mode and start frantically digging up baby toys and clothes from the garage. Washing everything in Dreft, sorting, folding, organizing. So who has time to talk?

Then it's Thanksgiving, and my parents are out of town again, this time in New Jersey to see my dad's sister, my aunt Diana.

I keep waiting for the moment when we will get it all out on the table. But then I realize that I'm waiting on one of us to open the discussion, to begin the conversation. Perhaps when the baby arrives, and Mom and I are actually sitting face-to-face, since my parents will be visiting, then maybe we can finally talk.

But how will we start? Talking has never been hard for me, but for Mom, it's an entirely different story. I guess I take after my dad, who's always cracking jokes with total strangers in the grocery store. When I was a child, my parents enrolled me in an experimental British primary school with the type of environment that encouraged talking. I don't recall having to sit quietly in class until I left that school and entered a strict Catholic girls' school for fourth and fifth grades.

I wasn't used to sitting quietly for forty-five minutes or longer. I remember my fifth-grade social studies teacher's voice, reprimanding me from way in the front of the room. "Alana, stop talking!" she would demand. The effect seemed to last only a few minutes because soon I would hear her voice again, directed at me. Then there was art class, which at my old school was a place that encouraged conversation. At this new school, however, I can still see my gigantic art teacher's huge dark eyebrows and artist's smock as he leaned over his desk, voice booming for us to be quiet.

Then there was seventh grade, in a new public school, and my science class. It probably didn't help that I sat next to my best friend, Erin, who always had something hilarious to say. I spent many afternoons writing "I will not talk in class" a hundred or more times.

I wasn't a bad kid. I just liked to socialize, make friends, fit in.

And now months have passed, and the baby is here. I can hear the impatience in my dad's voice as he asks, "When are you going to work on your book with Mom?" But all I'm thinking is how I'm going to recuperate from hours of labor and lack of sleep while trying to give my other two kids a couple of minutes of attention here and there.

My parents are visiting for three weeks. Plenty of time for Mom and me to talk, right? But somehow the opportunity never arises. Are we avoiding each other? How hard is it really to begin this conversation? I guess I'm waiting for her to sit me down and say it's going to start. That never happens. As soon as we come back from the hospital, the baby is diagnosed with serious conjunctivitis in her left eye. So I spend three days and nights with the baby at the children's hospital, followed by appointments with the ophthalmologist and a cardiologist—because the baby also has a heart murmur. As she improves, we all are grateful and relieved—focused on her care and comfort. And then my parents are gone.

"We will be back in March," they say.

March? That's three months away. Our talk can't wait until then.

After their visit, I finally bring it up while talking on the phone. "Mom, are we ever going to talk?" I ask, frustrated. "Isn't it weird that we haven't talked in person? How can we write without doing that?"

I can sense that I have made Mom very uncomfortable. She doesn't like to talk, in person that is. She's a writer to the bone. She would rather write you a perfectly composed essay response and present it to you in an envelope. I know I'm asking her to go beyond her comfort zone.

"I guess we should, Lana," she says hesitantly.

But she has the flu, so she's going to have to call me back. Four long days later she calls.

"When can I get on your schedule so we can have this talk?" she asks.

That's hilarious to me. I have to hold back my laugh. I can't believe my mom has to schedule our conversation like a doctor's appointment. I know she means well. She knows I'm so busy with the kids. But I can't help thinking that deep down she's freaking out and wants to avoid this moment. I don't want to wait any longer. This is what's wrong with us. This is why we have coexisted for years having level conversations. We can't keep walking around this topic.

"Now's good!" I say, catching her off guard.

"Okay," she replies in a shaky voice.

I'm feeling a little anxious as well. What have I done? I've opened the gates.

She takes the first step and asks me a question: "So when did this all start?"

And suddenly we *are* talking. Her question did it.

"New York," I reply. I feel ready to explain it all to her and relieved that it has finally begun. I was in the middle of my freshman year at Fordham University while pursuing a joint BA in dance at the prestigious Ailey School for the Alvin Ailey American Dance Theater. It was my dream come true to study at The Ailey School. I had worked so long and hard to get there. I had studied for years at dance studios in Denver, and then I made the cut for Ailey in national auditions. But now I was having doubts.

I had just left an intense ballet class, breathing hard and dripping with sweat. I sat in the hallway, taking off my ballet shoes and rubbing my sore feet. My dance teacher walked into the hallway. "Nice work today, Alana," she said. That was the first compliment I had received from her all semester, which was huge considering she didn't hand them out lightly.

Her comment caught me off guard, and I took a quick breath to say thank you in reply. Considering I had already made up my mind to leave the dance program and pursue a more academic path, her timing was ironic. In fact, I had an appointment right after class with the director of the dance school.

"I don't want to dance anymore," I said confidently, although inside I was scared and unsure about my decision. I still loved dance, but I needed more. I just wasn't sure what I needed yet.

Shocked and amazed, the director reluctantly agreed to remove me from the program. I hadn't consulted my parents before making this decision. I rarely did when making life decisions, out of fear of their disapproval. But now it was done, and I knew that my life would take a dramatically different path from then on.

"My mind wanted more, Mom," I explained to her over the phone. I had feelings of anxiety about my future in dance. What if I got injured? What about when I'm older and can't dance in a company anymore? I didn't want to teach dance class at a studio like so many former company members whom I saw at the school every day. I decided I wanted more of an academic education. These were the feelings and emotions running through my mind when I decided to leave, but I didn't anticipate they eventually would lead me on a journey to change my basic beliefs. I came back from New York that year searching and embarked on a spiritual journey that would change my life.

So I had answered her first question, but there were many more to come. I know we have to continue, despite how uncomfortable this may feel. I realize that this is the first time that Mom has heard this story. I'm proud of us, though, for taking these first steps. We can only go forward from here.

"This whole time I thought it all started in high school," Mom replies, surprised. "This whole time I thought that maybe your friends teased you about going to church?"

Church and faith were the last and least of my areas of concern in high school. Being a Christian was a natural constant in my life. An area that didn't need to be changed or even messed with. I had always been a

Christian and didn't know about anything else. Everyone around me was a Christian, whether he or she practiced faith openly or not. My friends and I never even talked about church, preferring conversations about clothes, boys, and music television instead. During the week, church was the last thing on my mind until Sunday, when my family and I fulfilled our routine obligation and attended the morning service.

Maybe the events in my life would have been different had my mother actually asked about this ten years ago. Maybe if our relationship had been one that fostered communication as part of our daily lives. Talking is a two-way communication, but instead of talking, my college-educated parents—both having master's degrees and working at the University of Colorado at Boulder—lectured me on those occasions when I made mistakes or disobeyed, which, to them, seemed to be a lot. Each lecture was like a well-manicured thesis in which I was supposed to be quiet and listen. There were no questions directed to me for us to discuss, and if I was asked a question, it was rhetorical.

I knew how to endure these sessions. Nod, say yes and no at the right moments. And then, finally, the lecture would end with a satisfied parent leaving the room and my flopping backward, exhausted, onto my bed, relieved for it to be over.

Real talking requires listening. Talking *to* each other, not *at* each other. To move forward, we must be ready to ask, then listen with open hearts, open minds, and then have the willingness to understand.

We are family, and I can't just give up on my family, no matter how hard it is for us to understand each other.

So many before me never gave up. There are so many stories in the Islamic tradition of prophets whose families were ripped apart because of the prophet's faith choices—including Moses and Muhammad, among others—but who, despite differences in beliefs, strove to maintain family bonds.

Muhammad was an orphan. His parents died when he was young, and he was raised by his kind and supportive uncle, Abu Talib, a devout polytheist who worshipped idols. After Muhammad's proclamation of faith, however, Abu Talib continued to help his nephew despite their differences in beliefs. Although Abu Talib never converted to Islam, he remained a loyal supporter of Muhammad and staunchly defended him from ridicule.

In a recorded tradition, called a Hadith, Muhammad said, "Whoever believes in Allah and the Last Day, should unite the bond of kinship."[2] He was also commanded by God in the Qur'an to give parents "good treatment" and to "accompany them in [this] world with appropriate kindness."[3]

Mom and I have to keep talking and continue to work through our relationship issues. I pray that as we talk, we are able to be strong enough to grow closer as mother and daughter and that our division, so wide and expansive, begins to close.

t w o
⟡

CAN WE LISTEN?

——————————— *Patricia* ———————————

MY LORD, WHAT HAVE I STARTED? I ASKED GOD QUIETLY. THEN I GOT
back to it. I'm determined, that is, to walk this whole journey. To come to
terms with my beloved ex-Christian daughter over her defiant choice of
faith. Even though it twists my thinking. Even though it stirs up fears. On
so many levels, indeed, I feel fear for what we're doing.

First, there's the big fear that stopped me in the first place. As I
explained to close friends: if Alana is granted a reason and a platform to
defend her chosen religion, she'll use it as ammunition, to put down her
family's faith. Even more, I feared she'd do a good job. That she'd make
Islam look good—while I'd fail to lift high the Cross. That pressure I
feel—to make Jesus and his good deeds and perfect life and extraordinary
sacrifice look phenomenal and far better than Islam—weighs me down
the most.

Because *I'm* not enough.

Not on my own. Not without Jesus. Or a miracle. Or both.

That's the voice in my head.

So I start scavenging for books on Christian theology—buying a
bunch online at a discount, checking out armloads at the library, grinding
down on apologetics and church doctrine; you name it. And struggling
to unravel most of it. Then one day, finally, I lay this burden down. Then
by God's good grace and mercy—and a dose of common sense—I stop

listening to the head voice. I figure that my words in a book won't count without the Holy Spirit anyway. So even as I acknowledge his beautiful help, writing it down right now in this sentence, I feel myself calming down. Resting. Believing. Hearing.

I got this, girl. That's how some church folks say it these days. God's got it. God's got my back. My words. My fears. My insight. My anger. My dismay. Even my funk. Or as the psalmists would say, especially my funk.

That's how I feel when I read the words of my precious baby girl—this daughter, born into the body of Christ and baptized in his name—quoting the prophet Muhammad on the importance of family. Family?

This child who spent her life acting independent of family? Who valued school friends more than relatives? Other people's "cool" parents more than her own? Or that's how she acted anyway.

Yet if I question this—the sheer irony of it—or even mention her prophet's name with *any* questioning, then I run headfirst into another layer of fear. It's dangerous, for me, to say anything at all questionable about Islam's prophet.

And I decry that threat. Abhor thinking about it. Loathe worrying about it. But I know that any casual, "wrong" mention of the prophet in a book can make even a struggling mom like me a target. Or these days, maybe we all are targets.

I mean, I'm supposed to be exploring here how Alana and I should hear each other better. But I'm thinking as much about some extremist cleric becoming offended and then branding one or both of us a blaspheming idol worshipper—or whatever we might be called—and issuing a fatwa.

And why do I know that term? Because I watch the nightly over-wrought news. Western-biased news, of course. But a fatwa is a fatwa. And these fanatic guys don't mess around.

They couldn't care less that a mother and a daughter just need to talk. And finally, now, we're doing that. We've talked more in the past month, it seems, than we have since she was a young girl living at home. Yet by trying to talk about the hardest thing—this faith dilemma that we've avoided for so long—we as women have opened ourselves up to other people's attacks, just by trying our darnedest to talk. About everything.

Big things. Little things. Everyday things. Then to talk about these things without argument.

Almost every day it seems we find ourselves checking in with each other to ask about one matter or another. Her search for the best kindergarten for her four-and-a-half-year-old. Her search for a graduate school program versus a job and a return to elementary school teaching.

Right away, however, I run into a faith wall. As she is talking about the frustration of wanting to return to school when she and her husband can't afford it now, I want to cry. No, to groan.

Why doesn't she know? Know this wonderful Jesus? Know this amazing Christ who can guide her through life's hard hurdles—lifting her over the frustrations and problems of everyday struggle? Didn't I spend her childhood trying to show her this glory, taking her to church every Sunday morning of her precious growing-up life?

I scream the questions in my head. But I know what the scream really means. I am angry at myself. I somehow failed to give Alana the priceless gift that my God-loving daddy gave to me: a saving knowledge of Jesus, not just as a good person but Jesus as the Christ.

Or maybe I'm the one who doesn't know him—who doesn't trust the Lord enough to know that if he found me on my Jericho road, then he can find her. And bring her and her family back.

Instead, I sit at my piled-up desk reading her words, hearing her voice quote a prophet who, in my mind, cannot even begin to compare to Christ. Especially when it comes to offering a theology for the awe and press of everyday living. But can I think that? Say that out loud?

I cannot.

Just ask fifteen-year-old Malala Yousafzai, the schoolgirl who took a bullet in the head from extremists for daring to think all girls should get an education. No, for daring to *speak* about it.

Fanaticism doesn't play, indeed.

Neither does doubt. Like Alana's Pakistani coworker who told her Malala's story is a big hoax. That the brave teenager isn't a champion for girls' education but a pawn for the West. And her dad? A good salesman.

"So she doesn't believe any of it," said Alana, quickly adding, "but I do, Mom. I believe Malala's story, and I reject the conspiracy theory."

I try hard to listen to all of this. Just as I try to weigh and hear my fears.

But this is all too much to consider. So I go down to the kitchen to clean out a kitchen cabinet. Something I can handle. Something I can control. Something that makes simple sense. Or, at least, that's how it feels. I even watched a YouTube video on how to clean out your kitchen junk drawer. And while it may seem obvious to some, I was embarrassed to learn that the best way to clean a junk drawer is, first, to dump it all out. Just pour your junk out. Put it all on the table. As mother and daughter would do as they struggle to talk.

So there's a metaphor in my kitchen for this interfaith project of ours. But I can't figure out what it means if, after everything in the junky drawer is dumped out, most of that junky stuff can be thrown clean away.

Because it *was* junk. So you toss it in the garbage. Wipe clean the drawer. Then sort and put back the few things worth keeping. Nice and clean. Right and in order.

But the metaphor goes only so far. Life isn't neat. It's messed up, and it's arbitrary. It doesn't fit into cubbyholes and boxes. Or that's how it can feel. All the stuff we've jammed in corners and neglected for years to air out and pile into categories and store in reasonable drawers and closets—all our stuff—is still clogging our sight and stirring our fears and begging for our attention. So I have to hear it. To shut my mouth. To stop typing and pick up the phone and listen to my daughter talk about Muhammad whom I'm not supposed to trip up and say anything wrong about.

Or? Maybe I could show respect? Like a good Christian? Isn't that what Jesus would do?

I pause. Rub my forehead. Try to think. Not just about me and my family and our situation but about the countless families struggling with the conflicts of interfaith life, or whatever else families are fighting over, and would appreciate some fresh help.

So I vow to pray. Close my eyes. Quiet my noise. Ponder all this hearing and listening business. How did king Solomon put it? "Listen, my child" (Prov. 23:19 CEB).

Well, I'm trying. Because I sincerely want to think on such things. As a Christian. A mother. A woman. An African American. Black people, after all, are "Hagar's children," as my pastor likes to quip. More than anybody, I should be able to embrace this lineage of Ishmael that calls itself Islam and their prophet—and the fact that my daughter has chosen that clan over our less exotic one.

Then I'm supposed to hear about it. "Listen, my child."

So listen is what I will do now. Stop talking. Start listening. In that way I go to the telephone. With more questions. More dilemmas. More unspoken funk.

Now I will ask. Then listen like Jesus. He does it with such excellence.

"What are you discussing together," he asked two men on the Emmaus road, "as you walk along?" (Luke 24:17).

Simple question. No panic. No prompting. Even though he knew exactly what they were discussing. Even though he knew that walking along, discussing together, is a good way to go. So they responded in turn, asking their own question: "Are you the only one visiting Jerusalem who does not know the things that have happened there in these days?" (v. 18).

"What things?" Jesus asked (v. 19).

Beautiful questions. Oh, to ask and listen like Jesus. Even when somebody precious is saying she no longer believes.

Alana

MY MOTHER SAYS I NO LONGER BELIEVE.

How can I make her hear and understand that I do believe? I believe stronger than I ever have in my life. I struggle with the frustration of conveying to her that my walk in Islam has filled my heart with so much faith and love that I no longer feel the empty void that I once felt.

And then after she hears this, I wish she could be content and happy for me, that I found a love like no other. A love for God.

I wish I could plug her ears when she hears the news about terrorists and extremists. I wish I could press the mute button and cover her eyes. I don't want her to hear the news anchor saying the words *Islamic extremists* or *Islamic militants* and then relate the news of some horrific act of violence to the name of Islam.

But as soon as I click on the news, I'm reading about yet another

Muslim convert, a young British man, who joined the ranks of an extremist group.

I want to grab my mom and say, "That's not me! I'm not like that, nor is any Muslim I've ever met!" But those words would fall on deaf ears. While on the phone, Mom is frustrated. She doesn't understand. She can't help but equate the violence in the world with the religion of her younger daughter.

If only Mom could hear me, hear what I believe. Turn off the news, her friends, whatever else is feeding her information, and listen to me. Hear her daughter's experience firsthand. Shouldn't she ask me why I love Islam so much? I could tell her, if she would only listen.

I want her to hear that Islam is not what the media portrays it to be, maybe not even what some Muslims make it out to be. I tell her that if you judge a religion based on its followers, you will always be disappointed. The religion is perfect, the followers are not.

She knows that. She mentions the countless historical situations in which Christians have misrepresented their faith. But she still doesn't understand how Islam, if it is what I say it is, can produce people now who do such horrible things.

"They aren't following the example left behind by the prophets or their religious text," I say. But that answer isn't sufficient for her. It's hard to explain to her why it appears that the Muslims in the world are an emotional wreck. I can speak only for myself and the people I know who abhor violence in the name of religion. I start to tell her about a time when Muhammad showed patience toward a woman who constantly harassed him. But Mom doesn't want to hear that. I can hear impatience in her voice as she interrupts me. I want to tell her more examples of his diplomacy toward his critics, but she's not listening. She doesn't believe me. Yet.

I try to find the answers to tell my mom, but I don't know where to look. The Internet seems to be filled with either religious fanatics or biased lunatics who think they understand Islam. Frustrated and overwhelmed, I decide to contact a family friend with a degree in Islamic jurisprudence to get his take on radicalism.

"I need help," I say, explaining how this "talking" with my mom is harder than I thought. He confirms what my heart tells me, that extremism was never a part of Islam and some random, radical cleric can't just make a fatwa that goes against the basic tenets of Islam. Unfortunately, however, some Muslims, at least the ones who make it into the news, are ignorant of this fact and behave violently in the name of their faith. Mom needs to listen to my point of view, not those who are extreme enough to make it on TV.

And while she's listening to me, I want her to hear about how much I love Jesus. This is the touchiest of all subjects between us—the root of our division. She needs to hear, and understand, how much I love him and the other prophets from Abraham to Muhammad. I admire his tireless service and submission to God, and I cherish his mannerisms and the lessons he left for us.

But I don't worship him or see him as God incarnate, and that's what Mom doesn't want to hear. I read the book of Philippians as Mom suggested. Of course, I read it in my youth while in church. But this time was different. I read it as a Muslim, and I listened to the words of Paul. His faith and commitment for Jesus resonated through the pages, like so many converts to a faith.

And as I listen to Paul relate his message to his faithful followers, I think of my husband, Paul, who also loves Jesus. So much, in fact, that upon his acceptance of Islam he informally decided to be called Iesa, which means Jesus in Arabic. He didn't have to change his name, but he did because he wanted everyone to know that he wasn't turning his back on the prophet he was raised with. According to my husband, he was affirming everything Jesus stood for. By taking his name, he was saying loud and clear, I believe in Jesus' message of humility, peace, and submission to God.

The Arabic throws her off, though. These terms I use, and my husband's name choice, make her uneasy. She thinks I've joined a foreign clan, an Arab religion. Has she forgotten that Jesus lived in the Middle East and spoke Aramaic, a language closely related to Arabic? I try to dispel the myth in her mind—that Islam is an Arab religion. We're on the phone after I've returned from a baby shower at a friend's house, a Bolivian woman married to an Afghan. I tell her that my Muslim friends include South

Africans, Vietnamese, Malaysians, Dominicans, Colombians, Mexicans, El Salvadorans, Ethiopians, Anglo and African Americans, and, of course, Arabs—among many others.

If she were to go with me on any day to any mosque in Houston, she would see that I worship with people from all over the world. I didn't choose an exotic clan—I chose God, chose him above all others, even family and friends.

Isn't that what every mother should want for her child? A sincere desire to have a relationship with God—directly? I know I can't completely relate to her and how she feels about me and my faith choice. Now that I have children, I'm not sure what I would do if my children left Islam for another religion. Like her, I want my children to share my faith with sincerity and conviction.

"How could you not trust us?" my mother asks. Her quiet voice quivers as she looks at me from across the table. My parents are visiting again for a week, in May, and we have managed not to talk about religion for five consecutive days. It's the sixth day, and they're packed and ready for the airport. That's when Mom opens the door for discussion. "How could you not follow the faith of your family? Of your parents and grandparents? Of your ancestors?"

I want to reach over and tell her that I do trust them. I trusted them in their search and love for God. "It isn't about you or Dad or anyone else," I say. "It's about me and my relationship with God directly."

Shouldn't I listen to *my* heart?

I want to quiet those voices in her head, just for a moment. The voices that tell her that I can't experience God as she does. She needs to hear me say that I have never before felt more in touch with and in awe of God. My heart has been touched and moved by the powerful words in the Qur'an.

If she could, for a moment, allow herself to hear those powerful words of the Qur'an, maybe she could begin to understand me. If she were to open her heart for a moment, she might hear the truth that resonates off the pages.

It's the heart that, if ready, can hear the words of God and be changed profoundly.

The Qur'an speaks of the heart on many occasions when referring to listening. In Islam, one's heart has to be softened so that it can receive the words of the Qur'an, thus hearing the true meaning. In chapter 50, verse 37, of the Qur'an, Allah says, "Indeed in that is a reminder for whoever has a heart or who listens while he is present [in mind]."[1]

The heart is essential to being able to listen. It is mentioned in the Qur'an that the hearts of believers expand when the verses are recited, while the hearts of those who reject faith are covered or hardened. In chapter 41, verse 5, Allah speaks of people who cannot hear the message in the Qur'an. "And they say, 'Our hearts are within coverings from that to which you invite us, and in our ears is deafness, and between us and you is a partition, so work; indeed, we are working.'"[2]

Is her heart covered in a way that prevents her from hearing me?

I know I'm ready for her to hear me, but am I ready to hear her?

I've heard many things from her already about her faith, as a youth, in her books and upon my early conversion to Islam. And now as we begin to talk, I hear desperation in her voice and longing. She longs for me to join her belief, to experience Christ as she does. I also hear disappointment that I left our family's religion.

I'm used to hearing this from her.

I want to hear something different from her. I want to hear her say that she understands how the Qur'an has touched me. I wish I could grab her heart and soften it so that she could receive the powerful words from the Qur'an that solidified my faith. I wish she could hear the words that I heard when I was first studying the Qur'an. These simple words resonated so profoundly in my heart that I immediately accepted the faith. It is in Surah 112 that Allah speaks of the oneness of God. He says, "Say, 'He is Allah, [who is] One, Allah, the Eternal Refuge. He neither begets nor is born, nor is there to Him any equivalent.'"[3] The idea of God being one, without partner, associate, or any equal felt like such an obvious truth to me.

After hearing this verse, I immediately felt as though my heart had been filled with the truth it had been longing for yet somehow already knew. And so like many believers before me, who heard the words of the prophets of their time, I behaved in the manner mentioned in chapter 2, verse 285, which says,

The Messenger has believed in what was revealed to him from his Lord, and [so have] the believers. All of them have believed in Allah and His angels and His books and His messengers, [saying], "We make no distinction between any of His messengers." And they say, "We hear and we obey. [We seek] Your forgiveness, our Lord, and to You is the [final] destination."[4]

And as I read the rest of the Qur'an, I heard a truth that was undeniable to me. As mentioned in chapter 39, verse 23, of the Qur'an:

Allah has sent down the best statement: a consistent Book wherein is reiteration. The skins shiver therefrom of those who fear their Lord; then their skins and their hearts relax at the remembrance of Allah. That is the guidance of Allah by which He guides whom He wills. And one whom Allah leaves astray—for him there is no guide.[5]

I think of my mom when hearing this verse. I think of her reactions to what I say, and I wonder if her reaching out to me, her desire to talk, is in a way a sign that her heart is opening and becoming more willing to understand me.

I hope we can hear each other and come to terms with each other's beliefs. I hope we can listen to each other, with open hearts, and begin to understand the passion for God that dwells deep in each of our hearts.

Patricia

YOU ARE BEAUTIFUL, O DAUGHTER.

I ponder that when I reflect on Alana. A child of my home. A woman of my heart. A daughter of my faith.

That's still what I hear when I listen to Alana talk about Islam—not a Muslim speaking but a Christian who got lost somehow in Islam. Her words, her voice, her tone, her spirit reflect to me not her new faith but the home she was reared in, the church she was raised in, and the Jesus she first knew.

The one who still pursues her. He doesn't stop. That's what I want to tell her. Long to convince her of, to point her back to the Twenty-third Psalm—a scripture she heard countless times as a child—and its promise that "*surely* goodness and mercy shall follow me all the days of my life: and I will dwell in the house of the LORD forever" (23:6 KJV, emphasis mine).

Goodness and mercy. Surely. *Follow her. Follow her, Lord Jesus.* Come and follow.

I want to say those things to Alana now. But this morning isn't the time. It's a day instead to step back and consider everything. Not to stew in it.

It's early March, almost a year, amazingly, after we first agreed to seek common ground. But I'm knee-deep in common life. It's tax time, and I am trying to render to Caesar. To get our tax returns started—and finished. So Alana's response to my earlier thoughts goes back into its folder on my computer. I know I must give it attention. Yet for many reasons on this day, I don't feel the same worry, irritation, obligation to answer right away, to argue or to persuade her she has it all wrong. To show her that all those statements in the Qur'an strike my ear like a version of the Bible that missed the mark. Which is not proper to say. But that's how I feel. So I write it here, getting it out of my head and onto the paper. I also know, however, that scholars have long surmised that Muhammad heard the Bible—heard, since he apparently couldn't read. Then he appropriated its insight and wisdom as his own revelation. Or that's what scholars say.

And look how I write that. All snide and superior. *Since he apparently couldn't read.*

I seem to see the worst, that is, in Islam and its prophet. Alana longs for the opposite—for ecclesiastical harmony and mutual respect. But whatever is Islam—this religion that introduced itself to my world with 9/11 and now compels my daughter—I'm not feeling one iota of charity today.

Not yet anyway. Alana expects me to link hands, feel peace, and sing "*Kumbaya.*" But I'm not there yet. As a Christian, I know I should be. As a mother, I'm not.

And peace? It's hidden beyond some horizon I can't see.

Instead, I'm working on my taxes today. I'm not a scholar of religion. I'm an American taxpayer trying to finish her 1120S. I'm a struggling vendor worker, trying to outrun the piles of paper rising on my belea-guered desk. I will gain control of this chaos somehow but not today. It feels unconquerable—if that's even a word. So I don't read Alana's last entry again this morning. On purpose, I don't read it. I don't like thinking about things she has said in past statements that feel just wrong. Like her assumption that I've forgotten that Jesus was from the Middle East (that he was a Jew, which she doesn't mention) or that he spoke Aramaic. Or that she thinks my view on Muslims is based on what I see in the media. Or that the Qur'an is trustworthy when it claims that "Allah begets not."

Can anybody look at a sunrise and say Allah begets not? Or a blanket of stars? Or the face of a newborn baby? Or wildflowers in an open field? Or morning dew on spring grass? Or a double rainbow after a summer storm?

Allah begets not? Nor was he begotten? Of course, I know what it means—that Allah is one alone. Still, I read that, shaking my head, think-ing of the theological snarl Alana and I can't seem to untangle—which gets me thinking about atheists. No wonder they think we're all crazy, tied up in knots by this detail or that fact or that claim of our respective and zealous faiths.

But I turn away from such matters today. Instead, I sit back in the chair at my desk, feeling the morning's begotten sun slice through the blinds, warming the room. The sunlight points me to a reminder that no warrior fights battles all the time. And I am weary to my soul of fighting with Alana. More than that, however, it reminds me of the biggest thing of all.

I love her.

To my soul, its deepest parts, with every breath.

I love my child.

So this shouldn't even be a fight. And we shouldn't be warriors. Facing off across a divide. Rattling our spears and sabers. Attacking each other with scriptures and verses from our sacred books, determined to trump one another with what we view as our superior personal faith. Doing the exact opposite of what Paul the apostle urged: to avoid "foolish and stupid arguments." And here's why: "Because you know they produce quarrels" (2 Tim. 2:23).

Boy, do they ever.

No wonder we're getting nowhere fast. Or that's how it's starting to feel. So I know what that means. It's time to pull back. Get quiet. Shut my mouth. Cease my arguing. To "gently" instruct, as Paul advised (v. 25). Then to do the next best thing: let God have it.

I'm saying that, I guess, because I've been reading the Bible more.

I'm doing some freelancing again for *In Touch*, the magazine of Dr. Charles Stanley's In Touch Ministries—and I feel blessed to have the work. So I'm subscribing to the magazine to keep up with its step and flow, recommitting to reading the daily devotions printed at the back of the ministry's magazine. Really reading them. So I'm reading the daily scripture that goes along.

So here I am, after rather random, unguided Bible reading—not the orderly reading I know is best—back now with Jesus. Reading. Studying. Meditating. Abiding. Or trying to abide. So I look at different Scripture translations. Pondering hard as an article in the magazine sends me back to John 6:44, telling me that no one can come to Jesus "unless the Father . . . draws them."

I open my big study Bible, page over to the gospel of John. Find the scripture. Read the whole thing. Go back a few verses, trying to gain context. To hear God good on this. To understand this declaration by Jesus that nobody comes to the Lord without getting called to him *by* the Lord.

So is that my prayer? *Call her, Lord.* Draw her to you, dear Father.

I chew on that for a moment, weary of my questioning and my efforts to figure it all out and pray it up on my own. Just this morning I'd seized on a phrase Dan read from his little Bible app.

"Faith comes by hearing" (Rom. 10:17 NKJV). I know that scripture, but I wrote down the words anyway. That's how my mind is working now. Any little scrap that feels related to our story grabs my attention. So I wrote down the words. Faith comes by hearing. Underlined *hearing*.

Oh, Lord. What a journey.

Nobody comes to Christ "unless the Father who sent me draws them" (John 6:44). So cut the noise, Patricia. This business of interfaith life—of having a son or daughter reject the family faith—requires restraint. Trust. A deep layer of wisdom and common sense.

Thus, my sixty-some years of graced living, working, parenting, and praising are telling me this morning to give it a break. That's what I'm doing on this morning. Stepping back. Taking in a long breath. Enjoying the early morning sunshine, closing my eyes, feeling its beauty and warming goodness. I even congratulate myself a bit.

I'm stepping back. Murmuring not. Letting God be God, which feels great.

Then the phone rings. I check the caller ID, and I smile to myself, trying to pay attention. Because it's Alana, calling early on this Saturday-before-taxes-are-due morning.

"Hi, Mom!" she says.

I smile. I love it when my grown children call me. I absolutely exult in hearing their voices. Did Alexander Graham Bell expect this? That we would rejoice so much in just the sound of a loved one's voice? Still, I hold my breath. She's calling about something. I hear it in her sound. So here it is: "I want to apologize."

"For what?" I ask.

"That article I sent you."

Article? Then I remember. She e-mailed me a piece a few days ago—on reported death threats that some Christians made against a professor at a university in Florida after he'd asked students in his class to stomp on a piece of paper with the word *Jesus* on it.

"I shouldn't have sent it," Alana says. "I wasn't trying to say that Christians do extreme things too."

I listened. Thinking. Hearing. Remembering the article. The professor, following an instructor's guide for the course on intercultural communications, wanted to get his students thinking. About symbols. About the meaning we give the tangible things, in this case, of intangible spiritual life.[6]

"I found it interesting," I said to Alana. I actually was glad she'd sent it. "It's good food for thought," I said, "since we're trying to talk more about faith."

"Right," Alana said, "but we should be looking at us, at ourselves. Our family. At each other. Not at what other people are doing."

I try to hear. But typical for me, I want to hear myself think out loud. About the article. Because I actually enjoyed it. As a onetime university faculty member, I liked looking at the professor's dilemma as an educator. Plus I loved reading the remarks in the comments section. Some angry. Some diplomatic. It was the kind of school-daze dilemma I enjoy,

"We should be talking about us," Alana says.

I open my mouth. Then I close my mouth. *Lord, let me hear.*

"I wish we both could just turn off the TV for thirty days," she said.

I tried to listen. She was saying something that mattered to her— especially since she and her husband don't even have a TV right now—because they don't want their children watching TV commercials. But with laptops, phones, and iPads, the children are exposed anyway to the world and its messages.

And media messages were on Alana's mind this morning. So I sat quiet. Let her talk.

"I think," she said, "it's easy for us Americans to understand that most people in a religion aren't extremists. But when you see it in the media, we think it is representative of the whole group or religion."

I nod. She has said this before, including in her e-mail with the article about the college professor. This matters to her because she knows I have judged Islam, in part, by what I see in the media—images of violence carried out by Muslims around the world.

"It's not the same with Christians," I insist. "Well, the Crusades, no matter how they are measured, were violent. But when you compare Christianity with Islam today, the level of violence against other people just isn't on the same par. Not at all."

I'd given her an example in Nigeria. There, in a place called Jos, Muslims have burned churches, killed pastors, attacked Christians in their homes, and slaughtered thousands in recent years. It makes you sick, forcing reasonable folks to think twice about a religion that spawns such evil, I said.

Alana disagreed. "You can't judge a religion by its followers because they always disappoint you." As for Nigeria, she said, "The conflict is not purely religious, and the Christians are attacking the Muslims as well. It's not only the Muslims doing the horrible violence. But I'm not going to look at either side and judge them because I know that neither Christianity nor Islam promotes that type of behavior."

She pushed her point. "I mean, Mom, if I see Snoop Dogg on TV, rapping some bad song and wearing a cross, I don't think he represents Christians or that all Christians are like that."

I stay quiet. Thinking about what an atheist commented about the college professor and the article: "This whole story, for me, is a perfect analogy of what religion has done to the world."[7]

Religion has divided people. It has split apart families. It has torn apart mothers. Alienated daughters.

So right on cue Alana and I are arguing.

It comes out of nowhere.

I say something, I guess, about Islam. Or maybe Alana says something about Christianity. I remember I asked why Muslims say they "love" Jesus—apparently forgetting what Jesus said about love, namely that "anyone who loves me will obey my teaching." And the result of that obedience through love? "My Father will love them, and we will come to them and make our home with them" (John 14:23).

"But how can you worship him?" Alana asks. "And pray to him?" Her volume climbs a notch. "And how can you think God needs a partner?" she asks. "God doesn't need partners. God is God alone."

I take a deep breath. Diving in. Watching us go down the black hole of interfaith-family conflict. Where no light escapes. Hard as we try, we know exactly where this is headed. Miles from the sunshiny, warm morning I so longed to enjoy. But we've fallen in mouth-first and can't stop.

So I throw out the gospel of John on this point, that point, any point, every point. "In the beginning was the Word, and the Word was *with* God, and the Word *was* God" (John 1:1 NKJV, emphasis mine).

I'm running hot.

"And the Word became *flesh*," I say, hanging on that word, "and dwelt among us, and we beheld His glory, the glory as of the only begotten of the Father, full of grace and truth" (John 1:14 NKJV, emphasis mine).

So stop messing with me, Alana Raybon.

I say that in my head. Appalled to feel this anger at my daughter. Appalled that I can't pull back. Or won't.

Instead, we go on for a good hour. Debating like the irritated readers of the "Jesus stomp" article. Arguing Christianity versus Islam. Islam versus Christianity. Before long, of course, we're debating the Trinity. And it's all making me plain nuts. Why are we doing this?

I try to halt. But I won't.

"You want proof," I observe for Alana. "Proof of Jesus?"

Proof that's he's more than "one of the prophets," as Muslims say. So Alana wants proof he is more than a wise sage. More than a really good guy. More than some odd visionary who said he was God's Son sent from heaven—and, indeed, God who came in the flesh. "Either he is God," I say to Alana, "or he was plain crazy."

But proof? I don't have it. I'm not a theologian. Not a seminary graduate. Not a bona fide Jesus scholar. I'm only a sinner saved.

So I just say—with the confidence of an A. W. Tozer—that when it comes to God, only by "faith and love" do we "enter and lay hold on Him."[8] Tozer quotes the lovely Frederick Faber on this paradox, of knowing God in "tender personal experience" while remaining "aloof from the curious eyes of reason." Thus concludes Faber on Christ: "Darkness to the intellect / But sunshine to the heart."

Proof? Forget it. Faber says, "Just believe the Word and press on."[9]

The apostle Paul offers this: Gently instruct. Especially those who oppose Jesus as the Christ. "In the hope that God will grant them repentance leading them to a knowledge of the truth" (2 Tim. 2:25).

Well, Alana's not having it. So for now, anything I say about Jesus as the Christ will to her sound simple. Maybe even ridiculous. Or not enough. Or not logical. Or not justified. Not even the scriptures I cite are enough for Alana, which shouldn't surprise me because Muslims are taught the Bible has been "changed" and isn't reliable. Never mind the existence of ancient texts of the Bible, as old as dirt, that verify just how accurate the Bible remains. Not to mention the Dead Sea Scrolls.

But Alana doesn't want to hear any of it.

The real truth, then?

Following Jesus is a journey. By faith. Tozer said it way before me. And better. Still, I try to find the words. "So it's not a religion," I finally say as my defense. "It is a faith." Following Jesus is a leap, I say. "The most exciting leap you'll ever take in life."

Even better, I make the leap every day. In this way, every morning feels like a priceless gift. Another day with Jesus. *And what are we doing today, Lord?* I ask. *Teach me. Show me. Lead me. Guide me. Let me walk alongside and discover. Discover with you.*

Yep, it's that relationship thing.

Jesus people love it. Know it. Try to explain it. But on the bottom side of the leap, you can't get it.

I want Alana to get it. To leap. With her husband. Her babies. Their friends.

The next morning at church, my pastor and shepherd—Dr. Timothy E. Tyler—preaches about this same thing. It's the week after Easter, and he's preaching about doubt. On how the disciples saw the resurrected Jesus. "But some doubted."

He's reading from the gospel of Matthew. Preaching like the smart black man that he is. "Any doubters up in here?!"

Folks are on their feet. Shouting "Amen!" Loving the honesty of our Bible.

"Any doubters in *this* place?" Pastor knows the answer. That we doubted when bills weren't paid. When jobs were lost. When Jim Crow got ugly. When we got ugly back. When we got ugly with God. We are loving this message. Some doubted. Indeed. We have doubted. Up to our worries. Down to our questions.

But we know, as my pastor also says, "If your God isn't big enough for your worries *and* your questions, your God isn't big enough."

Some white families from another church are in the audience this Sunday morning. Some of them are on their feet too. Saying amen too. Doubt and questions apparently cross the color line. And my pastor has put the cookies on the shelf, as he likes to say, where everybody can reach them. Any age. Any color. Any doubt.

"Because here's the thing," he says. He's walking the pulpit. Then he suddenly stops. Normal voice. "The best thing about Jesus? You can come to him even *with* your doubt." Even doubt of him.

Scared to leap. But diving anyway. Uncertain about believing. But yielding anyhow. Then you leap. And glory to God. Jesus is already there, arms outstretched, waiting. Catching you. Walking with you. Working with you. Loving you.

So in this post-Easter Matthew story, Jesus doesn't even speak to the doubt problem. Instead, with doubters right there, he starts to preach. Preach to everybody. "Doubters included!" my pastor says. "And what does he preach?"

We know the story. But we love hearing it. So Pastor tells it good—that "Jesus says: Go! Teach! Baptize! In the name of the Father, and of the Son, and of the Holy Ghost." But Pastor isn't finished. Because when we go into the world for Jesus, Pastor reminds us, we don't go alone. So when Jesus says, "I am with you always," that's exactly what he means. "Even," says Pastor, "unto the end of the world" (Matt. 28:20 KJV).

Despite my doubts. Or my daughter's doubts.

So I have to stop arguing and just listen for why she won't yet leap. She says it's because, in Islam, she has found a love for a God who doesn't have partners. Which makes me sad. Because I love and serve a God who calls me friend.

Alana

WHY WON'T I LEAP? BY FAITH? I FEEL LIKE I ALREADY HAVE.

But when I get off the phone with my mom, I realize that we are not acting like people who have taken a leap. People who are content with God in their lives don't spend hours debating theological ideas.

People who have leaped are empathetic.

We're supposed to be listening, my mom and I, to each other—but we're not. Listening requires empathy. Right before I hung up the phone after that exhausting conversation, I asked her a simple question, "Why don't you ever ask me about what I believe?" *Isn't that part of listening*, I thought, *to ask—then listen without throwing in our own opinions, perceptions, or beliefs?*

I'm guilty of that. I know it. I always want to say my two cents and get a word in when we talk. It seems that we both just need to be quiet and try to empathize.

What's the point of all this talking anyway, to convert each other to our faiths—or to understand each other? Isn't that the key element missing in the world—listening? Religion isn't dividing families—it's our inability or unwillingness to empathize.

I am reminded of my elementary students, when teaching them Stephen Covey's seven habits—listening with empathy being the last and hardest for them to understand. One student summed it up so eloquently when she said, "It's like putting on someone's shoes and really trying to *feel* like them for a day."

If fourth graders can try to empathize, then surely my mom and I can.

And so now here's our chance, in a few hundred pages or less, to say what we can while we "seek first to understand, then to be understood," as Covey puts it.[10] We have to give each other the chance to speak, though, without putting in our own two cents or thinking about what we are going to say in reply. Real listening requires the listener to silence his or her own thoughts while hearing the speaker. This is how we will mend our division.

Mom's response to my question?

"Well, to tell the truth, Alana, I'm not that interested in Islam. But I'll try to write down some questions to ask you."

I was a little hurt by that remark because I didn't mean that I wanted her to ask me Islam 101 questions. I want her to try to understand me. I want her to appreciate that although we differ in our beliefs, I have every right to proclaim to have a relationship with God, just as she does.

I stew over this for a moment and get ready to write down all the questions I wish she would ask. And then she calls. It's a Saturday, and as usual, my toddler and almost five-year-old are eager to contribute to the discussion. I'm shouting over them and trying to hear what she has to say. I can hear worry and uneasiness in her voice. She is frustrated because our writing feels negative. She's not sure we're heading in the right direction. She doesn't think we're listening either.

It seems as though God has intervened with us at the right moment, like he always does. He's put both my mom and me on the same page. He's slowed us down and woken us up. I express my desire to listen as well as share my thoughts about empathy. It hits right at home for Mom, and I can feel a sense of relief in her voice. I don't want to give up, and I know that she doesn't either.

And so as readers of books by Covey—yes, a Mormon—we both decide to try to apply what we've learned. We have to ask each other about our experiences and then listen without trying consciously or sub-consciously to think about all the rebuttals we're going to make. I have to listen intently and sincerely until she feels like she has been understood.

I'm excited because I know it's going to make her feel great. She loves talking about her faith and sharing it with others. I know it will be an affirming experience for both of us.

And then, as untimely as ever, my husband returns from work and mumbles something about the bomb in Boston. "What bomb?" I ask, stunned. My heart stops its beating. I hadn't read the news all day, and since we don't have TV, I hadn't seen anything about the Boston Marathon tragedy. I open the news on my phone and immediately feel sick to my stomach. A sour taste begins to form in my mouth. Two dead, one an eight-year-old boy, and many more maimed and hurt.

My shock turns into worry. Although I don't want my mind to lead me down this path, I can't help but worry that if the bomber is a Muslim, the backlash will be terrible. I begin to breathe quickly. I don't think that I can take another ten years of being the villain in the news. I didn't experience many problems after 9/11, but because I wear a *hijab*, I feel constantly in the spotlight, under the microscope. Maybe I'm paranoid, or I read too much news on the Internet, but I always feel like I'm being dissected and analyzed by onlookers when I leave the house.

My heart grieves for the parents of the eight-year-old boy, who I'm sure never imagined having to bury their child. I look at my children and cannot imagine the pain those parents must be feeling. All the while the feeling of dread continues to creep up inside me as the authorities get closer to identifying the bombers.

I keep checking the news for updates. Then I see one news outlet mention that the bombers' identities will be revealed at five p.m. I check my phone. It's 4:45. The minutes tick by like hours. As I read the report my heart drops. The revelation affects me instantly. I'm angry at first because each new suicide bombing or act of extremism tarnishes the image of Islam that I know and live. Then I'm frustrated because I want to do something immediately to polish the perception of Islam. I want to erase the negative view of Islam so many people now have.

I don't want to leave the house, and every time I reluctantly do, I think, *Does everyone think that I am like that?* Every weird look makes me wonder, every questionable glance makes me hold my breath, praying the person won't say something rude or, God forbid, try to hurt me and my children. "They're not us!" my husband proclaims, referring to the bombers. He tries to convince me to quit worrying about what other people think and just be myself.

I don't speak to my mom during this time. I think I'm afraid to call her. I know she is confused and upset—just as I am. She makes a comment on her Facebook page about how she and my dad are reading about Chechen history, which spills over into a heated debate beneath her Chechen post. The commenters spew out bunches of angry statements about all kinds of crazy, unrelated topics. My mom intercedes to try to diffuse the argument. Through her words, I sensed what she was doing. She wasn't defending the bombers, she wrote in her post, just trying to widen her understanding of the world around her.

After a week or so the phone rings. It's my dad calling because he's cleaning out the basement and wants to send my daughter Laila all of my old Barbie stuff they had saved. We talk politely, on and on, about the usual small-talk stuff. But, as usual, the elephant remains in the room, staring us down and asking why we're not talking about the bombings.

I know my mom doesn't want to bring them up either. Maybe she's not sure what exactly to say, as if she'll come off as insensitive. I send her a documentary, based on a Gallup Poll study, about the Muslim world. It puts the extremist percentage of the Muslim population at 7 percent.[11] She thanks me for sending it and says that it was interesting.

Another week or so later we talk again. I tell her how I was stuck, frozen in time after the bombings. Unable to proceed with our project because of the tragedy and even more traumatized to discover that our family members—on my husband's side and my own—had expressed concern that our faith might lead us to do something radical. Their comments were based on fear that surfaced after watching media outlets question how some normal teenage American kids could become radicalized.

It was so shocking to me that our families would think we could ever do something so incredibly horrific. That people who have known us our whole lives could even begin to worry that we might become murderers was heartbreaking to me. I was speechless, and crushed by this revelation. I thought of my husband, who has dedicated his entire career to integrating the Muslim community into America and working toward interfaith and multicultural relationships. I thought about myself and how I had spent the past nine years of my life teaching America's children and raising my own. And then I thought of the many verses of the Qur'an that clearly describe the sanctity of life and forbid the taking of life, even our own.

It became obvious that the division in our family was not just between Mom and me but encompassed my father and sister, and it was in my husband's family as well. A whole herd of elephants was trampling through the rooms of our immediate and extended families, and no one was tackling them head on, except Mom and me.

This can't be good. We can't be the only ones trying to heal this rift while everyone else is either ignoring the problem or pretending it doesn't exist.

I read an article about a non-hijab–wearing Pakistani American woman who, while attending the White House correspondence cocktail party, was treated rudely by the door security. After crying and ranting about her frustration with people who unfairly judged her, she eventually decided not to let it get to her anymore. That if the world doesn't want to give her a chance, it is their problem, not hers.

This hits me hard, and it begins to hurt. I start to feel the last ten years of being scorned, not just by the media but also by my family. Mom in particular. I feel upset; despite all the positive things my husband and

I try to do in our lives, and despite a lot of crazy stuff other family members have done, we are still the black sheep of our families.

I realize that it has affected me and my self-esteem. It hurts to think that all of the good that I have tried to do in my life seems trivial in my mom's eyes because of my faith. I think about each article she has written, sections of books and lectures done on topics relating to me and my decision to convert. I realize that I am tired of being disapproved of and shunned as the poster child for what, in her eyes, was a failed attempt to raise me as a Christian.

And so we go through another spell of not talking. I'm avoiding her again because I don't know how to tell her how I feel. I can tell in her voice mails that she knows something is up. I call her back but decide not to bring it up. A mother's intuition kicks in, though, and she asks me what's wrong. I tell her about my hurt, and she listens. She's really listening, although it's hard, and acknowledges my feelings. It feels good to be heard. I know she is trying to empathize. She is hurt, too, and has been for years. I realize what we are doing and how far we have come. We're listening to each other, we're hearing each other, and that gives me hope.

"So do you want to stop?" she asks. I reply with a definitive no. I want to continue but in a more positive way. I want to step out of the divide and begin healing the rift. I want us to become the model for a successful, happy interfaith family. Getting out of the ditch we were in will take a while, but I'm more than willing to hold my mom's hand and climb with her.

three

FAMILY MATTERS. WELL, DOESN'T IT?

Patricia

OF COURSE, IT'S RAINING NOW. RAINING HARD. POURING LIKE crazy. No mercy. Another soggy, rainy day in Big Sky Colorado—where we count it a divine right to get three hundred days of sunshine a year. A rainy day in Colorado? Looks wrong. Feels wrong. Is wrong—so wrong that on cloudy days in Colorado, the roadways are filled with drivers shining their high-beam lights. And if it's raining too? Folks get downright offended at the sun, that it failed to shine—high beams notwithstanding.

So during this summer and early fall of 2013, with one cloudy, rain-soaked day following the next—or that's how it feels—the sun-starved people of Colorado are driving through the days with lights on bright, but not too happy about it.

That includes our house painter guy. He's called to put off, again, painting the wood siding on the home of my beloved late mother. Mama lived nearby, a quick five minutes from where Dan and I live, and even after ten years' gone, I still miss her. But that's emotional stuff. On a practical level, and on this day, her house needs a good painting.

"Too wet," the painter tells me. He sounds grouchy.

"I understand," I say. I'm not angry.

I'm just trying to be a good daughter. Mama was big on home maintenance. No raggedy grass. No dirty windows. No unpainted siding. If God blessed you and your people with something as materially wonderful as your own house, you and your people had better take care of it. That's just how she saw things.

So that's my role now. Trying to take care of her house. To do right by family. To honor what my parents worked a lifetime to build—that's now in my hands to keep and protect. Or that's how this painting project feels. Less about home maintenance. More about family.

Except it keeps raining. And it won't stop.

And I haven't talked to Alana.

So I turn to something I can control—or think I can. I'm on the schedule to teach next week's adult Sunday school class. Topic: God's Rainbow Covenant with Noah. A rain story. A flood story. Like most of us in the class, I already know the Noah story. Or think I know.

Yet I can't wrestle out a hook. Something to ignite class discussion. Something, again, to honor Mama and Daddy, who took me to Sunday school every single Sunday of my growing-up life. So *surely*, as good Psalm 23 says, I ought to know enough to wrestle out the Noah hook.

I flip through lessons from *Precepts for Living*. Scour my *NLT Study Bible*. Plant myself in the book of Genesis and read chapters 6, 7, 8, and 9—word by word, line by line. Read stuff on the Internet. Make notes in a spiral notebook. Listen to Dan's assurances that my teaching "will be fine." Finally I fall asleep on a Thursday night with my notes and Bible piled high on my nightstand.

Around midnight, I wake up. Listening.

Rain.

Well, this is more than drizzle rain. This is wild rain. Gushing. Gurgling. Pounding. All at once from the skies. And "all the fountains of the great deep were broken up, and the windows of heaven were opened" (Gen. 7:11 NKJV). God unlocked the oceans and the skies.

Didn't it rain, children?[1]

In the Spirituals Project Choir, a community, interfaith choir in Denver in which Dan and I used to sing, we belted out that song with strong confidence and love.

Didn't it rain, children! Rain all night long!

In fact, the storm on this night was downright biblical. That's what the TV newspeople kept saying the next morning. "A *biblical* rain." Sounding dramatic. "A thousand-year flood." Gripping microphones. Wearing their TV-news storm gear. Standing in front of devastation that shouldn't ever happen anywhere on God's green earth. But in pretty Colorado, with our three-hundred days of sunshine and our pretty wildflowers and our clear mountain creeks trickling through picturesque mountain ravines, the biblical rain turned creeks into raging wrath.

Many Coloradans died. Swept away. Drowned. Gone too soon. Too fast.

Tens of thousands of homes were damaged, many washing away all in a piece. Here one minute then gone. Forever. Total property loss was $2 billion plus.

The phone rings. It's early. Barely dawn. The rain still wild. I look at the caller ID. It's our tenants at Mama's house. I draw a deep breath and pick up the phone.

"Hi, Shweta," I say, whispering, holding my breath. Knowing something is wrong.

Shweta is a beautiful engineer who lives with her engineer husband—both thriving immigrants from India—and their adorable three-year-old daughter. But right now, Shweta is frantic.

"It's raining inside your house!"

Lord Jesus. Mama's house. I sit up straight.

Listening to Shweta tell about the rain pouring. "It won't stop!" Raining into the basement. Right through the basement windows.

Into my *Mama*'s special place. Her Christmas place.

Yes. I'm thinking about Christmas in a wild September rainstorm because Mama kept her Christmas—as she called her lights, glitter, manger scene, tree stands, garlands, and all of it—in her basement. That stash was family.

So when Mama carried that glass nativity scene up from the basement every year, tinsel dragging happily behind her, Mama was carrying up family.

"Is this your house?"

My house? It's a short while later, and the handyman we contacted is calling from Mama's. Still raining biblically outside. He sounds drenched.

"Not much I can really do here." He tries to explain: "The ground is soaked. Just can't hold any more water."

So rain is pouring into Mama's basement from *under* the window wells. Shweta's husband is using buckets, pails, bowls, whatever he can find, to shovel up rainwater, climb the basement steps, slosh through the living room, and pour water out the front door. Dan is rushing us to get to Mama's, but I'm standing with the phone in my hand, not moving. I can't face it. *Rain, rain, go away.*

"The storm is stalled," says the handyman.

The storm that won't move. No end in sight.

"Nothing I can do for you." I hear him sigh. "I'm real sorry, ma'am."

I'm sorry, too, because when I open our basement door, water is also gushing into a northside window of our house. The hand of God pouring down rain like nobody's business.

In the Noah story, when it started to rain, Noah had been sitting in the ark first for seven days. No rain. Waiting. But he wasn't alone. All those animals and birds and creepy crawlies were locked inside with him. But so was Noah's family. And I struggled to pay attention.

This old Bible story is about rain, for sure. But more than rain, it's about kin.

As old Genesis says, "This is the account of Noah *and his family*" (6:9, emphasis mine).

Because that's how faith works. As family.

That's not me talking. That's God. "Look! I am about to cover the earth with a flood that will destroy every living thing that breathes. Everything on earth will die. But I will confirm my covenant with you" (vv. 17–18 NLT).

So, therefore, God tells Noah, "Enter the boat—*you and your wife and your sons and their wives.* Bring a pair of every kind of animal—a male and a female—into the boat with you to keep them alive during the flood. Pairs of every kind of bird, and every kind of animal, and every kind of small animal that scurries along the ground, will come to you to be kept alive. And be sure to take on board enough food *for your family* and for all the animals" (vv. 18–21 NLT, emphasis mine).

Then what happened?

"So Noah did everything exactly as God had commanded him" (v. 22 NLT).

Oh, this story. It's about God. It's about obedience. It's about rain. It's about *one family.*

And in our one family, Mama's Christmas was stored for years in the now flooding basement. My stomach churned at the thought of it.

Christmas was big to Mama because when she was a child, it served as her birthday. Born the day after Christmas to her truck driver father and her homemaker mother, Mama knew any birthday gift among her five siblings was precious. But a birthday gift around Christmas—during the Great Depression—was downright priceless.

Still, each of Mama's beloved four siblings—two brothers and two sisters—managed to get a gift from their parents on their birthdays. Not a fancy gift, of course. But at least a piece of chocolate because their dad drove a truck for a candy company. (And to tell the truth, sometimes he brought home "extra" pieces.) But on Mama's birthday?

"It was just so close to Christmas," Mama always explained.

So no birthday candy. No little party. No purloined chocolates. Instead, like her siblings on Christmas Day, she got one orange and one apple, plus they each got one pair of shoe skates—their transportation around town for the upcoming year.

Then Christmas Day ended. Apples eaten. Oranges peeled and devoured. Everybody happy and filled with turkey and feeling warm and grateful. But the next day? Mama's birthday? Nothing.

"Well, it was so close to Christmas. Really it was," Mama explained.

Indeed. She wasn't bitter. But she had worked so hard her entire life, especially after her beloved daddy died in a trucking accident when she was just twelve years old—and her mama had to find work as a house-maid. Mama did day work to pay her way through college. When she finally graduated, getting a teaching job up in fancy Westchester County, New York, Mama earned her first, real, regular paycheck. And *then* Mama could have Christmas. *And* her birthday too.

She made the season her own. It was her own time of year, and anybody who knew my hardworking mother and may be reading this now will be nodding and agreeing. Mama and her Christmas were one.

So at Christmas, her house that Shweta now lives in with her family—this house that needs painting and is getting flooded—would be dripping in holiday lights. Front door to back. Roof to sidewalk. Mama's random and ever-growing collection of unrelated holiday lights of every color and size and shape draped her house. Her front door. The fireplace mantel. The dining room table. Kitchen counter. Bathrooms. Bedrooms. Foyer. Staircase. Any otherwise clear surface was fair game.

And Mama couldn't be happier.

But we all were happier then. Weren't we? It was Christmas. Who doesn't love Christmas? The baby Jesus. The wise men. The star in the East. Our God Incarnate. The Savior. The Light of the World. In a summer when it's flooding where it's not supposed to rain—and high-beam lights don't really compensate—and Christmas is a season that embodies family like no other, what now shall I do?

Why, indeed, does it matter to me so much? This longing to keep Mama's basement dry, the lights twinkling, and our family's traditions alive and going?

After the flood and the basement cleanup and the digging of new landscaping around Mama's house and the building of sump pumps and drainage systems and the putting back together of everything, I typed the question to Google. Why does family—and why do family traditions— matter so much?

For an answer, a psychologist answered: family traditions protect us.

If you look at the way rituals developed, said this psychologist, "they really served to protect the family from the forces of the outside industrial world that was pulling them apart."[2]

I nod. Thank you, Dr. Barbara Fiese, the psychologist.

In that way, said the doctor, holiday traditions are glue.

Tradition says we *are* a family.

So now, looking at my household, what are we? People who don't do Christmas? People who don't store Christmas in the basement? Thinking about Mama and her flooded basement and our dying Christmas tradition, I feel lost and off-kilter and angry too.

I want Christmas back.

Even more, I want Christ back in the center.

Because he comes before everything. That's what Paul told that early church—the one at Colossus. "He is before all things, and in him," Paul wrote, "all things hold together" (Col. 1:17).

And that's what I want. Jesus holding us together as family. It's what I desire. For family to matter. For family not to die on my watch.

Isn't that what Jesus meant? Nailed on a Roman cross, what was his first concern? His mama. *Take care of her.* He spoke those words to his disciple John. "Behold, your mother!" Don't you dare leave her out in the rain. "And from that hour," the scripture says, "the disciple took her to his own home" (John 19:27 ESV).

And likewise, Noah went into the ark with his household. Because in an evil world God was pleased with this Noah, "a righteous man, the only blameless person living on earth at the time" (Gen. 6:9 NLT). So God blessed Noah to get in the ark, not alone but with his family. Even the brazen and squabbling relatives too.

Because without them Noah would be not quite whole. Because family matters. And so do family traditions. And family beliefs.

And the rotating lights and the plastic Santa singing "Rockin' Around the Christmas Tree" that Mama bought from one of the zillion Christmas catalogs she got every year in the mail. And the church—our praying ground. And the gospel songs we sang. And the baby Jesus in the manger. And the faith in him that was real, sustaining our little clan across time and pain and deliverance.

It all mattered. And it matters. Well, doesn't it?

That's what I will ask Alana.

If it doesn't, I'm left in the flood, trying to do the next best thing. Trying to honor Mama and Daddy and the faith of our fathers and the baby Jesus by at least painting the siding on Mama's blessed house and wrestling out the right hook in the Noah story.

Because, indeed, who else but a family of God can stop rain?

Alana

DOES FAMILY MATTER?

I should answer that now. But it's bedtime at my house in Texas, and the ritual of family commences. My children are scrubbed clean, teeth brushed, hair shampooed, and wearing fresh pajamas. The younger son decided on his matching *Star Wars* set—my elder daughter, her purple-and-pink ice-cream-cone pj's. Hair has been brushed and socks are on. "Pick a book!" I yell down the hall as I slowly coach my newly walking one-year-old along. She babbles happily and waddles with me, holding my hand as we go. She knows it's time to read and settle down for the night. She enjoys this treasured time together as much as my other kids.

"Laila, do you have your book?" I ask. The room has already been tidied from the day's fun, but there are still remnants of playtime on the floor. My daughter's super-fancy white dress from my mom—the one Laila wears to her tea parties—plus a couple of stuffed elephants the baby loves, along with three or four cars strewn here or there, cover the floor. I quickly scoop it all up, toss everything into the nearest basket, and hang up Laila's dress.

"What about you, Noah? Did you pick a book?" My son, with his usual toy car in hand, hops over to the bookshelf. This particular December night the children are choosing from our own stash. We recently returned the forty or so library books that we check out every two weeks, and we haven't had time to check out more. But since our Islamic school is off during the Christmas holidays, we will have plenty of time to go.

Tonight, the children choose from the stash of books that have been read and reread many times in our house. "This one!" Noah exclaims excitedly, holding up his book. He's picked one of his favorites, *Noah's Ark*.

We've already read it at least fifteen times. Noah loves this book because of the pop-ups. The cute animals spring out of the book and wiggle around when you tug them. It's remarkable that so many of the pieces are still in the book, considering how much the book has been loved.

"All right!" I say and plop down beside him on the floor. The baby waddles over, snuggles into my lap, and immediately goes to work on her bottle. Before I open the book, I pause and ask, "Do you know who Noah is?"

My daughter, very well-versed in religion for a five-year-old, pipes up from across the room. "A prophet!" she yells. I give her my let-Noah-answer-the-question look. I realize that I haven't ever explained the book to him.

"What's a prophet?" I ask Noah.

He looks at me innocently and smiles. He doesn't know.

"A prophet is sort of like a mailman, but he brings a message from Allah," I say slowly.

Noah smiles, his eyes lighting up.

"Do you know the message that Noah gave to his people?"

Noah shakes his head.

I continue. This time Noah's face is eager. Laila is too immersed in writing in her diary on her bed to answer this question for him. "He wanted people to worship Allah alone and to be good to each other."

"Yay!" Noah responds, excited.

"And so," I continue, "Allah told Noah that he was going to wash away all the disobedient people from the earth and that Noah had to build an ark to be safe from the flood."

"Oh, like this!" Noah says and points to the cover. It has a picture of an old, gray-bearded man, standing in front of an ark, surrounded by an assortment of smiling animals.

At this point my husband, Iesa, comes in, ready to participate in the nighttime routine.

"I want Daddy to read it!"

Noah jumps off my lap and immediately hops right into his dad's. They commence reading the story, but this time I think Noah is listening even more.

The book we own tells this story from a Christian perspective. So as we read, we change bits and pieces here and there to fit our Islamic understanding of the tale. According to the Qur'anic version of the events, Noah warned his people for many years until he finally asked God to bring an end to the disbelief that had spread over the earth.[3] He boarded the ark with his family and a few believers in his community, but one of his sons remained behind.[4]

As I listen to my husband read the story, I realize how far my mother and I are from understanding each other. In her view all of Noah's family believed and were saved. But in my understanding, Noah's family was torn apart. A division occurred among them, and Noah had to choose.

When faced with choosing God or the disbelievers in his family, Noah chose God. My mom thinks I chose to divide the family, but I chose to follow my heart.

The Qur'an explains the moment in which Noah's son was lost in the waves.

> And it sailed with them through waves like mountains, and Noah called to his son who was apart [from them], "O my son, come aboard with us and be not with the disbelievers." [But] he said, "I will take refuge on a mountain to protect me from the water." [Noah] said, "There is no protector today from the decree of Allah, except for whom He gives mercy." And the waves came between them, and he was among the drowned. (Qur'an 11.42–43)[5]

Noah and his son had a mountain of water between them, separating them from each other and tearing them apart. Similarly, my mother and I are calling to each other, trying to get the other to understand, yet the divide remains. My mother doesn't understand that I didn't choose to divide our family. I chose a path. A path that allows me to worship God alone. My mother claims that I'm not following my ancestors' religion, but I beg to differ. I follow my fathers of faith—Adam, Noah, Abraham, Isaac, and Jacob. Their families were angry with them as well, for tearing the family apart and not following their families' faith. The communities in which these prophets lived were angered also. It seemed as if mother was turning against daughter, and son turning against father, all because of belief.

The Qur'an mentions many examples of community members lamenting the divisions that were forming in their families. In chapter 14, verse 10 of the Qur'an, Allah addresses mankind by refuting an argument made by people opposed to the messages of the prophets:

> Their messengers said, "Can there be doubt about Allah, Creator of the heavens and earth? He invites you that He may forgive you of your sins, and He delays your death for a specified term." They said, "You are not

but men like us who wish to avert us from what our fathers were worshipping. So bring us a clear authority."[6]

A divide existed in families after Noah's time, during the prophet eras of Abraham, Lot, Joseph, and Muhammad. Each man was faced with a family member who didn't believe and who was angered that the "religion of our forefathers" was not followed by the prophet. In verse 74 of chapter 6 in the Qur'an, Abraham questioned his father's worship of idols, pleading with him to worship God alone. "And [mention, O Muhammad], when Abraham said to his father Azar, 'Do you take idols as deities? Indeed, I see you and your people to be in manifest error.'"[7]

I understand how much traditions such as Christmas mean to my mother. I get how important Christmas was to my grandmother, and I know that my mom desperately wants me to share her faith. But what she doesn't get is that just like every other human being on this earth, I have a right to follow my heart. I have a right to find my path with God even if it differs from hers. I don't mean to hurt her feelings, and I am not trying to disrespect our ancestors.

Story time is over, and my husband and I take turns snuggling with the kids and tucking them in. This time I tell Noah an exciting story about Lightning McQueen as he lies sleepily in his blue race car bed and stares up at the automobile decals on his wall. On cue, the baby says, "Done!" which indicates that it's her time to be put to bed. We switch off the light and leave the room.

A few nights before this one, Mom had called with my sister, Joi. They wanted to brainstorm about a time when we all could reunite, creating a new tradition of getting together.

"Since Christmas is out," my mother states in a matter-of-fact voice, "we need to create a new time to meet up."

Is Christmas really out? I question myself. I don't remember actually stating that my family and I would not get together with the rest of our families on Christmas. But we rarely all get together anymore anyway, at least, not all of us at the same time.

It used to be nice, spending Christmas with my family in our warm house in Colorado. The snow was always thick and white outside our windows. The house was filled with the warm glow of the tree with lots of brightly wrapped gifts underneath—some marked "From Santa" in my dad's handwriting. There was love involved. The smell of Christmas dinner and eggnog filled the house. Then we'd open the presents, and I'd get tons of toys, many of which were on my ridiculously long Christmas list.

It must be hard for Mom, to be alone with Dad on this treasured holiday. They've resorted to spending it with friends of the family. I feel a twinge of guilt that I'm not there. But then I think, *If I were there during this holiday, who would I be aiming to please?* My mom will not be at ease until I share her faith. And so, as I sit down to write this on Christmas Day, I realize that we are physically and spiritually a world apart.

Patricia

WHEN YOU'RE IN A STORM, GET IN THE ARK.

That's the first thing I learned from Noah.

So that's where I go—crawling into the bosom of Jesus, hungry for comfort, looking for answers. After a rainy fall filled with repairs to Mama's basement, including dirt grading around the home's foundation, I want to take a breather. Or try. But all my Christmas emotions are running high, threatening to take me over the edge. I'm primed to react as I have these last several years ever since Alana converted. Moping around. Feeling lousy. Missing my grandkids. Missing my daughters. Longing to see them all gathered around a family Christmas tree. Singing "Silent Night" and reading the Christmas story and being joyful together, the children's little faces aglow. But that won't happen. Not this year. So this year I vow to wrestle a victory.

I sign up with my husband for Christmas caroling at our church, which is less about singing in tune and more about visiting home-bound seniors who like the caroling and company. Led by our Visitation Ministry pastor, our group presents a Christmas stocking filled with fruit and nuts to each senior. We visit awhile, and then we end with singing carols. We follow the same order at the retirement home next door to our church—even helping the church-sponsored Girl Scout troop serve Christmas dinner to the residents. Stay busy, in other words. That's how I will deal with Christmas. Praying that being busy will carry me through the holiday.

But I'm sulking and trying to hide it. Dan isn't. "Make a wreath," he tells me. I know what he means. Making wreaths at Christmas has been my hobby for years. But not just any old wreaths. I pile on the Christmas. Candy canes. Santa dolls. Angels. Glass ornaments. Glittery this and that. The more sparkle and thingamabobs the better. So my Christmas wreaths are steroidal. And I've loved, absolutely loved, making wreaths for people and sharing them. Selling them sometimes. Giving them away more often.

So make a wreath, Dan says. I understand. It's a week until Christmas, and our house in Colorado is still bare of any sign. I pull out a miniature gingerbread house—a gift from a family friend after Mama died—set it up on a table, and plug it in. It looks a little mopey too—especially compared to Mama's excess. But the little lights in the little windows shine on, making me smile. I call our friend who gave us the house, checking in for the first time since last Christmas. And embarrassed about it.

But she laughs, knowing why I'm calling. "Oh, it's great to hear your voice."

"Yours too," I say. I tell her I just plugged in the little house and thank her for her Christmas card. We talk about our mothers, now both in heaven, watching down. When I hang up, I call a few more people. "Merry Christmas!" The words sound right. People love hearing it. Most people? I believe so.

So I will make a wreath.

Never mind it's like pulling teeth. But I get in the ark. Reflect on Jesus. Mary's little baby. He's at the center of our family problems anyway. Because of him "I can't say merry Christmas to you," Alana tells me. As she puts it, "It would be like encouraging your faith in something I don't believe."

I nod, trying to listen to this argument. But when you get in the ark with him, everything looks different. Better. Maybe even ordained. For certain, that is, I miss Christmas as a family. But I take comfort in knowing the Comforter.

In that way, even when the storm is shaking and rolling, I find a home at the feet of Christ, hearing a Christ promise. That in this world, you will have trouble. Or as Eugene Peterson, that robust theologian, argues, we're each and ever on a battlefield. In fact, we were chosen by God for it. "Chosen out of the feckless stream of circumstantiality for something important that God is doing," Peterson says.[8]

And what is God doing?

"God is out to win the world in love," Peterson declares. "There is no neutral ground in the universe. Every square foot of space is contested."[9]

So we each get our portion of trouble. In spite of it, says Jesus, "Be of good cheer!" (Matt. 14:27 NKJV). Despite everything, have hope. "I have overcome the world" (John 16:33 NKJV). Inside of families. Outside of families. Jesus overcomes.

And my job? To accept the second thing I learn from Noah: when God makes a promise, count on it. Seated at the feet of Christ, that is, I start to see.

I will never get from Alana the satisfaction of a faith decision for Christ. Even if and when she returns to the family of Christ, my hope should be not in her but in him.

And that's how I revive my Christmas. Well, it's how I start. By understanding that the first way for a Christian to have Christmas is to receive it from Christ. To receive his birth, then live like I opened the gift. In the storm. Which may sound like a cliché. But that's how I prayed it on this Christmas. *I receive you, Jesus. In the storm.*

So just love, Patricia.

And trust me.

And make your doggone wreath.

So I make it. And it's gorgeous. Oversized plastic glory. Covered in shiny, red thingamabobs. Candy canes and gingerbread houses and little packages wrapped in shiny red foil. Not one environmental anything about it. Mama would've loved it. I love it, too, especially the new Christmas balls that won't break if you drop one. Thank you, Hobby

Lobby. And forgive me, environmentalists of the world. Just this one time, please.

The big wreath glitters on the brick aside our garage door. Dan helps me tie it down, safe from wind, rain, and stormy, raging downpours.

I post a photo of it on my Facebook page. "Ran out of red thingabobs for my wreath. But I still like the way it turned out."

Folks love it. Even though I spelled *thingamabobs* wrong.

"It looks great!"

"BEAUTIFUL!"

"Great job, Miss Pat!"

Then we had Christmas. I bought gifts, as usual, for all our grand-children—but didn't add "Merry Christmas" to the gift tags. In return, I got photos and videos from Alana on my cell phone of all my little progeny wearing their new Christmas outfits, loving on their new dolls, showing off their toy cars, and saying "I love you, Grammy."

So the storm didn't take me down.

And that's the Noah story hook. That's how I taught it in Sunday school. That God promised: *Never again.* I won't send a storm that takes you down. That wipes you out. That scrapes what I've poured into you off the face of the earth.

In phone calls I had promised Alana I would respect the boundaries she deserves as an adult. How? I would do it by letting Christ be Christ. And Christmas be Christmas. By letting him overcome the world with his love.

That's how I went singing on the Christmas caroling night. With his love, we stopped at one senior citizen's apartment or home after another. Denying the snow and cold. Bringing love. In one high-rise place, an eighty-seven-year-old church member showed off her family's genealogy —a painting of her family tree hanging on her living room wall.

Pointing to one son, she said, "And this is my middle son and his family. He follows that fat man. What's his name?"

"Fat man?" my husband asked.

"You know the one," she said, raising an eyebrow.

"Oh!" Dan said. "Buddha."

"Yes." She shrugged. "He follows Buddha."

Then she pointed to another son. "And this is my youngest son and his family. He's a—what do you call it? Muslim. He's a Muslim."

I listened, nodding. Not responding. And on it went—her litany of adult children who'd made their own choices of faith. Finally I asked: "So how do you deal with that?" I pointed to the photos. "With your children—your family members—leaving the church?"

This aging mother laughed. Standing in her apartment, ready to sing Christmas carols, she stood next to her family-tree picture and laughed, telling me an aging mother's answer.

"I don't deal with that, honey. God deals with that." She shrugged. "I did what I was supposed to do. Took them to Sunday school. Took them to church. Sent them all to college. Every single one of my children has a college education. This one is a doctor. I did my duty. So when I stand on Judgment Day before almighty God, I have nothing to fear. I took them to Christ. They turned Christ down. That's not on me, honey. That's on them."

Does she still see them?

"Oh, yes. We'll get together on Christmas Day. We'll have dinner together." She and the children she prayed for from birth in the name of Jesus will come home. At her table, however, they won't bow their heads to acknowledge her faith or Jesus' name. "And that hurts," she admitted.

Still, I envisioned her then. Not skipping a beat. Letting Jesus calm that storm. And she'll roll on. She'll love. In the same way that she gestures me to her dining room and says, "C'mon, honey. Let's sing!"

We help the aging mother to a chair of honor, borrowed from her kitchen table. The pastor presents her with a Christmas stocking. Gives her a communion wafer and grape juice. We all pray together. Then our little band of carolers sings "Silent Night." A couple of other sweet songs follow, "The First Noel" and "Joy to the World" for starters.

Then, burrowing into our coats, preparing to go out into the cold night, we sing "Go Tell It on the Mountain." The strongest voice in the room is the aging mother's.

"Go tell it on the mountain! That Jesus Christ is born!"

He is born, the Scripture says, to take on the waves that would kill us. To calm even the waves we've stirred up. To be God—so we won't push folks away trying to be God ourselves. Especially in storms.

I send a text to Alana: Thanks for the pix! Love you guys!
I mean every word. Will she believe me? Jesus will help her to know.
One Christmas down. An eternity to go.
Joy to the world!
Oh, yes, Jesus is.

------------------------------ *Alana* ------------------------------

IT'S CHRISTMAS DAY, AND I HAVE A HEAVY HEART. HAVE I CAUSED all of these problems? I can't help but wonder if I am the one who is at fault. A twinge of guilt sets into my heart as this thought resonates.

I haven't felt guilty on Christmases before this one, but for some reason, today especially, my mother's statements are stuck in my mind. Her repeated frustration and sadness for being without family on this holiday are directed at me. Am I the one who is breaking the family apart? The lone, frazzled string that won't stay interwoven with the rest? I can't help but feel bad.

A few nights before this one, when Mom called with my sister, Joi, she seemed so certain when she said, "Christmas is out." Maybe she's right after all. Thinking about our family void makes me feel empty.

A visit to a friend's lunch party on Christmas Day adds to my pain. Somehow the topic of my family dilemma comes up. The women encourage me to at least call my mother on Christmas Day. Some say I should visit. They don't understand. None of them come from interfaith families. It all seems so easily fixed in their eyes.

I regret telling Mom that I went to that party. It came stumbling out of my mouth during our phone conversation. I could hear the hurt in her voice as she asked why I could spend time with friends on that day and not her.

So I ask myself, *why don't I celebrate the Christmas season with my family?* Why is it so hard for me to wish Mom a merry Christmas or a happy holiday? I have Muslim friends who send out Christmas greetings, love to sing Christmas songs, and tour the city's display of lights. These are friends whose families are Muslim, of course. Am I so intolerant that

I can't even call on her special day and wish her the best? Why can't I shake that feeling I have inside about encouraging something fundamentally wrong? That somehow, by expressing a desire for her to enjoy her holiday, I'm admitting that I endorse it.

Christmas was a treasured holiday in our house when I was growing up, but so were Thanksgiving and the Fourth of July. We had traditions that we stuck to and repeated every year. They made me feel safe, together, and whole. They were normal, and what everybody in my close-knit, African American community was doing.

Then Christmas Day would end, and the regular routine would set into place. Dance practice, school, and ice-skating lessons. The normal stuff many American families experience. But what was the glue—the hidden and invisible bond that held us all together and kept us from falling apart? Was it these traditions, was it Christ as my mother suggests, or were we even glued together at all?

Growing up, I knew there was a rich history behind our family's faith. The history of Christianity and the African American experience had been passed down to my sister and me through stories, church, movies, and art. During my childhood, two things were repeated to me often: I was African American, and I was Christian. These two went hand in hand in our community. So of course, as a child, I saw myself growing up and continuing to follow the age-old black tradition and staying in church.

The songs of the slave spirituals, sung deep and low throughout the church service, told our history as well. At home we had tons of pictures and statues of historically black Christian situations. The walls and shelves of my grandma's house were filled with scenes of church. Some pictures were portrayed as hot, sweaty, summer Sundays with congregants raising their hands in the air or fanning their sweating brows. Other images had most of the congregation on their feet in an enthusiastic display of praise. Black Jesus statues and pictures were interspersed with the rest. I had watched *Roots* and *The Color Purple* countless times. The scenes of black churches with all the praising and singing were very similar to my church.

This is the faith of my forefathers, the faith that my mom says I've abandoned. I wanted to hear what my dad thought, so I called him the next day. Dad's father, who passed away when I was a toddler, was the family outlier—the "three times a year" type of Christian. Grandpa Jesse spent his Sundays at home doing house maintenance, Dad told me, while Dad's mom (Grandma Laura) dressed my dad and his sister, Diana, in their Sunday best, marching them down to the "meetin' house," as Dad jokingly calls it.

As he recalled, Grandma Laura—whom I never met because she passed away before I was born—had the type of strong, solid faith that held the family together. Her faith got the family through the trials of enduring Grandpa Jesse's alcoholic addiction and through the test of her cancer. Tragically, she died from this disease when my dad was only in his twenties. Grandma Laura was the spiritual rock that stood firm in their lives when the weight of Jim Crow and racism pulled them down. When she died, my father and Aunt Diana went separate ways spiritually, both remaining on a Christian path yet choosing different denominations. (She married a Roman Catholic man—Uncle Mac—and was married in that church.) Still, their mother's spiritual strength remains in their hearts.

Even so, "you can't go to heaven on your mother's religion," my father said over the phone, explaining that he had to find his own path to Christ. He doesn't seem as hurt as my mother over my choice, or maybe he just doesn't show it.

And here I am, with parents who both had ancestors who believed strongly in their faith. Yet I don't share their belief. I have broken away from the family religion, and hurt my mother in the process. My father said it would "be nice" if I shared their belief so we could do more things together, but he seems to understand that I have to find my own path to God.

And so my mother and I struggle to mend our hurts, to find a way to reconnect.

Somehow, after the Christmas holiday, we manage to schedule a conference call to discuss how we are going to unify as a family and commit to get together. Iesa begins by calling my parents. Then he calls me to connect. Then I conference in my sister, and with modern technology, we unite. Everyone is feeling in high spirits and cracking jokes. My dad is eating in the background, which means he will definitely be in a good mood. I sing the song "Let's Get Together" from the original version of *The Parent Trap* to add to the atmosphere. We're all openly optimistic.

My mom starts, in her usual hesitant manner, but I hear hope in her voice. I sense that she knows God is with us on this phone call when she begins the conversation in an optimistic tone. She wants to make sure that we're all in—that we all actually want to get together. I joke about how ridiculous that sounds, as if we wouldn't want to see each other, then realize that might be the case for some families.

We debate times to meet up during the year, finally deciding she and Dad will hook up during Christmastime with my sister and niece in Dallas, then drive down to Houston for New Year's Day with us. We even decide to get together in June for a family vacation in the Colorado Mountains.

We're especially careful not to schedule the summer visit during Ramadan—which, this year, starts on June 28—or during my niece's volleyball tryouts in early June. My dad mentions we need to make a calendar of important religious holidays. It's miraculous how well our discussion goes, yet somehow I'm not surprised that we accomplished this goal. I can hear the relief and joy in my mom's voice as we end the conversation, promising to talk again with updates.

"All good action is bound to bear fruit in the end," according to Gandhi.[10] We all want this to work, and we are all willing to try. In the back of my mind, though, I can't help but worry about how Mom will feel next year during Christmas when I'm not there. Even though she'll have my sister and her precious preteen granddaughter to share her joy, will she feel as sad as she does now? I hope that meeting up with her more often will help fill part of the void in her heart.

For now, I guess, we'll take it one year at a time. Yes, one small step. But is it a victory?

What's wrong with saying yes?

four

NOW, WHY ISLAM?

Patricia

THIS ISN'T A WEATHER REPORT. BUT LET ME JUST SAY IT'S COLD. Frigid and January. Temperatures dropped to minus ten degrees overnight. With Christmas barely over, the cold can make everything feel wrong and regretful. But this is Colorado, so the morning sun is blazing bright, strong as a torch—making the day and the daughter and the struggle over our faiths feel not as bitter and hard and cold as they might.

Next to a sunny window, I read what Alana has written so far. I'm trying to learn, and not just feel—a process reminding me of my late pastor, Rev. J. Langston Boyd Jr. A Harvard graduate and onetime factory worker before that, he always said if a faith can't stand questioning, it's not much of a faith.

So I'm trying to listen. Listen hard. To hear why my daughter chose to believe Islam. Why, indeed, do any of us need to believe *something*? How will Alana explain? Will she say of Islam what C. S. Lewis said about the cross? That "I believe in Christianity as I believe that the Sun has risen, not only because I see it, but because by it I see everything else."[1]

Or would my daughter, in the words of Muslim poet Muhammad Iqbal, declare that "Islam is itself Destiny and will not suffer a destiny."[2]

Mercy. I read the poet's tough words and sigh. When it comes to faith, everybody's got his or her backup. Me included.

Still, I'm finally vowing as a Christian to learn more about Islam. A reasonable goal for a brand-new year. Yet as I confess my intent, I expect a pushback. Christian friends will rise up in protest. "Learn about *Islam*?" They'll say it like that. Some of them anyway. "Are you crazy?"

But that's not what they say at all.

The social justice minister at my church, hearing about this journey, gives me a whoop and a big hug—plus a copy of the Qur'an.

Another friend offers to connect me with two missionaries, just back from Pakistan, who worked for fifteen years among Muslims before being forced to return home to Colorado when their son needed heart surgery.

Every Christian friend I tell about this journey wants to know more— well, not so much about Islam per se, but they ask to know more about a mother and a daughter's faith struggle. During dinner at a recent wedding, two friends leaned in to share struggles with their grown daughters. Listening, as I described what Alana and I are attempting to unravel, the mother sitting next to me whispered, "Is the book coming out soon?" She laughed. "I really need it."

Or as the social justice minister at my church told me, "I'm not looking for your theology. I want to see how you and Alana work this thing out!"

We laughed too. But like anybody who's ever lived inside a family, she knows family business is tough work.

I know I have to learn more. Islam sits like a quiet stranger in my house. I have to learn more. So I try to start, thumbing through the paperback copy of the Qur'an given to me by the social justice minister. It's hard to read. Teensy type. More than that, to even handle it feels odd—yes, odd—or to even consider what others believe. It's uncomfortable. Plus, like other copies of the Qur'an I have considered, the content doesn't compel me.

I'm not supposed to say that. Muslims get crazy, it seems, when Christians comment on their holy book. I'm just trying to draw the line of this process. So I do the next thing.

I go to the Internet and order a passel of books about Islam. Some by famous authors. Some by obscure scholars. Some pro-Islam. Some questioning Islam. I also dig out a hardbound copy of the Qur'an from the back corner of a bookshelf, placed just as I left it almost ten years ago when my son-in-law gave it to me as a gift. Inviting me to read it. But after thumbing through, I didn't.

Now, however, I will read. To learn more. To know more. So I can love more.

What I am saying is this: I love you, Alana. I'm your mother. I carried you nine months in my belly. I nursed you. Weaned you. Fed you. Led you. Taught you. Prayed for you. In Jesus' forever name. By faith.

I owe it to myself, and to you, to understand what changed. Why people choose. And how. How people decide. And why. Why people hunker down in their faith—as I hunker down in mine—refusing to budge. And why, when we hunker like that, our determination on faith can feel so right.

I believe. We say this. Not moving one inch. Repeating the Apostles' Creed on Sundays at church. I close my eyes—speaking, feeling, and loving not just the words but also the sheer sound of the words.

> I believe in God the Father Almighty, maker of heaven and earth; And in Jesus Christ his only Son, our Lord: who was conceived by the Holy Spirit, born of the Virgin Mary, suffered under Pontius Pilate, was crucified, died, and buried . . .

Church folks love this creed. Know it by heart. The whole thing. This is just a portion of it, but deep believers love every single syllable of this declaration—and never mind the pundits who say it was mandated onto Christians by a crooked church process.

Say what you will. Nobody cares anymore. We love the words anyway. The meaning of them. The story and glory of them.

And yet, on this morning, I find myself pondering faith in general. Why, indeed, do we believe by *faith*? Is there really a "God spot," as some people claim, plunked down deep in our souls? Like some headquarters for God that's desperate to make a connection with the Almighty?

That idea of a God spot went viral a few years back. On talk shows and Twitter feeds, the talking heads went wild with it. Then finally researchers confirmed there's no single God spot per se in the brain. Instead, a neurophysiologist, whose sublime name is Brick Johnstone, declared that spirituality is "a much more dynamic concept that uses many parts of the brain."[3]

That wasn't just fancy talk either. Johnstone, in fact, did all sorts of research to confirm his theories. Chair of his department at the University of Missouri, Johnstone studied a place in the brain called the right parietal lobe. When the area is damaged, patients show less concern for themselves—feeling more connection to a higher or bigger thing. Such as God.

And this is where the God spot stuff gets interesting. Interesting to me anyway. Because as Johnstone learned about the right parietal lobe, it's not a God spot. It's more like a "Me" spot. The place in the brain that makes us aware of ourselves. As in Me the Body. Me Writing This Page. Me Reading This Page. Me Eating My Lunch. Me at the Thrift Store Buying This Really Pretty Blouse for Me. And Yay for Me, indeed, shouts the right parietal lobe.

In spiritual folks, however, our sense of Me is tempered. Turned down. Dialed back. Then a feeling of something transcendent or higher or bigger—such as God—grows larger. Studies of healthy Franciscan nuns whose brains function normally showed that the Me parts were not as active. Same with healthy Tibetan Buddhist monks. As if they'd learned to deny that egotistical part of their brain function. Low Me. High God. That is, a heightened sense of spiritual connection.

And here's the thing. Spiritual people *like* this feeling. Of being connected to something larger. Of believing in something bigger we know to be real. And to gain that feeling, we don't have to be brain injured.

We just have to believe. And pray. And serve. And help. Then we scale back our *self*-awareness for the greater glory of *God*-awareness.

As the disciple John testified about Jesus, "He must increase, but I must decrease" (John 3:30 KJV).

But what about a mother and a daughter?

Do I pull out all this stuff so Alana and I can talk about it? To point her to the Bible, where John's followers were jealous because "that man"—this Jesus—attracted bigger crowds by healing all the people (John 3:26)? And John answered: "'I am not the Christ, but I have been sent before him. . . . Therefore this joy of mine is now complete. He must increase, but I must decrease'" (John 3:28–30 ESV).

On a practical level, here's how C. S. Lewis put it: "It is better to forget about yourself altogether."[4] Lewis was speaking of humility, of course.

Well, did anybody in the history of the world exhibit more humility than Christ? I say no. But I'm just a mother who prays, sometimes to quiet my Me.

Maybe Alana can tell me something different. About her faith. Her choice. Her life. That place, that spot, that landscape in her soul that receives her God. And maybe, this time, I will listen.

Listen with love?

Yes, I can try.

Amen.

Alana

IT'S JANUARY NOW, SO I JOINED THE YMCA. I NEED TO EXERCISE. To burn off stress. To spend this one morning doing just one thing. No extras. No add-ons. Just one clear morning doing one clear thing. But I'm thinking about my mother. I know what she's going to say: the Y is a Christian organization. As if I don't already know. Or as if it matters. Like the time we were together at a Chick-fil-A, and I mentioned how polite and helpful their staff was.

Then Mom looked me dead in the eye and said, "Well, you know they're a *Christian*-owned business."

We both sort of laughed, but mostly I felt hurt.

I know she was trying to make a point. But a part of me feels as though she is always trying to prove her religion is better than mine. And so when she calls me in Texas on this January morning, while I'm on my way back from the Y, I don't want to answer. I do anyway because it's time for me to tell my mom, and the world, why I became a Muslim. So I'm actually hopeful that for once I'll get a chance to share and that maybe she will listen with an open heart.

In fact, she is listening.

"I joined the Y," I say.

"Really?" she asks. But no snide comment. So I go on.

"They have a women's room," I say, and I explain the layout. Workout room. Pool. Child care for kids.

We talk while I gush about the facility—about how nice it is.

Then I joke about the Muslim woman I saw come in, wearing full *abaya*, a long, modest robe worn by many Muslim women, and hijab.

"I was going to introduce myself. But when I got into the workout room, I couldn't recognize her. She'd taken off her covering." The woman had switched into leggings and T-shirt—better for working out.

"Oh, no!" Mom says, laughing with me.

I can tell she wants to mention that the Y is Christian-based, so I finally say, "Aren't you going to tell me that the Y has a Christian philosophy?"

Mom pauses. I hear her breathe. Then she says that Christians are doing great things in the world, the Y being one of them.

In her mind, though, she's probably thinking of all the bad things she's heard about Muslims.

But I didn't choose Islam for the people. And although Muslims in America aren't opening awesome gyms with pools and child care—at least, not as far as I know—there are good things being done by Muslims in the world. But I'm tired of having to defend Muslims. So I decide to tell her exactly that.

"I just wish . . ." I try to find words.

"Wish what?" Mom asks.

"I just wish the news stations would come to my school where I teach, just for a day. Our Islamic teacher is so good about teaching kids about tolerance. About peace. About compassion." Then they could see that each class has a yearly charity project and the theme for this year's fundraiser is based on being leaders of tomorrow.

But no one is talking about what our little school is doing, despite our PR attempts. The rest of the world drowns us out.

Then as I listen to my mom go on and on about Jesus, I interject. "Isn't this supposed to be my turn to talk?"

She stops, explaining that she was just answering a question. But part of me thinks that she is avoiding the topic. I don't think she really wants to hear about my journey. "Just listen for a second," I plead. She responds with a quick okay, and I begin.

The reasoning seems simple enough to me. Four short Arabic words sum up my conversion in a nutshell: *la ilaha il Allah*. It means "there is no God but Allah." This simple phrase is the foundation of my faith, of my belief. Yet in some way it has become the source of our division.

Bottom line: The concept of oneness draws me to Islam. One God, without partners. No divisions, no shared power or authority, no intermediaries either. Just God and God alone. It feels right to me. It feels pure.

This idea of God's singularity holds me together when life seems to pull me in so many places. I often feel like I can't seem to focus on just one thing. With four kids, a cat, a neglected husband, a writing project, and a classroom of students, it's hard not to feel unraveled. Now I've even added tutoring to my schedule. There is so much on my plate it's hard to tell if I'm doing any of it well.

"Thanks for taking the dishes out of the dishwasher," says my husband one night. It's late, and the kids are sleeping, but we're still up, working and cleaning. The housework never seems to be all done. He overheard me talking to Mom one night about how stressed I am. He knows I keep adding responsibilities at work, and I am overloaded at home. I smile and say, "Sorry I didn't finish. I got distracted by the kids."

"Thanks for *starting*," he replies, smiling.

I pause, reflecting on the idea of starting. We start things with the intention of finishing them, but when we don't, somehow, I think God must appreciate that we began the process. We fall short of completion while God is complete—the source of completeness, in fact. In my eyes God is the rock that remains steadfastly there to help us find a center in our lives.

That's why it's hard for me to wrap my head around the Trinity. It seems divisive. I'm familiar with the arguments and reasoning behind it, but it seems to separate God into three parts. That doesn't seem right to me. It feels unnatural. I've read and heard so many explanations about the Trinity that I can probably explain it as well as any Christian. I'm not faulting Mom for believing in the Trinity; it's just not for me. I've had to follow my heart.

As a child I tried extremely hard to understand the Trinity. I would stare endlessly at the three banners hanging from the ceiling in our church. *Father*, *Son*, and *Holy Spirit* were intricately woven in gold letters. For some reason I couldn't wrap my head around God being the Father, the Son, and the Holy Spirit all at the same time. I would stare in wonder at the elder members of the congregation jumping and shouting, waving their hands in the air. Their faces would be glistening with sweat as they raised them in praise. I would listen to the singing and all the emotion that comes along with it. Yet I wasn't able to accept it. I never felt ready to proclaim that Jesus was my Lord or even my Savior. That job was taken already by God. I used to wonder when I would get the feeling that would change my mind. I used to wonder if something was wrong with me.

I felt God's presence, though, and I always believed in him. As a young adult I began to actively seek God. I was sick and tired of the way my life was going. I was twenty and had just come back from a reckless year in a Manhattan college. I wanted to come home. But, most of all, I felt empty inside. My soul felt hollow.

I was searching. I was starting. I could feel myself drawing closer to God. I came across the Qur'an and read many parts with the words *la ilaha il Allah*—there is no God but God. This kept me going and searching. I wanted to follow the religion that believed this statement.

And so I read—the Bible and the Qur'an at first, then the autobiographies of Gandhi and Malcolm X. I read books by Elijah Muhammad and about the Nation of Islam. Religious anthologies by Karen Armstrong, Martin Lings, and Fazlur Rahman, among others. I regularly attended Bible study at my college and went to the small storefront mosque near school. My college apartment, though sparingly furnished and without a TV, was filled with books.

I read and read—and my soul began to fill. I held on to the idea that God was One. And then one day I decided that Islam was the path for me.

A part of me feels as though I always knew God in this way. I just needed him to help me sort it out. I needed God to lead me on my journey of untangling and removing the distractions in my life so I could reconnect with him.

That is what I tell my mother. It's both difficult and freeing at the same time.

Sometimes that's what I need—to get away from it all.

It's finally Friday, and I try to do just that—to escape from my hectic week by attending a family night in the mosque. I heard there was going to be dinner and a moon walk. It sounded like a great break from cooking dinner and entertaining the kids at home. While sitting in the prayer hall after the evening prayer, a woman approaches me and asks, "Is there going to be a lecture tonight?" Before I can answer, I'm immediately approached by another woman who asks, "So what are they doing tonight, just dinner?" It seems that everyone is expecting a buffet of entertainment choices.

I check the mosque's Facebook page. Family night will consist of dinner and a craft for the kids, if needed. No fluff, no extra stuff, just one thing. I sigh in relief, smiling at the irony of the situation. It's nice that whoever organized this event realized that it's okay to do just one thing at a time.

The following Monday my husband calls while I'm on the way home from work.

He's made dinner—chicken breasts, salad, and spaghetti sauce.

"All you need to do is make the noodles," he says. "That'll make it easier. Easier for you tonight."

Then a bonus: "I'm making steel cut oatmeal in the morning for the kids," he adds.

I sigh, gratefully, not exactly knowing how to express my thanks. I love when he cooks, but this time I know he's trying to lessen my load and unclutter my plate.

One less thing to do tonight.

"Thank you so much," I say later to Iesa, trying my hardest to show my sincerity. I'm grateful for his help, but more important, I'm glad to share my life with someone who sees God the way I do.

Mom doesn't understand my point of view, but will she try? I'm hopeful that she will at least meet me at the door. And listen.

Patricia

Did you ask God?

That's what I'm tempted to say. Say to Alana. Say to my child of God who struggled—as most of us do—to figure out the mysteries of faith. The Trinity? I could dive in. Offer a sweeping answer. Or say faith doctrines are easy. Or say they make perfect sense. Or fit our logic.

Oh, I could talk. Argue. Speechify. Roll out my reply. Quote my scriptures. I'm locked and loaded. Ready to aim. Set to fire.

But that's the problem with too many peace talks. Nobody listens—starting with me. Yet that's my first job now. First to listen. Then to learn. Then to let the Holy Spirit lead.

That was my official prayer for this new calendar year. To let the Spirit lead. *Lead me, Holy Spirit.* Lift my questioning, testing, busy self ahead of my noise and set me down with you.

So instead of talking back, I lay in the cold and turn the covers back on another icy morning. The temperature in Denver this February is seventeen degrees below zero.

"I'm freezing," Dan says. He sits up in bed. Puts on his glasses. Squints at the tiny thermometer on top of the TV.

"I'll turn up the heat," I tell him.

Downstairs, I peek through the blinds. Outside it's cold, black, and quiet. It's barely five a.m. and arctic. Our street is iced and snowed under. No neighbors out yet. No cars moving. So I click up the furnace. Head back up. Crawl back under the covers. Then Dan has a better idea.

"The fireplace." He pads downstairs. Hits the switch.

"Love that thing," he says, climbing back up. He crawls in bed. Pulls the covers around us. Inches closer to me. "Let's feel some *heat.*"

I laugh. Liking our waking-up closeness. Liking the covers. Liking the warmth we're trying to build. This is morning time. The time that keeps marriages cooking and alive. The time when, after thirty-eight years, I can look at Dan wearing crumpled pajamas and socks and a plaid Eddie Bauer jacket—and he can look at me wearing long johns, a quilted robe, and a scarf on my head—but we see only grace.

We talk. The house creaks in the cold. We talk about family, love, and charity. We reminisce about the Saturday food bank at my childhood church, where we had recently helped out. When we arrived, thinking we'd be the first ones there, we were surprised to find one woman already in line, smiling, waiting for the food pantry to open. She was quiet and polite enough. But preoccupied. Finally, she said, "I got here early." A look crossed her face. She shrugged. "But my dad always taught us, wherever you go, make sure you go early."

Dan grinned, nodding. He told her his dad, a mailman, always said the same thing. *Don't be late.* So then my extroverted husband and the woman waiting for food talked about dads. How they teach us. How they lead us. How they pass on their best.

Introverted me listened. Charmed by how Dan understands people. How in minutes, he'd connected. How when he and I talked a week later about this woman at the church, that moment taught me what to say to Alana.

So here it is. Father knows best.

Especially when we're confused. The Father says it this way in his book of Proverbs: "Lean not on your own understanding." Old king Solomon recorded the words:

> Trust in the LORD with all your heart
>> and lean not on your own understanding;
> in all your ways submit to him,
>> and he will make your paths straight. (3:5–6)

Because when we don't trust and ask God, the gospel and its mysteries can seem—to human minds—like so much foolishness. The apostle Paul, who made that claim, wrote it as a question: "Where is the wise? Where is the scribe? Where is the disputer of this age? Has not God made foolish the wisdom of this world?" (1 Cor. 1:20 NKJV). Was Paul attacking human intelligence? Or did the apostle nail it—that *"the foolishness of God* is wiser than men, and the weakness of God *is stronger than men"* (1 Cor. 1:25 NKJV, emphasis mine)?

Irish theologian Alister McGrath argues this same idea, especially when it comes to the Trinity. "Our misgivings about the Trinity arise," he says, "mainly because the reality of God does not map easily onto our natural categories of thought."[5] And that's the whole point.

God simple? Simplifying God "leads to reduction, and reduction to distortion. And that's just not acceptable," says McGrath. Think instead, he says, of an iceberg; "nearly 90 percent is below the waterline. We can't see it—but it's there, supporting and upholding the part of the iceberg that we do see."[6]

So it is, indeed, with our Trinity. Too vast to reduce. Too marvelous to simplify.

My husband and I talk about this mystery under the icy covers. Before the sun rises outside, we've given our early moments to this reaching for this same exceeding God. Not with our thinking. But with God's. With, indeed, the mind of Christ.

So Dan grabs our daily devotional, delighting with me that the focus for this day is on "The Holy Spirit, Our Teacher." This is Dr. Charles Stanley teaching, and Dan and I marvel at the timing. At its gentle reply to Alana's concern. At how the eighty-two-year-old Stanley is simply saying this: stop relying on your own thinking to figure out God.

"Even the most admired human thinkers cannot begin to grasp the mind of the Lord," writes Stanley.[7] Blaise Pascal, the French theologian, came to this: "In faith there is enough light for those who desire only to see, and enough darkness for those of a contrary disposition."[8]

Finally, Tozer: "There is no truth apart from the Spirit. The most brilliant intellect may be imbecilic when confronted with the mysteries of God."[9]

So ask God.

That's what Dan and I do. We huddle under the covers—praying, not on our knees as usual but drawing in close to thank God for the fresh day. For his blessed help. For being our holy teacher. For giving our weaknesses his strength. For gracing us to hear our daughter—then let her go her own way, which is what she's asking us to do. *Let me go.* As we release her to God, we thank him for blessing us with something else to put in our hands. On this day, that new thing is our assignment to buy warm gloves, scarves, and personal care items—the basic stuff of life—for the homeless women sleeping on cold winter nights at my childhood church. But more than all, we thank God for granting us by his Spirit his priceless peace. Amen.

Dan then shrugs out of bed to the floor, to lift weights, trying to warm up in our cold bedroom. "When I read the book *The Shack*, I really got it," he says.

"Got what?" I ask. I haven't read that book yet.

He holds a barbell over his head. "Got," he says, grunting, "the idea of dimensions of God. The Trinity. And that one of them—the Father's Holy Spirit—lives inside of us."

He puts down the weights, turning to me. "*Inside*. Right here." He holds a hand to his chest. "All the time. He's our guide. He's our teacher."

"But we have to ask," I say. "Ask him to teach."

"Right," Dan says. "Then listen for his still voice to answer."

Then you don't get all lost.

That's why folks praise God in churches, Alana. They're grateful. They didn't get lost. Didn't get dead. Didn't get broke. Didn't fall off a cliff. Got stupid, but God saved them anyway.

It's not because you understand everything God is and God did. Every mystery of faith. Boil it down to human understanding? To one thing? This God who does so much? In so many ways? Sometimes for no reason? Or that's how it looks to our human minds?

That's one way. To figure out everything for ourselves. Check a list. Say okay, now I get God. Or we could go the way of the author of faith and just ask first.

When we do, he invites us to be still. I'm trying to do that this year. To be intentional. On some days, in fact, I actually do that. On other days, when I'm not intentional—not asking, not listening—before noontime hits, the day is flying apart.

So today I ask for grace. A good prayer. Not a "fix my daughter" prayer. Or a "help me" plea. I just ask for grace. A mother's prayer.

Praise God. In so many ways he is answering.

Alana

I LOVE THE STUDENTS IN MY CLASSROOM. I LOVE THEIR DEDICA-tion, their joy, and even their constant curiosity. What's interesting is never once have I heard a student ask about who God *is*. Maybe the idea of God is already clear to them and unquestionable. Perhaps they don't know how to word their questions. If they are confused about God, they don't show it. But then again, not many preteens are willing to admit their intimate confusions. We try to encourage them to think and ask questions, though many of them are written on the classroom "parking lot" for further discussion later—when the topic is more connected to a lesson.

"Greek mythology is like the opposite of Islam," one student remarks during a world history lesson on ancient Greece. They're all avid readers of the new young adult novels based on Greek mythology. "It's still fun to think about, though," she says with a smile. The other students nod their heads in agreement.

My own children also seem to understand God's singularity. They ask me questions about his attributes and behaviors, but they haven't yet shown confusion about the concept of oneness. While I'm driving home, my three-year-old son asks, "Who made us, Mommy?"

I say Allah, of course.

He follows with, "Then who made the buildings?"

"The construction workers," I reply. He's too young to get it.

Before I continue, my daughter pipes in knowingly and says, "Allah made everything on the earth that the construction workers use to make the buildings."

My son is satisfied with this answer for now. More questions will come later, and I welcome them. I want them to understand the singular-ity of God, to ponder his magnificence and wonder at his creation. More important, I want them to know that it's okay to think and to question. They need to know that Allah encourages thought and reflection—espe-cially about him.

We arrive at home. Soon, it's time for me to pray the evening prayer. "I wanna pray too, Mommy!" my son says enthusiastically. He aligns his mini prayer rug with mine and carefully straightens all the edges and fringe. I've already begun praying by then, beginning with the words *Allah hu Akbar*, or God is Great. He hurriedly stands up and comes as close to me as he can. Then he copies me as I recite chapters from the Qur'an, bow, and prostrate.

The whole time I can see him eyeing me, watching my every move so he can follow. We bend in prostration with our heads touching the prayer mats and then sit to continue the prayer. I whisper in Arabic a declaration stating that there is no deity but Allah, tapping one finger on my right thigh to demonstrate this concept. He follows my lead, tapping his finger, and looking over at me every now and then to make sure he is doing it right. I know he's too young to understand, and he does this to please me, but I'm happy nonetheless. I continue to pray quietly, asking Allah to guide and protect him and to put a love for God in his heart.

When prayer is over, he looks over at me, beaming, knowing that I am proud. I hug him tight and tell him that he did a good job and that Allah is happy with him too. We laugh as we watch the baby "clean up" the prayer rugs by waddling with them over to the basket in front of us.

Eventually the evening winds down. The kids have finally been put to bed. The dishes are done, and the high chair is wiped. "We've got to find a way of getting them to bed earlier," my husband grumbles. He's right. It's 9:30—way later than any book on child rearing would recommend putting kids to bed. I don't answer because I'm lost in thought, staring at my notepad. "Helloooo?" Iesa prompts, coming over to rub my shoulders. "Um hum," I mumble absentmindedly.

Pretty soon he's shaking me, rousing me from sleep. I've fallen asleep in front of my computer again. "Don't forget to pray *Isha*," he reminds me. He's referring to the last prayer of the night.

I'm groggy but compliant. Somehow I wake myself up enough to perform ablution and wipe cold water over my face, arms, head, and feet. He's already prayed, so I pray by myself. I don't bother to turn on the light in my room. The only sound is the baby's soft snores. I place my head to the ground and say, "Glory be to Allah the Most High," three times. Then it hits me. When it comes down to it, it's all about me and Allah. Just him and me—no one else—and I like that.

five

⚬

AND WHY THE CHRIST?

———————————— *Patricia* ————————————

JESUS.

I stand at my kitchen sink and call his name. Looking out a sink window at cold sky, I place my hands in soapy, hot water, searching for soiled plates that need cleaning. So I whisper his name yet again—a long sigh that lets him stop my pity party: Maybe I didn't pray enough. Or take Alana to church enough. Or care enough. Or love enough. Or die enough. All those things a Christian mother wants to ask when a child of her home rejects the Christ.

I could ask with anger, indeed. Or with this sadness.

But Christ leads me to a dish towel instead. Wash down the counter, Patricia. So I wash down our determined beige laminate—holding to my promise to God and myself to do a strong job of keeping up with my kitchen. So I don't just clean it. I categorize my kitchen now by contents. I even bought one of those label machine gizmos. Then I spent a solid week cleaning out cupboards—throwing away dated cans, including pumpkin pie filling from 2008 or some long-gone year. Then I labeled each shelf: Canned fruit. Green peas and beans. Tomato sauces. Pasta products. On and on, down the line. Finally I installed a spice rack with eighteen pull-out shelves, each one also labeled—niche by niche—for every spice I'll ever need.

Dan laughed, hugging me. Thinking it silly, I guess, that I need the order when, in fact, I need certainty. After decades of ups and downs—including

79

the real silliness of trying to cook in a kitchen with jumbled-up cabinets and outdated canned goods, I took a breath. Then I emptied every drawer, shelf, cupboard, and cubbyhole—scrubbed, vacuumed, washed, and dried—and, with God's help, I created some kitchen assurance.

So now I know: This can *is* this can. This box *is* this box. This spice *is* this spice. This shelf *is* this shelf. No surprises. It's the kitchen that makes sense. Everything in its place. Well, most things. Okay, many things. A small matter? I'm not sure how to measure order in life. I just know I like the feeling of investing in something that returns what you expect. Something that stands, in a crazy and confused world, like a rock.

And that's just one thing I love about Jesus.

If I'm making a list about Jesus, the rock factor is near the top. Not first, necessarily. There are so many things to love about the Lord. And every believer's list would be in a different order. That's because he knows us one by one—down to the hairs on each of our mixed-up heads, according to the scriptures. And in that same way, beyond the knowing of us, that's how he loves us. One by one.

Knowing even me by name. So he knows the pressure I feel on this page to explain with care and love and accuracy the mystery of the Christ.

But he points me first to the kitchen counters. Inviting me to hand over to him the rubble of all that I'm thinking: Maybe we gave Alana the wrong things. The ice-skating lessons. The private coaches. The sparkly dresses. The sharpened blades on the brand-new leather skate boots. The early morning practices. The trips to competitions. The private schools. The cheerleading camps. The dance instruction. The four years of college, plus the fifth year to figure out life. The cars. Two of them. The decision, midway, to settle for buying my work clothes in thrift stores so my daughter and her sister could study without worrying about tuition, books, plane tickets to and from their universities, and then open their dorm-room closets and wear new.

All wrong, it turns out. And, yes, that *is* guilt-tripping. And anger. And sadness about all we gave as parents, to get back what?

My head wants to understand. And I need my head because I am committed to talk here about Jesus. But Jesus already knows more than I could say: that, after reading Alana's last section, with her beautiful rendition of her Muslim family life, I can't do that yet. Well, I can. I can do all things through Christ who gives me strength (Phil. 4:13). But first, Jesus, let me whine a minute. *Then* I'll try to sound lucid, calm, and ecumenical. First, however, I am heartbroken. Jesus understands that.

And that's what I love about Jesus. He understands.

Because he gave. Gave all. And what did he get back in me? A good Christian? Well, no. Not all the time anyway.

Jesus.

I look through the glass of my sink window at fallen snow, thinking on his name again.

Then as Jesus people know, the hurt eases. Or if not the hurt, the nagging, grating of it eases. Then I can take in a breath, pushing away the need to argue here for Christ and, instead, just talk to Christ while I wash a plate. So I finish the dishes, leaving everything fairly sparkling and clean. Down the drain goes the hurt of a daughter who turned the Lord down without spending even one second to ask her give-it-all mother what I thought.

And that hurt.

And of course, Jesus knows. He understands. He feels it too.

So he lets me talk to him. And maybe that's the first thing I love about the Lord. He allows the talk. Then he listens. Somebody on Facebook put it this way: "I talk. He listens. He answers. I praise." So I'm at the talking stage, grateful he will wait until his listening and answering turn into my praise.

Then with the turning, I can head upstairs to look for his tough love. Before long, I find it in obvious places. In the Bible, of course. Always so good for heartbreak.

I also follow the Lord to a research study. So, yes, I am procrastinating. Because I should be calling Alana—or getting on a plane to go look her in the eye—not reading a research paper called "Tensions in the Parent and Adult Child Relationship."

But this isn't a Hollywood movie. I don't get on a plane. Not today.

So for this moment I read and read—because it's a big study. Lots of words. Thankfully, there's a bottom line: tensions in parent-child relationships are normal. Normal over all of life. Always tension. Parents pulling. Children pushing away. The key trouble? The power struggle over children's need for independence.

Everybody needs it. This drive to be our own person. To be left alone. Let me live my own life, *please*. No surprise there. Alana has been saying that for years. Let me be me.

But look what I didn't know: Tensions feel worse to parents. We invest more. Those ballet lessons. Those sparkly dresses. All the rest. Cars. Vacations. College tuition. Attendance at every dance recital, school program, high school game. You name it. Parents give it. We gave too. The Good Parents' story.

And like all good parents, we want return on investment.[1] *ROI, God.*

More time together. More phone calls. Even a text every once in a while. Like one Alana recently sent early one morning to share photos of our grandkids. That same morning she called early while Dan and I were still in bed. And when he saw her phone number on caller ID, Dan started crying. "This moved me so much," he said.

He said the same a couple of days later when our older daughter called, also from Texas, while I was out doing errands, and the two of them just talked. "And we had the best time just laughing and talking," Dan said. My husband, who gets weepy in a second, then added, "She even said she and Nia miss us."

More than that, however, as parents age, we want assurance we've passed on our deepest family values. The adult child's need: to be her own person. The parents' need: to pass on their knowledge, values, and beliefs. Indeed, their faith.

Yet Alana is saying no. Declaring no. Insisting no. Writing no. Jesus? *No.*

So what's a mother of faith to do? I will buy warm gloves.

Soon it will be Tuesday night, and I promised to buy the gloves and scarves and hats and toiletries to take to the homeless women who sleep at my childhood church one night a week. If I give, I feel certain the homeless women will appreciate the gifts. Or even if they don't appreciate them, it can't possibly hurt like a daughter whose stake is to go her own way. To "simplify" God. To push back so hard she has washed from her life every semblance of the family traditions her dad and I worked so hard to create.

And my God?

He's *not*, Alana insists. He's not a father. He has no son. End of discussion. So we could get stuck there. Instead, on this bitter cold day, I buy gloves for homeless women. My $120 budget—an expected payment for a short writing assignment—doesn't go far. The travel-sized toothpastes and lotions and such, along with the gloves, eat up the money in no time flat.

Yet as I stand in the grocery store checkout line, I forgive myself. Running out of money isn't wrong. Loving Jesus isn't wrong. So loving a daughter and wanting her to love her Savior, too, aren't wrong either.

But when you're feeling wrong, nobody helps better than Christ.

Here's his modest invitation: *come to me.*

Not deep theology. Not apologetics. Not the argument of Muslim-turned-Christian Nabeel Qureshi who, at his moment of crisis, turned to the Qur'an, "but there was no comfort there. It felt like a dead book." In contrast, while in Christ and the Gospels, he sought Jesus, and "in my pain I knew him intimately."[2]

In his book, *Seeking Allah, Finding Jesus: A Devout Muslim Encounters Christianity*, Qureshi recounts it all—explaining better than I am—all the good theological stuff an apologist is supposed to say. He's trained. He's a medical doctor. He's a theologian. He can do those things well.

And me? I'm just a mom. But when my heart breaks, I know the doctor.

The Healer Christ tells me to love my daughter. To look at the extraordinarily great person she is: A teacher. A mother. A wife. Not unlike me. So be glad for those beautiful things, Jesus says. Be of good cheer! In this world, you will have trouble. "But be of good cheer, I have overcome the world" (John 16:33 NKJV).

So I can do my good deed. Which feels great. Nothing kills a pity party better than helping somebody else. So I return home, leaving my purchases on a bench in my newly clean kitchen. Then I head to my office to finish a writing project for my church. I edit the yearly *Lenten Devotional Guide*, featuring personal testimonies from church members—and the stories are arriving now in my e-mail inbox. I read through the testimonies—soaking up the insights, enjoying the short reflections. I love the words of a young dad—a barbershop owner—who says in the fog of life and business, he stopped asking God for clarity. Instead, he finally prayed for more faith.

Then the fog cleared.

And that's why I follow Jesus.

He understands fog. Then at a kitchen sink, he turns it into love.

Alana

IT'S POP QUIZ TIME IN ISLAMIC STUDIES CLASS AT MY SCHOOL. THE students huddle over their papers, racking their brains. The teacher just instructed them to list the five books given to humanity by the prophets of God. The stress is evident in their faces. A few students look confident; others seem unsure. One student asks if she can write them in Arabic; another student accidently blurts out an answer.

Time is up, and the papers are collected. The teacher immediately reviews the answers out loud and the students chime in, "The Scripture of Abraham, the Psalms of David, the Torah of Moses, the Gospel of Jesus, and the Qur'an revealed to Muhammad." Some of the students sigh in frustration if they missed one book; others beam widely if they got 100 percent.

I smile while listening and think about my mom. She thinks that I reject Jesus. What she doesn't understand is that I don't reject him at all. In fact, I believe wholeheartedly in the message of the Gospels, and the messages in the books before it.

We just interpret the gospel differently. To me, Jesus is a messenger, a healer, a leader, and a teacher. Most important to me, Jesus—despite his virgin birth—is a servant of God, a man similar in status to the prophets of the past.

But I'm not trying to debate my mom. If we wanted to, we could go on for days citing verses and "evidences" to prove our cases. That's not what this is about. And as I sit in class listening to the students, I realize that I am greatly misunderstood by my mother.

To put it bluntly, I'm angry. Yes, I understand that we disagree on a fundamental issue in her life. I'm just sick of always being painted as the bad guy, the black sheep of the family who tore us apart. Is my life really that much of a disappointment? I wish that the highlights of my life—mother, teacher, wife, and college graduate—had more weight in my mother's approval. I thought she could see the difference between my life now and my life before Islam. I wasn't "bad" before Islam, but I did my share of partying, drinking, and dating shady guys. And now that I'm "cleaned up," so to speak, it's not enough. My modest, God-conscious way of life is not enough.

Too busy to ponder these thoughts for long, I continue typing a letter to my classroom parents about our next field trip. The students have been studying world history this year, and they read two novels about the Holocaust the year before. We've decided to take advantage of our amazing museum district in Houston by taking them to the Holocaust Museum, then to a local synagogue for a Q and A session. I type the parent letter, explaining how our school prides itself on educating students about diversity in local and community settings. An e-mail pops up. It's the rabbi from the synagogue, and he can't wait for us to visit. As I prepare my letter, I remind myself to have the Islamic studies teacher prep my students on asking thoughtful and considerate questions when they visit the synagogue.

My husband connected us with the rabbi from the synagogue. Iesa is known to have tons of connections with members of other faiths. On Monday night he comes home late again. This time it's because he was speaking at a Hindu temple. He spoke as he usually does about issues of faith, but he also spoke on how to work together on service projects with other faiths. At home, he's beaming—it went well. "I brought you a plate!" he says, enthusiastically. He always does that since there's always delicious food at these things. It's filled with a mixture of Middle Eastern and Indian dishes. The kids attack the chocolate cake, and I sample a spicy samosa as he recalls his experience.

"What's in the package?" I ask, noticing a wrapped box on his dresser.

"Probably a book on Hinduism," he remarks.

Sure enough, it's a book on meditation. I place it in our shelf overflowing with religious texts.

Whenever my husband speaks to groups, he sometimes explains the meaning of his name first. Mentioning that his name translates to *Jesus*

in Arabic is a good conversational starter with any Christian he encounters. He often goes on to describe the Islamic view of the virgin birth,
sometimes debating the issue of crucifixion and resurrection. I listened
to him once talk to a group of Christians. "We love Jesus too," he said to
their surprise. He explained that although we don't worship him or see
him as God in person, we believe in his message of humility, kindness,
love, compassion, and servitude to God.

In the car on the way home, we listen to a *nasheed*, a religious song. The
singer melodically chants the Arabic names of the prophets. My children sit in the back and daydream as they listen. I hear my daughter
echo the names she hears, "Ibrahim, Musa, Noah, Yousef, Dawod, Iesa,
Muhammad," among others. When we stop at the store, it's filled to the
rim with Easter stuff. My daughter looks at me and asks inquisitively,
"What's Easter, Mommy?"

She's looking at all of the pretty pastel eggs and baskets. I explain
it as best as I can, keeping my mother in mind. I wonder if she would
approve of my delivery or think that I misrepresented the concept. I go
on to explain the Islamic view, that Jesus was never actually crucified
and instead was raised up to Allah, where he remains until the Day of
Judgment. It's a fundamental difference between my mother's belief and
mine. It's an area of potential controversy between us.

I don't want controversy with Mom. I just want to be heard and
respected in my right to an opinion. We go to the masjid, and I listen to
the imam recite the Qur'an while we pray. He's reciting from the chapter
called *Surah Iklas*, translated as "The Purity" in English.

"Say, 'He is Allah, [who is] One,'"[3] the imam recites in Arabic.

My mom has heard me mention this chapter before. The last verse,
however, embodies the full realm of reasoning behind Islamic monotheism.

The imam completes the recitation in slow, melodic Arabic, "Nor is
there to Him any equivalent."[4]

I finish my prayer and think about my mother. She and I will remain
at odds about this particular issue, but I know where I stand. I just hope
that she will appreciate that I have a right to take a stance about my belief.

Patricia

NONE LIKE GOD. THE BIBLE SAYS IT TOO. SAID IT FIRST ACTUALLY. "No one is like you, LORD." That's Jeremiah 10:6. "You are great, and your name is mighty in power." So I read it again, this time in 1 Samuel 2:2: "There is no one holy like the LORD; there is no one besides you; there is no Rock like our God."

Then in Psalm 86:8: "There is none like you among the gods, O Lord, nor are there any works like yours" (ESV).

Then in 1 Chronicles 17:20. "O LORD, there is no one like you. We have never even heard of another God like you!" (NLT).

None like him.

I want to sing this out loud. But we're in Houston, visiting Alana and her family—and staying at her house. So I wouldn't dare go on YouTube and play out loud Richard Smallwood and the Richard Smallwood Singers. Then Walt Whitman and the Soul Children of Chicago. Then the Mississippi Mass Choir. Then the New Jersey Mass Choir. Then a young singer named Cora Hercules, belting it out of the park with a Praise Gospel Choir in a place called Brown Chapel at Point Loma Nazarene University.

None like him! *Jesus.*

Young Cora sings from the gut, a deep place. The others do too. But my YouTube stays silent on this day in March. So does my mouth. I want to celebrate triune magnificence and unfathomable love—this encompassing intimacy with Father–Son–Holy Spirit that blesses me so much.

But a daughter and a mother can't argue such matters. Not this day. And not this weekend. Already Alana has told me I have "control" issues. She'd read over my last section. Her response?

"You really have control issues, Mom."

Really?

I could answer like that. Yes.

But I shrug it off. Still, if wanting to guide my offspring to Jesus means I have control issues—then, yes, I have issues. But control doesn't work. So I'm prepared finally to give it up. Moreover, it would be nice to have a great spring break weekend in Houston.

So I try. But already I'm in hot water—trying just to get along with Alana and her Muslim friends.

Alana had arranged for us to go to an archery club with her children. It's their introduction to the sport. When we arrive, however, a small group of young Muslim women is standing outside with their children—a group of about twenty—all waiting to get into the archery center, which isn't yet open because the owner is late.

The group part surprises me. I thought just Dan and I with Alana and our grandkids were going. Now introverted me has to figure out how to switch gears. To socialize with strangers. It's a classic setup. My expectations out of sync with my daughter's. During marriage counseling, Dan and I learned these mix-ups are dynamite. Better to take a minute to get in sync, our counselor said. To say, here's what's happening. You okay with that?

At the archery center, however, I'm out of step from the get-go. Expecting one thing. Finding something else.

Then, sure enough, out of the blue one of the moms walks up and, after introductions, starts talking to me—not small talk, but she's talking about racism in Islam.

Set up.

I swallow hard, watching her talk. In her hijab and long clothes, this young woman of color approaches me as an ally. So she's ranting on about racism—and how "these Arabs" don't accept other Muslims.

Arabs?

She gestures at her kids. "Not even our children are accepted. They're unkind. Even to the children."

I nod, not sure why I'm nodding, trying to act like I agree or understand. Sure, I understand racism. But on this spring break morning, I don't understand Islam, and I'm not prepared to discuss bias with a stranger about a religion and a people I don't know. To Alana, I probably would sound condemning to Islam. To the women, I probably would sound knowledgeable of their situation, which I'm not.

As for Arabs, what about Alana's kind friends? Welcoming folks who have opened their homes, served us hot tea, cookies, company, and friendship—even when I didn't know how to reciprocate.

I sigh. I just wanted to watch my grandchildren try their hand at archery. To travel from Colorado to Houston to hang out with my sweet little grandbabies. I'd bought them all new outfits, and they were wearing their new clothes, looking sweet and fun and wonderful. But now I'm standing in a Houston parking lot—the only woman not wearing hijab and long, covered-up clothing—nodding but biting my tongue, my introvert's antenna on high alert to figure out where I stand. One of the women had purchased a Groupon discount for this whole group, which apparently now includes my husband and me.

But when this young woman takes on racism in Islam, I want to whisper *Jesus*. To ask this young woman to take her burdens to him. In this group, however, I can't do that. So I smile at the young woman, but I'm feeling out of place and confused.

I'd been reading Nabeel Qureshi's book, *Seeking Allah, Finding Jesus*—despite Alana's claim that Qureshi isn't reliable. Nevertheless, I'm finally learning in his book what Muslims are taught: That Jesus was never crucified. That God put Jesus' face on someone else and that someone else was crucified in Jesus' place. That this substituted person could've been Simon of Cyrene—the man who carried Jesus' cross. Or some "devout young volunteer," as Qureshi's book put it. Or even the betrayer, Judas—a popular view today, Qureshi says, because of its "poetic justice."[5]

But there's more. Apparently Muslims are taught that Jesus, even "if" he was crucified, didn't die on the cross. Instead, he "swooned" from the experience. Then—after being taken to the tomb by Nicodemus and Joseph of Arimathea and wrapped in cloths with one hundred pounds of aloe and other herbs—Jesus, some Muslims say, was healed. By God. And Jesus isn't God.

Jesus.

Bottom line: Muslims are taught that Jesus couldn't have been resurrected—a claim striking not just at the heart of who Jesus is but at the whole of Christianity. I hate even to write of such matters, feeling distressed to ask my publisher to reprint such claims. But to talk across faith, you have to know what's on the bridge.

So here is another of Alana's Muslim-convert friends, stressing to me the "similarities" between Islam and Christianity. But introverted me speaks up.

"No." I shake my head. "The theologies are *different.*"

The young woman looks perplexed. "Different? You think so?"

And here we go. I could let it be. Just compliment this determined young woman on the cross-cultural leadership program she directs in Houston for teens of different faiths. Say something kind about that. Then back off. Nice to meet you. Shake hands. See you soon.

But controlling me longs to set the record straight on Jesus. He's the redeemed, *resurrected* Christ. Shouldn't I defend that? To speak of his cross-defeating love. His grave-ending power. His intimate helping. His prayerful power. His uplifting joy. His friendship! His all in all.

But the young woman closes down. Besides, it's late in the morning—long after the archery club owner showed up and let everybody in. The children got several turns aiming bows at targets and letting the arrows fly. My little granddaughter Laila got a bull's-eye on the first try. *Go, Laila!* Which was fun.

But this isn't fun. The young woman is smart and nice and excited about her work bringing people together. Her talking across doctrines. But shared theology?

Controlling me can't accept it. The young woman's mother apparently thinks the same.

"That's what my mom says," the young woman finally says.

She looks sad. Raised a Christian, this young woman also converted to Islam. Now she and her mother can barely talk, she admits.

And it is time to leave the archery place anyway. So our talk awkwardly ends. Another mother's daughter at odds over faith.

Jesus. How did faith come to this?

He alone helps me with all this. And I'm grateful for the help, even if the daughter I love doesn't understand it in the same way.

A few weeks later Alana's birthday dawns. I send her a happy birthday text. Ask if her packages arrived. Sign it with my love.

I'd bought her three cute tunic tops in dark colors because she is a

Muslim. Extra-long because she is a Muslim. One of them black because she is a Muslim. Then sent the package with love because I follow Jesus.

And Jesus loves the little children. All the children of the world.

That was my first love song, taught to me by my parents and my childhood Sunday school teacher. They knew, as I learned, that Jesus' love is sweet when you don't know much love. In the Jim Crow fifties, during my childhood—and during the Depression years of my parents' youth—love seemed the hardest thing in the world for a black child to find. For me anyway, love seemed elusive and impossible.

But Jesus took away the difficulty. Even small black children could understand this: in the midst of conflicted life, Jesus loves.

So with Jesus' love I bought my baby Alana the cute, long, Muslim-appropriate tunics for her birthday. Sent them priority mail so she'd get them on time. Included a black one when I wanted to buy pink or orange or yellow or some happy color that looked fun. Then I waited. Didn't hear anything. So I texted: Do you like them? Praying. Hoping. Loving. If they don't fit, I added in my text, feel free to exchange.

In a few minutes Alana texted back. Saying, I really do like them.

I smiled. Grateful. Love never fails, wrote the apostle Paul. So I keep reading Alana's text: I'm wearing the black one right now!

I smiled again at Jesus. He lets controlling mothers love. A black tunic for a Muslim daughter? Doubters say no. But Jesus says yes.

Max Lucado puts it like this: "The more tightly we are attached to Jesus, the more purely His love can pass through us."[6] My pastor, Dr. Tyler, in a sermon on Luke 6, added this: "Pharisees want to argue for policies and procedures and protocol. But Jesus always argues for people."

So in his name, just *love*. I didn't do that well in Houston. Not at the archery place anyway.

Back home in Colorado, I try again. I call Claudia, the woman with the homeless ministry. She sounds sleepy. She's been at the church all night. But she remembers me. Hears my question.

"Are twenty little tubes of toothpaste going to make a difference?"

"Actually, that's perfect," she says. "Just what we need. The women are always asking us for toothpaste, lotion, deodorant."

Deodorant. Didn't buy that.

Back to King Soopers. I head for the travel-sized shelf. Count out twenty travel-sized Secret deodorant roll-ons. With about $32 to spend on this day, I pay for the deodorant, plus tampons and sanitary pads. Like my friend Denise says, when you help women with what they truly need, you change the world. God knows I hope so.

Two days later Dan drives with me to the downtown church. It's Saturday. The food bank people are organizing donations. Dan helps unload the truck while I carry in my King Soopers stash.

"You guys are just in time," says the leader and longtime church friend, Minnie Cullins, giving us hugs.

I head inside, carrying my items.

Claudia is there with other ladies I've known for years. So we talk family.

"Hey, Patricia! How's Joi?" one woman asks.

Fine, I say, and then ask, "And how's *your* Patricia?"

We laugh. Her daughter and I share a name.

So we go down the list of our children. Then she says, "And how's your baby?"

"Alana." I say my daughter's name. I smile. "She's doing fine. She's a schoolteacher. And a wife and a mom. Just had a birthday!"

Mothering Me could say more. But love is enough. So I hand over the toothpaste and deodorant and other items to the church ladies. They thank me. Bless me. We hug. All good.

It's time to do the same with Alana. To finally hand her over to Christ. Trusting him. I'm sixty-four. Too wise to keep battling. Too young not to love. To be content, as the late Dallas Willard said, "not to make things happen."[7]

Thus, I'm content to be out of control. But I'm scared half to death.

Jesus will help me figure out the way.

Alana

IT'S A LONG STRETCH FROM SAN ANTONIO TO HOUSTON. A GOOD time for me to process my mother's words. The long Texas road seems to go on forever, broken up occasionally by a sign for Cavender's Boot City and Posey Road. I look out over the landscape dotted with blue and red Texas wildflowers, and see God's creation, so peaceful and uncomplicated. Pretty soon a town rolls up, interrupting the serene, untouched scenery. We're in San Marcos, home of the famous Wienerschnitzel restaurant, fulfilling our family tradition of grabbing some hot dogs on the way back to Houston. I sigh, biting into my delicious chili cheese dog, wishing the short trip to my in-laws wasn't coming to an end.

Going home means returning to the normal routine and, most stressful of all, preparing for my parents' visit this week. It's weird having them come now, after reading Mom's words. She texted me, acting like everything was normal, using exclamation points and stating how excited she was to be visiting. It seemed fake, based on her recent comments. How could she be excited to come after what she said? I hesitantly write her back, trying to avoid showing my discontent. I add a smiley face to my text, trying to make me seem less cold.

The reality is much different. I'm going to have to face her again, after so many emotional moments have passed between us. It's going to be unpleasant, and I know it. The lull of the passing landscape soothes my worries as we drive on. In a small town I see a sign advertising pecans for sale and three consecutive churches on Church Street. "We believe in miracles," the sign says.

I do too, I think, wondering what my mom would say about the three churches lined up on the same street, yet not worshipping together. Something is dividing them, despite their similar belief in Jesus. It's hard to imagine why *they* can't even unify. Perhaps it's a disagreement within the leadership or small-town politics. Despite the purposed reasoning, seeing them all separated from each other sticks with me as we drive by.

During the trip, Iesa spoke at a local mosque's open house. The moderator, a geneticist, mentioned how the incredible similarities in the genetics of humans and chimpanzees illustrate the fact that humans should try to find commonalities in their beliefs. The audience members, a mixture of many religions and ethnicities from the local community, nodded their heads in agreement.

I thought of my mom and wished she was with me to hear this. Her claim that we are so different in our beliefs is divisive. We obviously disagree on Jesus' divinity, but shouldn't we try to unify on our common beliefs and not dwell on our differences? We have so much in common that it seems more productive to focus on the unifying principles of our faith. I'm reminded of my visit to the synagogue with my students during which the rabbi's presentation purposely mentioned nothing about Jesus. Instead, he focused on specific commonalities between Islam and Judaism.

Of course, it's ridiculous to act like these differences don't exist, and I'm not at all suggesting that. It seems necessary, however, to point out that at some point, Mom and I have to acknowledge that our understanding of Jesus can either make or break this project.

Chapter 109, verses 1–6, in the Qur'an give advice on how to handle this sort of stalemate. Allah states,

> Say, O disbelievers, I do not worship what you worship. Nor are you worshippers of what I worship. Nor will I be a worshipper of what you worship. Nor will you be worshippers of what I worship. For you is your religion, and for me is my religion.[8]

My husband mentioned these verses at the mosque's open house after sharing a fascinating historical presentation on Islam in America. He made some Texas-themed jokes, smiling charismatically at the audience, and then he surprised them with facts about the first documented Texas Muslims and Thomas Jefferson's Qur'an. He included these verses to emphasize the idea that sometimes we have to agree to disagree.

"Once we can get over this hurdle," he explained, "we can begin to learn about each other."

During his final thoughts, he paused, looked at the audience, and thanked them for coming, commending them for taking a step toward understanding their neighbors.

We went to the movies afterward to watch *Noah,* leaving the kids with the in-laws. It was a much-needed break from the hectic life of two working parents. I had heard that the movie was nothing like the biblical version of the story, but I was interested anyway. Toward the end of the film, the fictional Noah struggled to see good in any of the characters. Seeing the good in people is often harder than finding the bad. Even for my mother, what she perceives to be so bad may be blinding her toward seeing a solution.

Maybe we should drop the Jesus issue and move on.

Familiar landmarks start passing by as we near home. The baby sleeps soundly and the kids play loudly in the back. The road begins to congest with weekend travelers returning to my crowded city. My dad always complains about the traffic during their visits.

"It's ridiculous!" he laments. "You have to wait in line everywhere you go here, even in the car!"

It took me a while to adjust, but I'm used to it now. I actually enjoy the busyness of the city. In 2012, the *Houston Chronicle* reported that the Houston region had surpassed New York in its diversity. A woman mentioned in the article stated that she moved here so her kids could be around different people.

The crowded streets and diverse demographics are part of my normal experience. I'm not shocked to see a Hindu, Sikh, or Muslim walking down the street. I've grown accustomed to these differences. It seems as though people here don't deny the differences between each other but are able to coexist respectfully.

My thoughts are broken by the slowing of the car. We've arrived at the house, after a long four-and-a-half-hour drive. Now begins the daunting task of unloading the bags and four sleeping kids and then somehow getting them to bed on time. I'm tired, but optimistic about seeing my mother. Maybe we can use my city as a model for tolerance and understanding within our own family.

For now, I've got to get ready for their visit. I'll get up early and clean the bathroom and the room they sleep in. Then I'll wash some sheets and pillows. The kids will help me vacuum and pick up toys. I might even have time to get to the store for the Texas grapefruit my dad craves and my mom's favorite salad dressing. Then we'll welcome them with love and open arms, as I'm praying for peace and understanding.

six

LETTING GO

———————————— *Patricia* ————————————

HOLY WEEK IN HOUSTON. DAN AND I GET OFF THE PLANE, OUR
stomachs in knots. Well, my stomach is tight. He's carrying bags of toys
and goodies for our little grandchildren, looking for a direct path to our
rental-car shuttle. I follow, pushing a small suitcase, hoping I packed all
our toy stash but mostly nervous about seeing Alana.

Our work on the book, writing back and forth, has produced early
progress in our quest for peace, and I'm thankful. But now we'll be face
to-face, on Easter weekend no less, both of us looking to interact in a way
that is helpful. Even peaceful.

Yet how will we manage that? How will we talk? Talk about our hard
things? Our rough spots? The prickly points that send us reeling?

The Bible gives a warning: "Whoever loves a quarrel loves sin"
(Prov. 17:19).

But where does that leave divided families? Families who see God
with different eyes? Should we stay quiet? Should I act surrendered? *You
are the potter, Lord, I am the clay.* Then go silent but feel resentful?

That's how I managed conflict during our last visit to Alana's. I
asked her husband, a champion of interfaith relations, to recommend a
church where Dan and I could worship on the upcoming Sunday. But he
answered me with an odd look.

"A *church*?" He said the word, not with ecumenical peace but with
derision. So I dropped the matter unhappily.

Now, already on this visit, Alana and I are struggling to connect, too, even using the kids as buffers.

Alana: Tell Grammy what you did at school today.
Me: Ask Mommy if she needs help with dinner.

Our meal is pleasant enough, the kids keeping everyone engaged. Later, however, while washing dishes, I can't bear the tension. I turn to Alana: "So are you nervous about me visiting?"

She lets out a breath. "Yes!" She sets down her dish towel. "Are you?" She laughs.

"Nervous? About visiting?" I laugh too. "Yes!"

Then like that, we both drop guard, talking at once, trying to explain our anticipation, trying to align, to live through this Easter.

A small moment. But good. Positive. In that same way, I won't bug Alana's husband about finding us a church. Instead, I'll do a relationship thing—call a friend who lives in Houston, asking if we can tag along with her on Resurrection Sunday.

"Up from the Grave He Arose." Do churches still sing that sturdy hymn? Not all of them. But maybe they should. To be as one. All churches, indeed, aren't alike in tone and style. As for Islam, no matter what Alana claims about unity, mosques differ too. Then there's the conflict between Shia and Sunni Muslims, among other divisions.

So let's be real.

That's what I'm asking of Alana. That we not settle for a fake peace based on untrue reality. Or to claim "common" bonds between our faiths that aren't common at all.

Or to act as if Sunday hasn't been the worst day for her parents to visit her home in Houston. Because on Sundays at her home, her father and I have been in mourning. Yes, we get up early; we put on church clothes, eat breakfast alone, and quietly leave the sleeping house to find a church. With pain, we've done this for ten-plus years. Missing the Sunday morning bustle. Missing children getting dressed in their church pretties. Missing our family piling into one car to drive together to one church to worship the one risen Christ. Together. As family.

On several Sundays, while visiting without Dan, I drove around Houston by myself, looking for a church in a city I don't know. Once I got lost, turning down a street called Fondren—on my way to an A.M.E. church near Reliant Stadium—not realizing Fondren tracks diagonal, not parallel like many other streets in Houston. And the getting lost felt wrong.

Why should I be driving around Houston by myself, looking for a church address, when I have a daughter who lives here and could be driving me—or better, worshipping with me? But she sleeps in. And I drive hurt, going to worship while angry.

Then I remember what Thomas Aquinas said of harmony: "First, we need to know we are all madly in love with the same God." In fact, "We Are Fields Before Each Other," wrote Aquinas, asking with yearning:

How is it they live for eons in such harmony—the billions of stars—
When most men can barely go a minute without declaring
    war in their mind against someone they know.
There are wars where no one marches with a flag,
Though that does not keep casualties from mounting.
Our hearts irrigate this earth.
We are fields before each other.
How can we live in harmony? First we need to know
    we are all madly in love with the same God.[1]

In my family, since this isn't true, and our mad love refuses to acknowledge the same God, I decide to redeem this Sunday anew. So I don't call my childhood friend.

Instead, this Easter I listen to my husband.

"Keep it simple," he tells me, unpacking the one Sunday shirt and tie he brought.

So we choose a nearby church, where we don't know a soul, but it's not far from Alana's house—and where the church ushers welcome us with warm Resurrection Day smiles. Alana's husband, this time, recommended several churches—all pastored by friends he knows and admires. Alana urged him to help, I guess. I didn't ask, still tiptoeing around our ground. None of Iesa's picks are close, however. So Dan and I head for the nearby church, grateful to find Alana up early to help us with our breakfast and see us off.

And yet? "What shall I do then with Jesus?" (Matt. 27:22 KJV).

Pontius Pilate asked that question in Jerusalem, probing the masses on whether they were calling for crucifixion. Now every Easter since, people across history have asked it as well. What shall I do about Jesus?

On these pages, where I'm supposed to write about Muhammad—whom I can't write about because I'll possibly say or ask something wrong—I will instead look to the peace of the servant Christ.

What shall I do, Jesus?

On Easter, when I long to have a united family that celebrates your risen servant's heart, Jesus, what shall I do? Do about a beloved daughter who, as religious sociologist Rodney Stark says, has rejected her parents' mainstream "lower-tension faith" for "high-intensity" religion.[2]

What I do is sit on a pew in a welcoming church among families where nobody knows me, listening to a sermon that comforts and assures me. The pastor's sermon—"A Love That Makes You Forget"—starts with his description of things people have forgotten and left behind on commercial airplanes. A wedding dress. False teeth. Cell phones. Passports. iPads. Eyeglasses. The congregation laughs, nodding. We've all left things behind.

At the tomb of Jesus, however, when the women came with spices and herbs to embalm Jesus' dead body—but found the tomb empty, his grave clothes laying there—the women left behind the spices and herbs, the pastor recounts, but also their doubts.

"Now, what about you?" the pastor asks the congregation. "What will you leave at the empty tomb? Unforgiveness? Bitterness? Hate? Doubt? Fear?"

Your sadness, Patricia? I wipe away tears, listening to the question. Can I walk away from my grieving and mourning? From this crushing disappointment that my family's faith is so disjointed?

To answer, I accept the pastor's challenge—deciding then and there to reclaim the strong promises of the Bible, starting with Nehemiah's plea to the weeping Hebrew exiles: "Don't be dejected and sad," Nehemiah urged them, "for the joy of the LORD is your strength!" (Neh. 8:10 NLT).

On my own, I can't turn from my dejection. On my own, I can't convince Alana that what Islam says about Christ are calculated untruths. On my own, I can't convince Alana that what Islam denies about the Holy Bible are painful fabrications. On my own, I can't persuade Alana that the Gospels of the Bible aren't invalid or "changed"—that, in fact, more than twenty-four thousand ancient manuscripts of the New Testament still exist, so many manuscripts that any blatant variations among them would've been exposed generations ago. On my own, I can't point her to all those acrostic patterns in the Old Testament—so carefully constructed that each section corresponds to a different letter in the Hebrew alphabet, with each verse beginning with the letter of its section. This mode of repetition helped God's people memorize his Word and pass it along orally and accurately across generations.

On my own?

I can't convince Alana that sweet Jesus is the Creator God, come to earth as a servant, making it possible to know him for ourselves.

On my own, indeed, I can't make my family whole in our believing.

But the joy of the Lord *is* my strength.

And while she chooses others' claims over family, I will leave behind my sadness over this and live in joy. Isn't that what Alana wants? For me to "get over it" and be happy?

On my own, I can't do this thing at all. But with Christ, I can do all things. So after church, I suggest we all go to see a Disney movie. Happy? Well, for now, close enough. We agree to see *Bears*, a Disney story about a bear family. But first we agree to go out together for dinner.

Alana jokes with her dad about going to Luby's, the cafeteria restaurant—a style he likes. In the end, however, we go to a Persian restaurant, a place on Westheimer Road called Kasra.

"Persian?" I want to say. But I don't bother. We're going out together with our younger daughter and her family on Easter to eat dinner. In a world where people are starving and families are fighting and wars are waging, can't I be happy about that?

Once we are seated at the restaurant I am, in fact, more than happy. The food is excellent. We dive in to warm *taftoon* bread. Its own kind of heaven. I order chicken with saffron rice and roasted tomatoes. Fabulous.

I enjoy the atmosphere. The Houston diversity. The comfort of scores of families with women dressed pretty much like me, in familiar Western clothing.

The meal is wonderful. We enjoy each other's company. My grandchildren are adorable. Alana's husband helps us understand the food. The only blip is when a family enters the restaurant with young women dressed head to toe in hijab bling. Full makeup. Smoky eyes. Glossy lips. Bedazzled eyebrow to toenail. Sparkly, floor-length abayas. But not shapeless cover-up abayas. This is blinged-out glam. One outfit shimmers with shiny gold coins, sewn front to back on the skintight midriff. My little granddaughter does a double take, eyes growing wide.

She whispers to her mommy, asking Alana and Iesa to take her to a store right now to buy a hijab to wear to the movie.

So after we ate, that's what they did.

Then we sat in the movie, Alana and her firstborn in their hijabs—all of us too full from our Persian dinner to even think about eating popcorn—and we enjoyed a Disney story about bears.

It is my interfaith life. Do I understand it? No. Will I be happy about it? With Christ, here's the answer: if this life is God's will, I will live until I die with the strength of his joy.

So two days later Dan and I returned home by airplane. By mistake, I left behind my Kindle in the pocket of seat 14D—marveling how easy it is, indeed, to leave a thing behind. Am I sad? Not this time. Instead, I go online and submit a lost and found report to Frontier Airlines. Within twenty-four hours, Frontier Airlines e-mails me back. "Kindle found."

Driving out to pick it up at the airline's Denver headquarters, Dan and I talk about the difference between leaving something by accident or on purpose.

"To the person who found it," I say to Dan, "it looks the same—whether you left it on purpose or by mistake."

"But the main thing," Dan said, "is that the other person sees what you found."

So I will find joy. Hope. Goodness. Contentment. Trust. Then leave behind my stinking sadness. My bitterness. Confusion. Grief. May Alana see this changed path. Then lead me, servant Christ, to the next step on this journey. And where will that be? I don't know every step. But with you, the walk is always lovely. I finally recognize that. With you, shepherd Christ, the joy is to follow.

Alana

EASTER HAS PASSED, AND WITH IT A WHOLE NEW SET OF EMOTIONAL events. I knew it would be hard for Mom to visit during this time. Somehow, she tolerated the awkwardness of staying in a Muslim house during one of the most holy days in Christianity. She donned her smile for my daughter's sixth birthday, but she seemed sad the whole visit. I could see it in her eyes. Each time she smiled or laughed, the pain showed through. Every time I put on a hijab for us to go somewhere together, she paused for half a second and stared, as if not wanting to believe her eyes. I wore bright colors on purpose, to offset her misconstrued perception about Muslim women and dark clothing.

My daughter surprised us all by asking for a hijab so insistently after dinner at the Persian restaurant. I snuck a quick glance at my mom to gauge her reaction. Mom didn't know that we had already passed some of the dressed-up girls while leaving the restroom. My daughter's eyes shot open wide, and her jaw dropped the minute she saw them. She loves fashion, and I knew she was admiring their long colorful robes and sparkly hijabs. It's not that far off from what she sees at her school, where stylish modesty is somewhat of a competition among teachers and color reigns supreme.

We left the restaurant, headed for the movies, with my daughter insisting on a hijab. The whole time, I'm reading Mom's reactions and body language. She seemed tense and uncomfortable, trying her best not to look it. I'm sure the day turned out to be nothing like she expected. The Persian restaurant and my daughter's desire to wear a hijab must have affected her holiday spirit.

The day before, we were in the car, and my daughter said, right out of the blue, "Grammy, I want to go to church with you, just to see what it's *like*." Tension filled the car as Mom paused and cautiously answered, "Okay, but you have to ask your parents." My husband casually replied that we'd go together one day. Deep down I wondered if Mom was hoping we'd go for Easter and that the family would get dressed in their "Easter best" and head down together, almost like old times.

My husband and I talked about it on our date night that same evening. "Should we go for Easter?" I suggested to him. "If we do go, it would illustrate confidence in our faith." But I had worries as well. Although my daughter is so mature and conscientious for her age, she is also extremely impressionable. The music and performances of the church plus the extravagant Easter activities would be alluring to any child. It just didn't seem fair to expect a child to understand the religion behind all the pastel colors and chocolate eggs.

We hadn't purposely avoided going to church with them. We were just going to wait a bit until the kids were able to have a mature conversation about their experience. I didn't expect our kids to ask to go so soon. We decided to postpone the visit and go another time to a church run by a minister pal of my husband. Then we devised a plan to avoid my parents in the morning, especially the awkward moment when my mother might sadly look at my daughter when she asks to go to church. We conspired to go out and eat breakfast early or go to the park. Ironically, Iesa and I ended up being too tired from our date the night before to accomplish anything like that. I woke up feeling stupid for even suggesting such a ridiculous plan.

On Easter morning the kids woke up early and zonked straight into the iPad. My parents dressed in their Easter attire and quietly left for church. When they returned a few hours later, my daughter asked Mom where she had been. Although I didn't hear the response, I'm sure my daughter was disappointed that she hadn't gone.

We've taught our kids about church and the differences between Islam and Christianity, and always in a respectful manner. My husband and I don't put other religions down at all. We teach monotheism to our kids and point out that other views are different for specific reasons. Never once have we put down my mother's way of thinking. I try patiently to explain Easter and Christmas to the kids since these are the most visible holidays in the stores. We talk about St. Patrick's and Valentine's Day, too, even though they are more commercial than religious.

At school they now learn only about Islam. Occasionally, other religions are brought up within the contexts of the prophets who are associated with them. Never once has my daughter mentioned anything negative that she learned from her teachers of Islamic studies.

The kids know there are differences between the prophetic traditions of Islam and Christianity, mainly from our discussions about Jesus, but we don't dwell on them, nor are we preoccupied with disproving other beliefs. My mother continues to persist in discussing the differences within the stories of the prophets as if it hinders our dialogue. From my point of view, it's irrelevant to debate about the story variants within the Bible and Qur'an because many of the moral lessons within the two books remain the same. And I'm thankful that some of the bizarre and inappropriate parts of biblical lives mentioned in the Bible are left out of the Qur'an.

The Qur'an focuses on the concept of monotheism and holds that all prophets, from Abraham to Muhammad, were sent with the same message of proclaiming monotheism and condemning immorality. Other Muslims might talk negatively about other beliefs, but isn't this supposed to be about my mother and me, not everybody else?

My husband and I agree to take the kids to a couple of churches he knows. "To take the mystery out of it," he says. He has tons of connections with ministers in the city who would be more than welcoming to our kids. It's probably better that we go without my mother at first to avoid any discomforting emotions or, even worse, her tears.

The perfect opportunity arises. A local minister invites my husband to his church for a "peace rededication garden ceremony." As a means of outreach the church invited people of other faiths to worship and picnic with the congregation. My husband forwards me the e-mail, "*Assalamu alaikum*, sweetheart, I think we should go to this if we can," he types. I reply with a definite yes. It seems like a great chance to expose the kids to church. The church's website states, "We respect all world religions and encourage cooperation between all of God's children." I'm excited and optimistic about this opportunity.

On Sunday, however, our plan is halted by sickness. The kids and I are feeling ill with coughs and runny noses. We decide to stay home and rest, so as not to miss school the next day. I'm disappointed. I pick up my phone and find a text from my dad: We're on our way to church. Have a great day! He asks about our plans for the day. I almost fill him in on our previous plan but then decide against it.

Later he sends another note: We're at a Lebanese restaurant! It seems like today is their day for trying something new. Soon I hope, for reasons of my own, I'll be able to text him back and say that we've experienced something new too.

Patricia

WE'RE BACK HOME. THE AIR SMELLS LIKE SPRING. TREES ARE DARing to bud, ignoring the springtime truth—that before summer Colorado will see more snow. But it's warm on this back-home day. Sunny enough for gardening. So I head out to our brown front yard, which over winter has taken a beating. Our clematis vines, facing south, are thick with last year's dead growth. I grab our old garden scissors from the garage and start chopping away at dead branches. Tenderly chopping—if there is such a thing. Green shoots are already sprouting through the dead stuff, so I try to avoid the new growth. A tender prune. But a tender prune won't do it. To bloom well in summer, the vines need hard pruning in spring. Right to the roots. Down to the ground. New growth and all. I chop but cringe.

"You won't hurt it," Dan says.

He's on the driveway, sweeping up a riot of pine needles from the shaggy evergreen tree that separates our yard from our longtime neighbor's. Together, the four of us—Dan and I, with our neighbor Nancy and her husband, Steve—pooled our pennies to have the tree trimmed last year.

"Let's save it," Nancy said. She's a retired United State Marine and decisive—which I admire, especially in a good neighbor. So we went with her plan. The tree took a hard pruning and found new life.

Now revived, the tree shed a carpet of needles and pinecones over winter—half of them lining our driveway in deep piles.

So Dan sweeps. I chop. We rake. We trim. We prune for all we're worth. So, yes, I think of the biblical metaphor of pruning—how only in pruning away our stuff does the Lord prepare us for a useful life in Christ. I've always called this "hard" gospel. It's good news but tough love.

It does seem harsh to hack things to the heart. But it seems the best route to new growth. So I dig deep and ask the Lord to prune. Prune *me*. My first real prayer on this journey? I'm not sure, but within days I feel my heart open a slice. Back in my pile of books, I try to read more on Islam. Still hard. But God knows I'm trying to understand. To get past the rejection of Christ. The refusal of his gospel. The tweaking of his stories. Then calling it "revelation." Or that's how it seems. And that drives me crazy still.

But my pile of books says hold up. I'm not a Jesus Avenger. I'm a Christian mom with a Muslim daughter. And in the pruning of *this* path, my Bible offers the Jesus way. So I dig deep again to read his gardening words in the gospel of John 15:1–2:

> "I am the true vine, and my Father is the gardener. He cuts off every branch in me that bears no fruit, while every branch that does bear fruit he prunes so that it will be even more fruitful."

Hard gospel? I read it again, abiding. So Jesus prunes away, declaring in John 15:5–6 yet more:

> "I am the vine; you are the branches. If you remain in me and I in you, you will bear much fruit; apart from me you can do nothing. If you do not remain in me, you are like a branch that is thrown away and withers; such branches are picked up, thrown into the fire and burned."

Reading these verses again I see something. That God *will* cut off my dead stuff—resentment, anger, bitterness, wrath. All my "clamor," as the apostle Paul described it when writing to the early church at Ephesus (Eph. 4:31 ESV).

Meantime, beyond cutting off the useless, God will prune those parts worth saving. My passion. My questioning. My yearning for family peace.

My longing for my daughter's understanding. My hunger for mutual compassion. My need to show personal respect. My need in return to earn it. With all of that, surely, the Lord can redirect me to *something* useful. "If you remain in me."

Within days, I'm poring over books on how to rebuild community from a broken heart—including *Reconciling All Things*, the beautiful reflection on justice, peace, and healing by Ugandan theologian Emmanuel Katongole and his American colleague Chris Rice.

As they put it, reconciliation is about "transformation of the everyday." But first, they say, "before reconciliation is about us, it's about God." It's God's mission, in fact. So imagine it.[3]

Imagine that reconciliation in our action-infected world is not hurling ourselves onto the center stage—asking "what we must do," jumping into action. Instead, they write: "The journey of reconciliation begins with seeing that reconciliation is not the goal of human striving but is instead a gift God longs for us to accept." Even more, it "gives birth to other gifts within the reality of God's new creation."[4]

So peace is not just about harmony? Not just about understanding?

Something stirs. But I get an e-mail alert. It's a message from a friend, Dr. Brenda Salter McNeil, who runs the Reconciliation Studies minor at Seattle Pacific University. She's sending a reminder that her class is reading my racial forgiveness memoir, *My First White Friend*, and I have agreed to speak by Skype to her students in a couple of weeks.

I reread her beautiful book, *A Credible Witness*, on the connection between reconciliation and evangelism. As Brenda puts it, reconciliation isn't about browbeating people to Christ. Instead, "our unity in the midst of our diversity" in Christianity "is one of the most powerful ways we reveal the reality of what Jesus accomplished on the cross."[5] And that is a credible witness.

Lord Jesus.

Is this also your pruning? Because my journey with Alana has taken me beyond the matter of peace within Christianity, or peace within our family, to a path that feels global. Is that why Gabe Lyons, who's also on the reading list for Brenda's class this semester, writes in his book: "There's no longer a geographical place where Christians can isolate, incubate, or regroup. Whatever they become, it will have to be within the broader context of life in America and the world"?[6]

A global gospel. Will I follow? *I'm trying, Lord.*

Within days, and under the pruning knife, I'm peeking into books on interfaith ministry—going to Amazon to order *Getting to the Heart of Interfaith*, cowritten by a Jewish rabbi, a Muslim sheikh, and a Christian pastor. Their snapshot is on the book's cover. The three of them stand, shoulder to shoulder, arm in arm—the Muslim sheikh in the center. They are smiling.

They are global. As they say in their book's first chapter: "If there is to be a solution to the problems of poverty, homelessness, and global warming, it will take all of us working together."[7]

And the true vine won't let go. I know it's a Jesus thing to reach beyond borders. Surely it's a Jesus thing to love the poor. Absolutely it's a Jesus thing to get over Alana's refusal to go into a church. It's a Jesus thing not to get stuck there—and not to try to control how, when, and where she goes. Because as much as I long to sit on a church pew once again with my family—even if they're there to observe, not to worship—it's a Jesus thing to let go of the details. To be okay if Alana and Iesa take their children to a Houston church and I'm not there to go with them.

Besides, over these ten years since Alana moved to Houston, Dan and I have managed to visit all sorts of churches there—a little chapel near the Galleria, the sprawling megachurch of Pastor Kirbyjon Caldwell, the stately sanctuary of First Methodist, the rocking downtown pews of St. John's, the southwest suburban joy of Church Without Walls. In the end, the small A.M.E. church near Reliant Stadium grabs our hearts. It feels like home. The music. The preaching. The people. The friendly ways. Big or small, however, churches in Houston have blessed us on every visit. Joel Osteen, with his big downtown stadium church, is even on our church-visiting bucket list.

"I like that guy," Dan says, not worrying for now about critics of the megachurch pastor.

"'Cause he's upbeat," I say. "You like that."

"Right," Dan says. "He's positive. I do like that. A lot."

And Osteen can preach an Easter sermon.

"It may be Friday," the TV pastor tells his stadium audience, "but Sunday's coming!" The crowd shouts, "Amen!"

Watching Osteen on TV in our kitchen back home, Dan tears up, grabbing a Kleenex. Sunday's coming. A Jesus thing? On this day, I'm not judging one bit.

I'm also, on this day, not judging Alana. So I let pass—for now—her argument that story differences about prophets in the Bible and the Qur'an are "irrelevant." To agree feels like the slippery slope of relativism, as theologians would say. But today I'm just a mother and a Jesus follower. I will let it pass. Remaining in the true vine. *Help me, Lord, to plant myself there.*

In that way I'm enjoying my returned Kindle.

"It feels like a new gift," I tell Dan, "like the first time you gave it to me."

We leave things behind. When we stick with them in love, however, they can come back. Jesus taught that lesson in parables. Beautiful Sunday school stories. The Lost Sheep. The Lost Coin. The Lost Son.

That prodigal son was especially a mess. Partying and drinking and squandering his daddy's money—until he came to his senses and came back home.

I used to think this prodigal story would be about Alana. As I reread it today, however, I see it's about me. I've been lost in my anger, bitterness, sadness. All my dead stuff. Squandering the Father's grace. Wasting God's good time with my sadness and sorrowing. But as I move through this journey, I am coming to my senses.

So Jesus can celebrate today. Patricia is coming home. Letting him write the rest of the reconciliation story. Moving off center stage, I can let him grace me with gifts. I'm scared to open them. But if I dare, I can do what he does best. I can triumph in love.

In a week it snows again. The winter's final icing. The next morning, blinding sun starts to melt the white. Our freshly raked lawn sends up green shoots through melting snow. The evergreen renders a spring pine scent. The clematis sprouts new tendrils. Green and able. From ground level the branches face a long climb to reach the roofline on the front side of the house.

But ground level is a good place to start. My path to peace can restart there too. Pruned and ready. It's the least a mother can offer a daughter. So, Alana, will you join me? Keep trying for our peace? I pray the answer is yes.

Alana

It's date night again, a once-a-month occurrence for my husband and me. We drop the kids off at a friend's and hurry down the highway. I take a deep breath and relax a bit, then hold on as my husband rushes us toward our destination. We're a half hour late for an interfaith organization's fund-raiser gala. I'm wearing the same outfit that I wore the last time I went to a gala, but I don't care. I didn't have any time this week to shop for clothes. We arrive at the hotel, check in, and sneak in the side door. Our table is obviously the Muslim table, full with bearded men and two women, one in a Pakistani *shalwar*. I'm the only female in hijab.

I look around the lavishly decorated room and observe people of different faiths. Monks clad in brown robes sit at the table to my left, and here or there I spot Hindu women in a full sari and men in yarmulkes. It's a real-live religious salad bowl, so to speak.

The moderator on the stage gives us an overview of the evening.

"We've reserved a room for those who need to pray the evening prayer," he states, wishing us all a bon appétit as the dinner is served.

The woman next to me smiles and claps quietly, happy that a room has been put aside for us. A volunteer comes over to make sure we know that guides have lined the hallway leading to the prayer room, so we won't lose our way. My husband laughs and mentions that we'll probably eat a little first and then pray. He thanks him for all the extra effort. The volunteer looks worried and notes that he'll make sure to have the prayer room guides wait for at least fifteen minutes more.

We head out to the prayer room after a couple of sips of the first course, a butternut squash soup topped with pastry. The guides have long vanished, and the hallway leading to the room is abandoned. Laughing, we find our way to a room and enter, only to find it filled with tables and a few banquet stewards.

"Can we borrow your tablecloth to use for a prayer rug?" one of the men in our group asks a steward, who immediately looks confused and clutches his impeccable and probably just recently folded tablecloth to his chest.

"It's that awkward moment when you have to explain to a non-Muslim why you need his tablecloth," I whisper to one of my husband's friends next to me.

We laugh to ourselves as the Muslim man tries to negotiate with the steward for the tablecloth. Eventually the steward escapes behind a door, and we resort to pulling off a cloth from one of the tables. We spread it on the floor and begin to pray. I'm the only woman praying so I stand alone. In a few minutes another woman enters and immediately begins to pray right next to me. I don't look up, trying to concentrate on my prayer, but for a moment, I think about how nice it is to pray next to someone who believes in God the same way that I do. We finish our prayer, and I look over at the woman next to me. I'm surprised to see that it's one of my friends. We laugh and joke about how we didn't know that there were any other Muslims at the gala, then head back to our tables.

The keynote speakers, Dr. John Mendelsohn, president of M. D. Anderson Cancer Center; and his wife, Anne Mendelsohn, take the stage to accept their honorarium. Mrs. Mendelsohn praises the organization for its ability to bring people together by "our shared values"—thus creating "a more peaceful, understanding world."

She mentions that she's experienced firsthand what it means to live peacefully with others because she is in an interfaith marriage. She doesn't elaborate on that point, but my interest is piqued because of my own situation.

Mr. Mendelsohn takes the microphone next and mentions that we should pay attention to the "core values that we all share." He cites the Golden Rule as an example of an ideal that exists in so many faiths. He reads phrases from the Bible, the Torah, and the Qur'an that echo Golden Rule–like messages. He goes on to quote Confucian, Hindu, and Buddhist texts with a similar theme. When he mentions "commonness" and "ethical reciprocity," I wonder how he and his wife rectified their faith differences.

All this kumbaya *sounds great when you're in a room full of strangers,* I think, *but it's a whole lot harder with family.*

One of the alumni from the yearlong youth interfaith program takes the stage next. He talks about writing an interfaith prayer with the students during the year. "We couldn't even agree on which name to use for God," he lamented.

I thought about our family dinner during my parents' last visit. We didn't even say a prayer before we ate, to avoid the awkwardness of it all. It might be worthwhile for our family to write a familial interfaith prayer to use for meals when we're all together.

The evening concludes with a bunch of handshaking and networking on my husband's part, one of the main reasons he wanted to come. We find the Jewish president of the organization. "I'm so glad that you made it," he tells my husband sincerely.

I'm introduced to a couple more Jewish board members and Christian ministers in the crowd. They hug and praise my husband for his community work and promise to continue their partnerships.

The next day is Friday—movie night at our house. Our daughter settles down after a busy day of school and Girl Scouts. "Can I watch *The Prince of Egypt*?" she asks. "It's about a *prophet!*" she pleads, trying to convince me to overlook some of the violent parts because it includes religious history.

Despite the obvious commercial embellishments, the story doesn't stray that far from the Islamic version of Moses' life. We gather our pizza and snacks and sign in to Netflix. During the song "Let My People Go," I'm reminded of the rabbi who sang his rock-and-roll version of the same song to my students during our synagogue visit. The students connected with him then, considering they were familiar with that part of the story. I'm sure he chose that song on purpose, hoping to find another common thread between us.

At bedtime we're reading nursery rhymes. On the page with a Christmas tree lined with presents, my daughter states, "We don't do Christmas, but I wish we got presents on Christmas."

"You do!" I exclaim. "From your grandparents."

She smiles, feeling silly for forgetting her Christmas gifts. We don't send our family presents on Muslim holidays, but maybe we should. For me, it was out of fear that I might offend someone, I guess, by sending them a *Happy Eid* card. Gift giving among family members is definitely a common practice, though, among Muslims during Islamic holidays. Even though my mother doesn't share our holidays, I'm sure she would appreciate a token of affection from her grandkids.

Finding a way to pray together and give together seems like a good starting point to mend our relationship. I think of the Lord's Prayer, the most common prayer among Christians, and the first chapter of the Qur'an called "The Opening," which is the most-often recited prayer among Muslims. Both prayers are so widely used within their religions and so similar in message and theme. Both praise God emphatically, acknowledge his sovereignty, and ask for his mercy, guidance, and forgiveness. Both prayers emphasize the need for mankind to turn to him alone.

Maybe if Mom and I start at these two prayers, we'll find a common thread that binds us. The thread may become twisted and frayed as we go along unless we choose to find more threads to hold on to. I'm sure we'll find more commonness if we search sincerely, but we both have to be willing to try.

So yes, Mom, I will try. And I'm thankful that you're trying too.

seven

ᔖᔕ

WALKING IN LIGHT

--------------------- *Patricia* ---------------------

THE LEBANESE RESTAURANT ON DENVER'S SOUTH SIDE ISN'T crowded. Just a few tables occupied on this Sunday afternoon. So it feels okay to send a text to Alana, telling her all about it.

"I don't have my phone," I say to Dan.

"Just use mine," he says.

He pushes his phone across the restaurant table. I send the text.

We're at a Lebanese restaurant! Dad ordered chicken koubideh. Mom's having hummus and pita bread!

Why am I texting in exclamation points?

This isn't earth-shattering news. But eating here is outreach. It is stretching. It is interfaith. Well, a first step. Of sorts. This isn't IHOP, our regular after-church Sunday stop. This is a Persian café near a Denver college campus. Far off our beaten track.

So Dan grabs his fork and digs into his chicken *koubideh*, asking between bites, "How do you say that again?" I also order a chicken kebab and saffron rice. Not as tasty as the restaurant fare in Houston—truly one of the best restaurant cities in the United States.

Back here in Denver, however, Dan and I know it means something—to us, if not to Alana—to move beyond our usual Christian circles to eat a Sunday dinner among strangers. To talk to the Lebanese waiter. To smile at the hijab-wearing woman sitting on a chair at the back of the restaurant.

115

"Is this the way to the ladies' room?" I ask her. I smile.

She smiles back but doesn't say anything. Instead, she barely shrugs, helping me understand that she doesn't speak English. Or that's what I assume. But we do smile. And in the big-small world these days, a smile can mean more than a little something.

Still, a smile isn't Christian missionary work. It isn't taking underwear on a winter night to homeless women. It isn't tutoring underprivileged children. It isn't being busy. But it is being kind—which I can stand to do more of. That is, I'm not unkind. I don't think of myself that way anyway. But do I make people feel better? Am I willing, as Alana says, to find more "commonness" across faiths? Do I worry less about witnessing for Christ—and aim just to be like Christ?

I'm thinking about that today. During this week, when I intend to recommit to living *rightly* in interfaith peace with my daughter, I plan to call an interfaith outreach place and volunteer where needed. So here I go again. Jumping into *doing*. In Christendom, we are experts, indeed, at the doing. And we do a heck of a lot of good all over the world. So I mark my calendar for doing. Write down the interfaith center's name and phone number. Set my mind to driving across town to work with people of different faiths.

Then my lower back goes out. Seizes up. Frozen. Or that's how it feels. I'd bent down to take a glass from the dishwasher and *pow!* So I sat for a week on a hard chair and thought about everything. About gaining in years. About being traditional and unbending. About being so inflexible when I bent down that I pulled a muscle on my spine. So I thought hard indeed. Then I prayed hard too. What, O Jesus of Nazareth, do you want me to do? Or *not* do?

I struggled to know, especially with Mother's Day bearing down. Thinking about it, seeing it come up on the calendar, I'd been holding my breath. Not afraid but curious. What will my Mother's Day this year bring?

No, wrong. What will *I* bring?

My daughters aren't big on gift giving. Not to me anyway. Sometimes on my birthday. Never on Mother's Day. So especially on Mother's Day, the non-gifts have left me adrift. Doubting myself yet again. Not good enough for some earrings from Macy's? A blouse from Dillard's? A card from Hallmark or the dollar store? Anything?

"Here we go again," I say to Dan. "Another year to navigate Mother's Day."

"Everybody loves you," Dan says, singsonging it. Joking. Reminding me to lighten up. Matter-of-fact. "*I* love you. We all do. A card once a year or not doesn't change that."

He's right, of course. Besides, I've vowed to leave my sadness at the *empty* tomb. If Jesus is alive, and he is, it's time I started acting like it. Especially since I already have the best Mother's Day gift.

Alana is saying we can pray *in her house.*

The Lord's Prayer. In Alana's house. If that's not a gift, I don't know what is. So I sit for a minute on my hard chair and let the goodness of it sink in. Thinking about the years Dan and I have felt wary about expressing any part of our faith around Alana and her family. Especially in her home.

In the oddest moments I'd felt the taboo. So standing under the shower one night in her kids' bathroom, I opened my mouth to belt out "What a Friend We Have in Jesus." But before the first word left my mouth, I bit my tongue. I can't sing about Jesus in Alana's house. Can't call him a friend. Surely I can't sing his name in the shower. Somebody might hear. Somebody might object. But now I can pray. Pray the Lord's Prayer. *In her house.*

Our Father.

The two opening words cut to the heart of it all. Cut to the core of what makes a Jesus follower a Christian. It's knowing God as a brother, a friend. In the person of Jesus. And knowing that God in Jesus personally knows you. Knows "the very hairs of your head," declares the gospel of Luke (12:7). Knows "my downsitting and mine uprising" (Ps. 139:2 KJV) and every "word in my tongue," wrote strong king David in the book of Psalms in the King James Version (v. 4).

"Before I formed you in the womb," God says in the book of Jeremiah, "I knew you, before you were born, I set you apart" (1:5). Hagar, delivered in the desert, rejoiced over this good love, calling the father *El Roi*: "You are 'God who sees' . . . the one who looks after me" (Gen. 16:13 ISV).

The prophet Isaiah rejoiced even more: "But now, O LORD, thou art our father; we are the clay, and thou our potter; and we all are the work of thy hand" (64:8 KJV). The God who made me. Who knows me by name. And, in Christ, loves me anyway. Plus there is that empty tomb.

Our Father.

I am ecstatic. Grateful. Common understanding. Are we on our way? One small step. Well, actually two. Alana also said I might even get a token from my grandchildren at Christmas. Isn't that right? "To Grammy. With love." Forget the earrings. Forget the blouse. *Any* token from my grandchildren at Christmas will say family. I'm too overjoyed to speak. Afraid to say too much here. Fearful Alana will take it all back.

My back eases up after a week. Fairly limber again, I'm ready to launch into our fresh, hopeful season. Our shared understanding. But what is God saying?

Tell a story?

That's what my book by the three religious guys says to do. In their five "stages" to interfaith understanding, they say start with stage one: telling each other your faith stories. In such stories we "move beyond separation and suspicion."[1]

That's what Dan and I did at the Lebanese restaurant. Dan chatted up the waiter. And the waiter chatted back. A few weeks before, I didn't blink when our Hindu tenants—living in my late mama's home—showed me the altar room they had created in an upstairs bedroom, explaining how they pray. I listened closer when an elderly Christian woman we pick up for church every Sunday told us about the Passover seder she had attended at the Jewish nursing home where she lives.

She was laughing. "Girl, I ate a big bite of horseradish and almost choked."

"Horseradish?" Dan asked.

"For the meat?" I asked.

"For the bitter herbs," said our friend. "It represents the bitterness of slavery the Jews went through in Egypt."

"So how was the horseradish?" Dan asked. He likes that condiment. On meat especially. He wanted to hear more.

"*Strong* horseradish, Dan. Extra-strong horseradish. I didn't know what it was. I just swallowed a big bite, and Lord Jesus, I thought I'd stop breathing. Never tasted anything so strong in my life."

"Bitter herbs," I said.

"That's right, sweetheart. But you know what? Slavery *was* bitter. Bitter for the Hebrew children. Black folks understand that, too, don't we?"

"Yes," I said. "We understand."

Common understanding. Our elderly friend said it this way: "I didn't like that horseradish, but you know something? I learned a lot." She sat up taller. "Even if they don't accept Jesus Christ as Lord and Savior, I learned a lot."

So we could start there. Telling our little stories. Said the late Dallas Willard, "The aim of God in history is the creation of an all-inclusive community of loving persons, with himself included in that community as its prime sustainer and most glorious inhabitant."[2]

So here's a story.

Not a Bible story. Quaker Richard Foster told it in one of his books on prayer. So it goes:

> A venerable, old sage once asked his disciples, "How can we know when the darkness is leaving and the dawn is coming?"
>
> "When we can see a tree in the distance and know that it is an elm and not a juniper," ventured one student.
>
> "When we can see an animal and know that it is a fox and not a wolf," chimed in another.
>
> "No," said the old man, "those things will not help us."
>
> Puzzled, the students demanded, "How then can we know?"
>
> The master teacher drew himself up to his full stature and replied quietly, "We know the darkness is leaving and the dawn is coming when we can see another person and know that this is our brother or our sister; otherwise, no matter what time it is, it is still dark."[3]

This week two hundred schoolgirls in Nigeria are kidnapped by Boko Haram, an Islamic terrorist group. But as soon as I think *Islamic terrorist,* I pull the reins. The two words together—*Islamic* and *terrorist*—are for

Alana and me our place of dark. Our fighting words. Our intergalactic black hole. And I'm not falling in. Not today.

So standing in the light—at the empty tomb—I pray with Dan for the girls. Later I go on Facebook, joining in the calls to #BringBackOurGirls.

Facebook is awash with Mother's Day messages, photos, emoticons, and more. Hearts and balloons and love wishes. "You're the best mom ever."

At the empty tomb I post photos of my late mother on Facebook. I tell a story or two about her life. Delight that others remember her. "Your mother was a wonderful lady."

I mail cards to my beautiful daughters, both hardworking great moms, so the cards arrive in time for Mother's Day. On Saturday I call church members whose children have passed away—or who are estranged from their adult children. I enjoy our chats. Pray they do too.

On this Saturday before Mother's Day, I don't receive any cards. Well, Dan gives me a beautiful card and flowers. At dinner with old friends, their daughter gives me a lovely box of chocolate candy. Nothing from my daughters. Alana was sick this week. With her full-time job, she probably didn't have time. But on Sunday she and her sister call me. Late at night my son-in-law calls too. I close my eyes while they talk to me. Letting their voices fill me. Grateful. I post a photo of my flowers on Facebook.

Then right before bedtime, on my e-mail, I read a message to me from Alana: "The Human Cost of Your Mother's Day Flowers." It's an exposé on the cut-flower industry in Colombia, where impoverished women working under horrific conditions, exposed to pesticides and worse, break their health for pitiable wages so American women can enjoy bouquets.[4]

So what would Jesus do? I write a letter to the CEO of Kroger and King Soopers, where Dan bought the flowers, asking him to sell only Fair Trade–certified arrangements in the floral departments of all of his stores.

The next morning I change the water in my flowers. Pulling off the dead stuff. Trying to give them light. Determined to do right by the impoverished women in Colombia. That afternoon a card arrives from our elderly friend whom we drive to church every Sunday. "Pat, you're such a blessing to me. Happy Mother's Day!" Two days later, cards arrive from Alana and her children. "Happy Mother's Day, Grandma!"

Standing in my clean kitchen, I read the cards again and again. Then I set them on the clean counter.

With my phone Dan takes a picture of me standing by my flowers and card.

"Stand in the light," he tells me.

"I'm trying," I answer.

I'm trying.

Alana

PHILLIS WHEATLEY WAS A CHRISTIAN SLAVE.

I'm dressed as her today for the Historical Figure Day of teacher spirit week. I tried my best to find some clothes that fit the image of a poor slave from the Revolutionary Period. In her picture she sits thoughtfully at a table with a quill pen, poised to write a poem. On her head rests a white bonnet. I couldn't find anything that matched her exactly, so I improvise. Over my long brown abaya, I wrap the only apron I own around my waist. The apron was a gift from my sister years ago, and the worn, African-style kente pattern completely clashes with my abaya. Over my shoulders I drape my most worn black scarf, and then place a hijab on top.

My students haven't heard of Phillis, so I fill them in. She was famous for her poetry, an unlikely poet of her time, considering her background. She was also a strong Christian, expressing her faith frequently in her poems, and referring to biblical events often. In her poem "On Being Brought from Africa to America," she suggests that she is grateful for leaving Africa because it delivered her from heathenism.

Slavery introduced her to Christianity.

My mother and I debated this theory once, how slavery was a blessing in disguise because it brought Africans out of heathenism and into Christianity. I was incredulous then, asking her how she could possibly believe that. I thought of the argument as I researched Phillis for my costume. It's been many years since that argument about slavery, and I regret responding the way I did.

I read one of Phillis's poems to my students, the beautiful "An Hymn to the Evening." During the second and third stanzas, she praises God and eloquently paints a picture of the night:

> So may our breasts with ev'ry virtue glow,
> The living temples of our God below!
>
> Fill'd with the praise of him who gives the light,
> And draws the sable curtains of the night.[5]

I explain the term *hymn*, which I'm sure few of them knew. My students love the imagery in the poem. We dissect the vocabulary and paraphrase the meaning of the prose. Then, I tell them to call me Ms. Phillis for the day.

Unlike many slaves of that time, Phillis could read. In her poems she narrates significant moments in the Bible, reminding us of the lessons in some biblical stories. I remember those stories and hymns growing up in the church. In Sunday school we would read the Bible, often literally, but also focusing on the underlying themes and messages within each story.

When I first became a Muslim ten years ago, I was very persistent about looking for verses to disprove my mother's beliefs. I was foolish and rude then. And looking back, I regret that approach. One summer evening, I stormed into my parents' house, ready for battle. I had been looking for Bible verses that I could use to prove my mother wrong. I was so intent on being right, blinded by my insistence on proclaiming Islam as the truth. "I found a verse that prophesies the coming of Muhammad!" I proclaimed defiantly. It was John 15:26. The passage speaks of a "Comforter . . . even the Spirit of truth" who was to come and "testify" about Jesus (KJV). I argued fervently that this Comforter was the foretelling of the coming of the prophet Muhammad, an opinion held by some Muslims.

My mother was furious. Her eyes were wide with disbelief and anger.

"That's blasphemy!" she cried, insulted at the audacity of calling the Comforter anything but the Holy Spirit.

We had many moments similar to this one, when I would cherry-pick random Bible verses to prove my point. It was a fruitless attempt at persuasion. I had to be *right*.

"How can Jesus be God yet pray to God when on the cross?" I argued one day after poring through the New Testament, looking for proof against the Trinity. My exhausted mother tried as best she could to refute me, but I wasn't listening to any of her arguments.

My naive strategy only widened the already gaping divide between my mother and me. We soon stopped talking about religion altogether. A dark hole opened. No light. I quickly realized that I played a large part in burning the bridge of understanding between us. Now I stand near the smoldering ashes of that bridge, looking for light, wanting to repair it, yet searching for a way to begin.

I take a break from the task of bridge building and attend family night at a local mosque. The mosque is so tiny that I need specific directions to find it. My husband forwards the directions to me from a friend at the mosque. "Just call me if you get lost," he writes. I park behind a couple of small businesses and find the small storefront door.

I knock because the door is locked with a special key-code entry attached to the knob. A small girl in hijab timidly opens the door. We place our shoes on the rack and head toward the small women's section, where a handful of women and children sit or pray quietly. I nod and smile at a couple of women, saying a general *assalamu alaikum*, or peace be with you, to everyone. It's already past time for *Maghrib*, the early evening prayer. I see a woman I know from school and greet her with a hug. She's brought her daughter. My daughter immediately locks eyes with her, planning to play as soon as the shyness wears off.

I stand up and pray the three *rakat*, a form of prostration, that make up the *Maghrib* prayer.

Then I hear my husband on the mic. His talk is the main reason I came tonight, despite the lateness of the event. He opens with a quick joke and a pop quiz. "Who here knows the Six Pillars of Faith?" he asks the audience. A couple of hands go up. He picks an older man who names the pillars in a thick Pakistani accent, "Belief in Allah, his angels, his books, his messengers, the resurrection, and predestination."

Belief in the books. This phrase echoes in my mind as my husband continues on with his speech. As one of the tenets of my faith, it's a critical part of my belief to hold that the prophetic books were sent from the same God, proclaiming similar messages to each specific group of people. The point of contention for my mother and me, however, revolves around the authenticity of the texts. A Muslim believes that the Qur'an cleared up any alterations or corruptions in the original biblical texts. My mother disagrees with me on this point and refuses to see similarities in the stories of our sacred books.

"The stories are so *different*," she claims over the phone one night. I don't notice the differences as much as she does. The stories of the prophets in the Qur'an affirm the childhood Bible stories of my youth. Yes, there are differences in the details, and the Qur'an focuses on moral lessons. However, many of the prophetic themes are similar.

And this is where the hard part begins. I'm no theologian. I don't want to debate with my mom about the legitimacy of the holy texts that make up the Bible or the Qur'an. I just want her to acknowledge that I also value the lessons taught by Abraham, Moses, Jesus, and many other revered figures mentioned in the books of our faith.

As a pillar of my faith, belief in these books means that I should be able to discuss faith with Christians and Jews. The Qur'an even refers to these people as the "People of the Scripture."[6] Our similar texts should be a point of unification for my mother and me, not contention.

Back at the mosque my husband continues with his opening thesis. "The six pillars define our religious identity," he states. "If we embrace our religious identity when we stand to protect our religious freedoms, we protect the religious rights of every American." The audience listens intently as he discusses political matters related to the topic. He closes in enough time for the last speaker, another political activist, to share some upcoming community charity opportunities.

Everyone is hungry by then, and the smell of spicy *biryani* flows into the prayer hall. We pray *Isha* together, the final night prayer, and make our way to the kitchen.

Huge platters of the flavorful South Asian rice-and-meat dish are served. My daughter loves this stuff. She opts out of the kid pizza, and prepares for the adult meal by placing a large glass of water at her side. The women are more than gracious and helpful, seeing me with a small baby. They know I'm not a regular here, and they go out of their way to make us welcome. They offer us more biryani and an extremely sweet dessert. A woman approaches me; we know each other from somewhere, but I forgot her name. We add each other on Facebook, and she invites me to join a small Muslim women's youth leadership organization in town.

"We meet about once a month," she says. I agree to the commitment and ask her to join a youth project at my school.

At eleven p.m. we call it quits and head home. The kids are sweaty and hot from running around with the other kids. They whine about not wanting to leave, but I persuade them with a reminder about soccer the next morning. When we get to the door, some women smother us with more kisses and hugs, thanking us for coming, and asking us to return. They hand my husband a bag full of more biryani in to-go boxes. I promise to come back, feeling satisfied that my kids got to spend some quality time around such nice people.

It's moments like these I wish Mom could see. The tiny mosque, buried in this huge city, is not making the front page for the good work it does. Instead, images of the horrors in Nigeria and Afghanistan make the headlines. The Qur'an, the book that my mother says falls short, guides these humble people at this mosque. It's the lessons of the prophets in this book that teach these Muslims to behave in this way. I know that they showed me kindness to please God, and I'm grateful for this reminder.

I try to get back to bridge building again, trying to find a way to make peace, but my obligations keep me too busy. At school I show a video about the collapse of the Tacoma Narrows Bridge to my students during science. The bridge sways and bows in the strong wind, creating a huge wave of concrete, and then violently collapses into the water below. "The bridge's natural frequency was amplified by the wind's vibration, causing an unsustainable wave," explains the commentator. I feel a twist in my stomach, seeing a metaphor in my relationship with my mother. Am I the external vibration in our family, causing the collapse? How can we rebuild after so much has transpired?

The collapse of the bridge inspired engineers to design better bridges able to withstand multiple frequencies. Perhaps my mother and I need to adapt as well, to accommodate the different ideologies that guide us. Like the bridge, we might have to redesign ourselves, to withstand the shocks of an interfaith family in order to remain whole.

Patricia

BUILDING THE BRIDGE. IN THE DARK? I'M DESPERATE TO TRY. Determined to heal what's broken. Then maybe I can make traction.

But first I'm at my late mama's home, where things are falling apart. Again. The roof is in pieces. Shingles on the ground. A gutter sagging. Underlayment exposed. Some twenty years of wear and tear have surrendered to age. A late spring windstorm ripped away the weakest links. Then Colorado hail finished off the work. A local roof guy, Tim, delivers the verdict. "This roof is *gone*, Patricia. *Done*."

I stand in my late mama's front yard, looking up at the damage. Knowing the cost. Feeling the burden of brokenness. But needing to rebuild right this part of her home. This is Mama's house. Whatever the cost, I have to set it right.

But today my head is anything but right. Alana and I talked the night before on the phone. Well, we tried to talk. To talk like a mother and a daughter. To talk calmly enough, as far as I know. To talk, indeed, like bridge builders—two people who love, respect, and believe in each other. Then suddenly we were *not* talking. Instead we're arguing. Back in our interstellar hole.

"I can't *believe* you would bring that up," she is saying to me—about something I thought was okay to say. I'd mentioned the Boko Haram terrorists.

Couldn't leave it alone? Couldn't leave it alone. Left the light. Stirred the dark. Insisted on making some point about Islam birthing such hating.

So Alana goes ballistic. She won't hear me. Then I won't hear her. So we're back in the interfaith rubble. I tossed all night. Never nailing down sleep. And now Tim, the roof guy, wants me to put my beloved dead mama's roof back together again. And not fall apart in the process.

Tim doesn't know my daughter. Doesn't know these rebuilding projects are grinding me down. Doesn't know the confusion of being a mother whose daughters no longer need her. About being a landlord who doesn't know how to repair. About spending time managing property instead of telling people about Jesus. But, in truth, I'm not a preacher. I just write down words by faith. But am I helping? What happened to light?

Jesus.

OK, Alana, I text my daughter. I wasn't trying to upset you. Wasn't trying to stir up trouble. I text her by phone, offering my mea culpa before the sun comes up. Just wanted to clear that up!

She texts back an hour later: OK, no problem.

I read her words. Stand back. Let her be.

Talk to our roof guy.

"So give me the number, Tim." I swallow hard. "Round house."

"Round house?" Tim squints. He's a tall, graying, sunburned white man with a day's stubble on his fifty-something chin. He rubs his stubble. Measures in his head. "Eighty-nine hundred."

I groan. Building always costs. Peter will rob Paul big-time for this. "When can you start?" I ask.

But Tim shakes his head.

"What, Tim?"

What now? What then? Why is fixing stuff so hard?

"Call your insurance," Tim says.

I groan again. "They never pay."

He shrugs. "You never know. See what they say first."

I stifle a sigh. Building up things and putting stuff back together is one slow Humpty Dumpty tap dance. Do this step. Do that step. Oops. Wrong step. Back up. Move around. Turn on the light. Leave the dark. Start over.

But I call my insurance man, who hands me over to an adjustor—a woman who can't fit us in for another week. Then when she finally gets to Mama's house, her ladder is too short.

I listen. Take in a deep breath.

Think about Jesus. Determine to act right. To be like Christ.

"Okay," I say. "When can you come back?"

But she can't come back. She has to put my name back in the system to assign me to a new adjustor. Somebody else with a longer ladder. I take a deep breath.

"Okay," I say again.

Then the new adjustor calls. "When can *you* come?" I ask.

"Sunday," he says.

I listen. Breathe deeper. Then I listen harder. Listen like I try to listen to Alana. Listen like I understand. Like I can handle new truth. Like I can accept that Sunday is no longer Sunday like I've always known Sunday to be—not even for an adjustor of a major American insurance company. With or without a longer ladder.

"Sunday morning," I say.

"Yeah. Between nine and eleven a.m. Will that work?"

Now this is when I'm supposed to make a speech to this guy. To say that we are followers of Jesus of Nazareth and we go to church on Sunday mornings. To say that Sunday is the Lord's Day. To say Sunday morning is the Lord's time. To say that the Sabbath, as Jesus said, is made for us not to work but to honor God. Then in saying these things, I could help reorder this man's thinking about Sunday until he gets the message and gets back to church. If he ever went to church in the first place.

Jesus.

When I pray about all of this, I sit with the Lord a long time. Not talking. Just quiet. Just waiting. Watching the sun come over the trees in my neighbor's yard across the street. Our house faces east and my little upstairs office room—which used to be Alana's big sister's bedroom—faces east too. So I sit in the little bedroom, and I look out of the window at my neighbor's trees, and I fall on God.

Light, Lord? Need you, Lord. Because your world is changing before I can stand it. Nothing stays the same. I get that. I even get that Alana wants to operate in her own frequency. To live her own life. To eat other families' food and join other people's religion—and for me to just go away. *Be gone, Mom.*

Well, I would do that. But I'm waiting for her to understand in turn.

The world *is* changing. For me, keeping up is gut-kicking me to my knees. I'm counting the days to marvelous sixty-five. Not old. But the "new" of today's world—with its terrorists and go-it-alone daughters and repair people who make calls during Sunday morning church hours—makes me feel used up and confused.

But build the bridge anyway?

In his thoughtful book *Why Buildings Stand Up*, architectural engineer Mario Salvadori quoted Leonardo da Vinci on the nature of an arch—a seminal bridge structure. Said da Vinci: "An arch consists of two weaknesses which leaning one against the other make a strength."[7]

I don't begin to understand the architectural rules of bridge building. But tension seems to play a role—overwhelming weak points with counterbalances that help built things stand without falling.

I think.

Either way, there's a bigger problem for bridges and buildings, Salvadori wrote. It's the dark tension in relations between people involved in doing the building. Said Salvadori, "Today's architecture requires the close collaboration between such a wide variety of specialists as to make the problems of communications between them unusually difficult."[8]

That Tacoma Narrows Bridge?

It collapsed, Salvadori said, due to the same failure that brought down several other flexible suspension bridges a century before. Yet lack of communication between quarreling professions kept the knowledge of the past from getting passed on. "In the history of science and engineering, facts and laws have been forgotten, which, if remembered, would have saved time, energy, and possibly, lives."[9]

For certain, nobody died in the Tacoma Narrows Bridge collapse. Well, one little dog, too frightened to leave a car that fell off the bridge, did lose his life. The dog's owner, Leonard Coatsworth, was paid $450 for his car and $364 for the car's contents, including the dog—a black cocker spaniel named Tubby.

After World War II, when the need for steel diminished, the Tacoma Narrows Bridge was rebuilt. The replacement bridge still stands. Looking back, one clear point emerges from the Tacoma Bridge disaster. In designing a bridge, work with others—but work especially with the wind. Saying that, followers of Christ will understand. Because wind in the Bible is an enduring symbol of the Holy Spirit. The Hebrew root for spirit is *ruach*— meaning "air in motion," which also means "breath" as well as "life."

Without this breath of God, nothing lives or stands.

Jesus told Nicodemus the same thing. To be born again—and made new in God—you must be breathed on by God's Spirit. Made alive with God's breath.

Charles Spurgeon, the nineteenth-century evangelist, wrote it like this:

> You may blow with your mouth, and produce some trifling effects upon trifles as light as air; man in his zeal may set the windmills of silly minds in motion; but, truly, to stir men's hearts with substantial and eternal Truths of God needs a celestial breeze such as the Lord alone can send![10]

As I consider this, Pope Francis is pleading with Israeli and Palestinian presidents to come to the Vatican to ask God for the gift of peace. Not to work for peace. Not to debate peace. But to pray. Together. In the light.

As Alana and I vow to make peace with each other's spiritual needs, the span between us that threatens to break won't fail after all. She needs to feel independent. I need to feel needed. More than all, however, we need to feel love. So let us pray.

Alana

"I GUESS I'M THE WORST DAUGHTER IN THE WORLD," I VENTED TO A friend at school, one of the few people whom I've talked to about this, our book. We were standing during lunch, discussing a Facebook post in which my mother praised my work on this project.

"Was your mom trying to indirectly make up for something?" she asked intuitively.

I laughed, surprised at her perceptiveness, and explained the comments Mom made about Mother's Day.

"Yep, I am the worst daughter," I remarked, after describing what happened.

"No, you're not!" my friend pleaded. "My mom always says, 'Don't get me anything! You already have so much on your plate!'"

"Must be nice," I remarked jokingly, but with some hidden jealousy. *Why doesn't my mom act like that?*

Another teacher piped in, overhearing our conversation.

"Not my mom! She would kill me if I didn't get her anything!"

It was news to me to hear that my mother was judging me based on my lack of Mother's Day affection. When I was growing up, it wasn't a part of our family culture to spend lots of money on Mother's Day. Even my dad didn't buy jewelry or fancy clothing from department stores for that day. The standard Mother's Day gift in our house was flowers and a card, nicely prepared on the kitchen counter for my mother to see when she woke up. We would go to church, with Mom, my sister, and me wearing red roses pinned to our dresses to symbolize our living mothers and Dad wearing a white rose to memorialize his deceased mother. After the service, we would celebrate by going out to eat at our favorite after-church cafeteria, Furr's.

"Mom doesn't even shop at Macy's!" I told my friend.

In fact, she and my dad are die-hard thrift store fanatics, and they buy lots of almost-new stuff by using their senior citizen discount.

"The card was late, though," I added.

My friend grimaced then chuckled.

"I'm sure that didn't help," I remarked.

Why should material things define our love for one another?

"Every day should be Mother's Day," my husband always says on that day. Yes, I appreciate the tokens of love from him and the kids on that day, but is it fair for me to be disappointed if it's not *enough*?

If that's what she wants, then I'll shower her with expensive gifts from expensive stores, but it won't change my status as the daughter who ruined our family. I'll still be in the gutter because of my faith choice.

I simmer down a bit and realize that my disgruntlement has caused me to forget a major part of my faith. As a Muslim I'm required to be respectful, devoted, and kind to my parents, to the point of not even saying "uff" to them when upset.[11] I also took a pledge when we first started writing our book to be empathetic, and now I need to put it into practice.

I get it now. My mom is feeling neglected and unappreciated. It took her twenty years to say it, but now's better than never. She was never one to express her feelings openly. So like a good daughter should, I'll reflect on myself and find a way to listen.

In fact, Islam commands Muslims to be dutiful and loving *especially* to mothers. A well-known saying of the prophet Muhammad explains that when he was asked who deserves the best companionship, the prophet replied, "Your mother." When asked twice more, "Who is next?" he replied in the same manner until finally upon the fourth question he answered, "Your father."[12]

"Your mother, your mother, your mother" is a common expression used among Muslims in reference to Muhammad's three replies. I am willing to admit that I need to show Mom more love.

On the afternoon before my daughter's kindergarten graduation, I'm focused on my *own* daughter. Feeling rushed, we hurry to pull together her "mandatory" formal outfit for the ceremony. My daughter is ecstatic, mostly about having an excuse to dress up. After walking for what seems like miles in the mall, we finally limp into Sears and find an ensemble she loves, an ankle-length, black, floral dress with a sweater.

From the look on the saleslady's face, I can tell she is dying to ask me something. She eyed me with intrigue, smiling strangely. "Excuse me, I don't mean to be rude," the lady started, "but can I ask you a question?"

I get that a lot.

I got ready to recite the same speech I say a thousand times to everyone who asks, "Why do you wear that scarf?"

This lady surprises me, however.

"I heard you say the name Noah. Is that your child's name?"

"Yes," I reply, wondering where she is going with this question.

"It's a nice name," she continues. "So do Muslims also have Noah in their religion?"

I smile, thinking of my mother, who claims to see hardly any similarities in our two faiths.

"Yes, Noah is a major prophet in our religion," I explain. "The Arabic name for Noah is pronounced *Nuh*, but there's no way my family could pronounce *that* since we're American."

I laugh, hoping she'll get the joke. It gets a chuckle out of her.

"It's interesting," she continues, "that there are so many similarities between Judaism, Christianity, and the Muslim religion."

She probably doesn't know to use the term Islam *instead of* Muslim, I say to myself. She begins to elaborate on the likenesses between the Jewish kosher laws and the Islamic version of food rules called *halal*. I deduce that she might be Jewish, but I don't ask. Instead, I nod and smile, agreeing with her on the many commonalities within these faiths.

How can this saleslady in Sears talk so openly with me about faith while my mother and I can't seem to discuss anything about it? Then again, working in my diverse town has probably exposed this saleslady to many Muslims, with whom I'm sure she has already sparked conversations. During this shopping trip alone, I had already passed by at least fifteen Muslim women, which I know wouldn't happen in Colorado where my mother shops. I start to leave the store, hoping that I have left a good impression on her.

"You have beautiful children," she says, smiling as we are leaving.

It's frustrating coming across people like that, who seem to get the whole interfaith relations idea, when my mother and I can barely talk about faith without an argument.

Next time I see my mother, it will be very close to her birthday. I always just send a card and call, but maybe this time, I'll spiff it up a little. It can be a truce offering, an expression of solidarity to open "diplomatic relations."

"Jannah (Paradise) is under her feet," Muhammad once said when explaining the importance of honoring one's mother.[13] I know it's the thought that counts, but actions speak way louder than words.

eight

⌒⊙⌒

PEACE. MAKING.

──────────────── *Patricia* ────────────────

DOES IT MATTER? MATTER THAT WE GET FACTS WRONG? THAT WE both say things the wrong way? That what Alana says about Christ and what I say about Islam may miss the mark? But does that matter?

Matter to a mother and her daughter?

Reading Alana's last entry, I ask such questions. Reading her words, I look back over those years when we weren't talking about faith—and got along fine. Or fine enough. As Alana would say during family visits, "Let's just have fun today." So if Alana, her husband, Iesa, and I kicked up some faith debate, she'd beg us to stop. *Can't we just get along?* So Iesa and I would back off, as best we could. Then we'd get on with our visit. And our family.

But here we are now in a muddle. Talking across faith has somehow raised the ante. Now every little wrong, every little fact, every other holiday sucks up my attention. Even Mother's Day. *Mother's Day?* When the founder of Mother's Day, Anna Jarvis, grew to hate the holiday—ruined, she said, by commercialism? All she wanted was for offspring to sit down once a year and write their mothers a letter of thanks. Bitterly, she scoffed at cards, candy, and gifts sold by merchants. Blasted Jarvis:

> A printed card means nothing except that you are too lazy to write to
> the woman who has done more for you than anyone in the world. And

candy! You take a box to Mother—and then eat most of it yourself. A pretty sentiment.[1]

Oh, Anna Jarvis. She struggled for years trying to convince Congress to repeal the Mother's Day holiday—dying penniless in a Pennsylvania sanitarium after spending the last of her modest income failing to undo what she'd unleashed.

Now here I am, caught in the tussle with Alana—wrestling as mother and daughter over holiday cards and religion—with every other word we speak sparking an argument. And I'm suddenly so willing to let that happen. To sabotage family peace.

But she's begging to make her own case. Writing me an e-mail to say she never said I could pray at her house. Or exchange gifts at Christmas. Instead, she explains in her e-mail,

> I said that we might start giving gifts during my family's holidays, meaning Eid, and I was trying to see if we could come up with a neutral family prayer for dinner that we would both be comfortable with saying. I thought I was pretty clear in saying that, and I don't think it's okay to change what someone actually said. Please let me know what you think.

Jesus.

What do I think? I think I'm disappointed. I think people hear what we want. I think mothers and daughters—and fathers and sons, husbands and wives, Muslims, Jews, and Christians—say what we want. And hear what we desire. But is this talking? Is this understanding? Is this peace?

Instead, Jesus is saying this: let go.

Stop pounding your daughter with facts and figures and history and harangues. Instead, *follow* me. Walk in Light. Then you can let go. Because in Christ, "when I am weak," as the apostle Paul wrote, "*then* I am strong" (2 Cor. 12:10, emphasis mine).

The embattled Bible, which Alana rejects, offers story after lovely story of the power of this kind of surrender. During a storm at sea, when Jesus' fearful disciples were tearing their hair, Jesus lay down in the boat and took a nap. Terrified, the disciples shook him awake. *Master!* "Carest thou not that we perish?" (Mark 4:37–38 KJV).

In this way they sound like me. *Master!* "Carest thou not that my daughter has turned away? That my daughter rejects your Word? That my daughter! My daughter! My daughter!"

But Jesus whispers to me as he spoke to the storm and waves: *Peace! Be still.*

Then at his voice, the Bible recounts, there is calm. A "great calm," in fact (v. 39).

So I sit down. I shut up. I listen to Vanessa Bell Armstrong go ahead and sing on YouTube, belting out "Peace Be Still" with the Detroit Mass Choir.

Then as I reflect on these things, I'm reminded why mothers and daughters find themselves in conflict. Not because one is right or wrong. Not because one is prodigal or pushy. Instead, as the apostle Paul reminded the persecuted early church in his letter to Ephesus: "For we wrestle not against flesh and blood, but against principalities, against powers, against the rulers of the darkness of this world, against spiritual wickedness in high places" (Eph. 6:12 KJV).

The enemy of God, that is, determines for people like us to fight. To fuss. To distrust. To suspect. Because if we ever worked together—and even loved each other together—the people of faith would be a positive force in the world to be reckoned with. Instead, we stay in the storm.

Half a world away in the Central African Republic, angry "Christian" youths in the town of Bangui destroy a mosque today. They are retaliating against "Muslim" rebel forces who attacked a church a few days earlier, killing fifteen people—most of them women and children taking shelter from the nation's ongoing interreligious violence.

The bloodshed is sickening. Beheadings. Machete attacks. Lynchings. Guns fired into markets. Grenades tossed into churches. Mosques defiled. In the year since Muslim "Seleka" rebels tried to take over the country, retaliations by Christian "Anti-balaka" have, in turn, engulfed the diamond-rich nation in bloody anarchy.

Who will bring the peace?

For good, both the town's Catholic archbishop and Islamic imam are calling for peace, with the archbishop opening his home to the imam and other Muslims as a safe haven. The peace gesture also underscores claims by both religious leaders that the uprising isn't a religious battle after all—that the violent groups are, in fact, neither Muslim nor Christian.

As the archbishop—whose name is Dieudonné Nzapalainga—told the *Vatican Insider* newspaper: "Not all men of the Seleka militia are Muslim, and not all Muslims are with the Seleka. In the same way their opposition, the Anti-balaka, do not represent the ideas and beliefs of us Christians, even though they are associated with us." Yet the "clashes, attacks and revenge killings have been going on for more than a year now, and seem to be gaining ever stronger religious connotations," the *Vatican Insider* reported.[2]

Reading about this anarchy in Africa makes my disagreements with Alana seem petty—but also sinful. If we allow religion to divide us, we're no better than the bullies in Bangui. In the comfort of my American suburban home, if I can't make peace with my daughter—living in the comfort of her American suburban home—then God help us both. Shame on us, indeed.

So I pull back. Go to my kitchen to make a veggie lasagna. Tasty and right.

"Great job, sugar pie!" my husband says. He goes for a second helping. Then he adds, "You should give this recipe to Alana."

"Yes," I say. "I should."

Because a mother and a daughter should be sharing recipes and giving each other tips—texting to say the oven-ready lasagna noodles that I tried for the first time worked great. Want the recipe?

To talk like that, however, I have to trust God. Then when my Alana tells me something that Muslims believe that I don't understand—like their claim that the apostle Paul was a "self-titled" messenger since Jesus "isn't" God and "couldn't" appoint Paul a messenger or anything else— well, I don't have to fight that. I can just tell God. Then leave the burden of our misunderstandings with him. Then in giving her grace, a daughter will discover my point of view—and I will discover hers. Then we can keep talking. Keep sharing recipes. Keep being family. Keep walking.

This is the mystery of God. If first we surrender to him, he dispenses the grace. Then we can give grace to others. No matter what they believe. In that way the impoverished early church in Macedonia "first gave themselves to the Lord," wrote our slandered apostle Paul in his second letter to the church at ancient Corinth. First to the Lord they gave, Paul said. "And then to us" (2 Cor. 8:5 NKJV).

And so must I. First to the Lord. That is the order. God first. Let me first give myself more to you, gracious Jesus. Then I can give the same grace to my daughter, as did the Macedonians—whose "extreme poverty welled up in rich generosity" (2 Cor. 8:2).

Talking about such things one morning, my husband broke into a gospel song—singing words that praise God for being so giving. So we start singing it together. Harmonizing. His strong tenor. My hopeful alto. Then during our prayer time, he confesses to God: "The world is so full of taking and very little giving. Help us to understand that it's better to give than receive." Better to forgive than fight. Better to love than lecture. Better to let go.

It's the way.

Alana

"ISN'T THERE SOMETHING IN THE WORD *ISLAM* THAT RELATES TO peace?" my mom asks on the phone one day.

"Yes," I reply, surprised that she has looked into the etymology of the word. "The root word *salam* means 'peace.'"

I wondered what she was thinking next, but she remained silent. The actions of Muslims haven't been exactly peaceful lately, and I waited for her to ask me about some recent event. Our general conversation was going smoother than normal, with me trying to be as outwardly loving as I possibly could. I was trying to stick to the promise I made myself to be a more loving daughter. We ended the phone call with my saying how much I loved her, and that I was grateful for all she had done for me.

"That means so much, Alana!" she exclaimed, sounding genuinely honored.

"Next, let's talk about peace in each of our faiths," my mom suggested before getting off the phone. My heart skipped a beat. With this request our short moment of repose came to a close as I realized the daunting task that lay ahead. I knew she must be curious to hear my stance on things, especially in relation to the violent extremism dominating the news.

I replied to her request with a nervous okay and then ran to my husband for advice.

"Read that little white book about peace on the right of the bookshelf," my husband suggested.

I scanned the living room shelf, found a book called *Peace and the Limits of War* by Dr. Louay M. Safi, and shut myself up in my room for an hour or so. Dr. Safi carefully dissects the idea of peace in Islam by refuting many of the misconceptions about Islamic law called *Shariah*. It's a scary word for many Americans, and one that I'm sure my mom has heard misused many times on TV.

In the book Dr. Safi states, "The term Islam essentially means to submit and surrender one's will to a higher truth and a transcendental law, so that one can lead a meaningful life informed by the divine purpose of creation—a life in which the dignity and freedom of all human beings can be equally protected."[3]

It's a beautiful statement but hard to believe if one is watching the news today. He goes on to explain in detail many of the ways in which the Qur'an has been misinterpreted by individuals to support an extremist agenda and how Islamic law should be used correctly to protect and defend human liberties. I'm sure my mom has heard this argument before, especially from me, and the proof is in the pudding, as they say.

The term *jihad*, which is often misused as well, embodies the internal struggle that a Muslim has with himself on the path of full surrender to God. Jihad has other "avenues," as the author calls it, in which peaceful resistance and repulsion of military aggression are warranted.[4] What should be noted, however, is that the violent acts perpetrated by some delusional Muslims today, such as 9/11 or the Boko Haram kidnappings in Nigeria, are categorically not jihad and go against the very fabric of Islam.

It's very easy for any person to find a random verse from the Qur'an or any other religious text and use it to promote his or her twisted agenda. Later, for example, I learned that this same expert, Dr. Safi, has been criticized for possible associations with people considered questionable. Meantime, he and others point out that atrocities aren't in any way Islamic—citing verses of the Qur'an that directly call for peace, tolerance, and the sacredness of life.

Such arguments are unconvincing to some non-Muslim critics, who also randomly pick verses of the Qur'an and interpret them without proper context. Many verses, for example, were specific to a unique situation or group of people, and cannot be applied to the general Muslim population. In one situation Muhammad and his followers were heavily persecuted in Mecca, so they were forced to migrate to a city nearby called Medina. Many years passed before they were given permission to defend themselves against the attacks of the Meccans, yet they were still required not to be the "aggressors."

Some verses in the Qur'an refer to these specific years in which the Muslims defended their homes and families from Meccan persecution. It's completely the fault of extremist Muslims today for not properly studying the Qur'an, within its historical context, and thus creating a fake reality in which horrific violence is allowed.

But I can't speak on behalf of the people who commit atrocities in the name of Islam. I've lived a sheltered life in America, unexposed to radicals and extremists of all sorts. Even now, as a Muslim, I am surrounded by people who demonstrate the complete opposite of what my mom sees on the news. My mom needs to know that I know firsthand about Islamic peace, through my own life and from the people who surround me every day.

It was just the other day that I ran into one of my close friends at the mall, a Colombian-American Muslim convert whose Arabic name means "tranquility." My heart swelled as I saw her, considering it had been a while since we had connected. She started to share about her most recent media project with her husband—a documentary about a Colombian

Mestizo Muslim who is in a campaign to make Colombia and Earth more environmentally friendly. *Now that's peace*, I thought.

"It's part of our faith to take care of the earth," she explained, describing how the indigenous people were so in tune with God and their surroundings.

I reflected on my friend's words, then searched online for the verse of the Qur'an that embodies their media work:

> O mankind, indeed. We have created you from male and female and
> made you peoples and tribes that you may know one another. Indeed,
> the most noble of you in the sight of Allah is the most righteous of you.
> Indeed, Allah is Knowing and Acquainted.[5]

What better way to "know one another" than to document the amazing civil service of this humble Colombian? My friend and I parted ways that day, with me wanting to visit this remarkable place she spoke about and feeling so proud to be her friend.

"*Assalamu alaikum waramatullah wa barakatuh*," she said while hugging me good-bye. It translates roughly as "Peace be unto you and so be the Mercy of Allah and his blessings."[6]

It's the universal greeting for Muslims, and a beautiful way to address someone. I replied in a similar manner, and while reflecting on this, I marveled about how many times I say *salam* during the day at my school.

My mom already knows about these basic tenets of my faith, I say to myself. *She probably wants me to dig deeper, so she can really find out why some Muslims in the world are not peaceful.* But before we cross thousands of miles to analyze some foreign land unfamiliar to both of us, I invite her to join me here in my town, where every day Muslims are real-life peacekeepers.

If Mom could meet my daughter's Girl Scout leader, for example, she would see how peace plays a part in the life of an everyday Muslim.

"It's a way for me to give back to the community," the troop leader explained to me one day, after discussing the possibility of my helping out more next year.

142

I hesitated at first when she asked me to help, considering my overwhelming load of teaching, grading, and rearing kids. Her words changed my mind, however, when I thought of how her full-time job and kids didn't prevent her from devoting so much time to Girl Scouts.

On the last meeting of the year, I pulled up in my van with my son and baby, ready to pick up my daughter. The kids were all grimy and flushed from planting flowers in the ninety-degree heat.

"Do you girls remember the three Rs?" the troop leader questioned them, reminding them to reduce, reuse, and recycle.

She wiped the sweat and dirt from her brow, and looked totally surprised when a parent gave her a thank-you gift recognizing her year of devotion.

Her humble spirit and lack of desire for compensation are part of Islam. This is Islam in action, not the nonsense propagated by sensational Muslim fanatics. The Qur'an and the sayings of Muhammad require Muslims to serve their community and promote peace. I'm just glad that my daughter got to witness this firsthand.

I finish reading and rejoin my family in the living room. My mind is swirling with ideas of how to explain Islamic peace to my mother. Then I realize that I need milk for the baby and race to the store with my daughter. We rush past a woman in the aisle who is eyeing me warily. I smile and nod a hello, catching her off guard. She looks startled, but her expression softens a bit.

"Do you know that a smile is a form of charity?" I ask my daughter after we pass the woman.

My daughter nods. Her teachers have already told her that in class. They've mentioned the famous saying by Muhammad, which notes some ways to perform good deeds. According to the recorded statement he said:

> Your smiling in the face of your brother is charity, commanding good
> and forbidding evil is a charity, your giving directions to a man lost in
> the land is charity for you. Your seeing for a man with bad sight is a

charity for you, your removal of a rock, a thorn or a bone from the road is a charity for you. Your pouring what remains from your bucket into the bucket of your brother is a charity for you.[7]

My daughter has this idea down pat. She smiles and greets so much that I decided it was time to have the "stranger danger" talk with her.

"But they're not strangers!" she protested. "They live in our neighborhood, so they're our neighbors."

It took a couple of conversations to convince her to be friendly but safe.

We return and unload the groceries, and she goes off to play with her dolls. I pause for a moment, milk in hand, and realize that my mom doesn't need to search any further for a definition of Islamic peace. Right before her stands me, her daughter—a living embodiment of one striving to walk the path of peace.

As a teacher I have devoted my life to the development and growth of America's children. I have dedicated countless hours to help each of my students succeed, all with the intention of pleasing God. It's through this desire to be a servant of God that I found my calling as a teacher. That's Islam, and that's how I find my inner peace. I feel sorry for Muslims in the world who don't experience Islam in the same way, but I know enough people whose actions prove them wrong.

I check my phone and see a text from a friend who started up a daily Qur'an study group on a social media site. She mentions that her friend initiated the movement, reaching out to more than one thousand women in more than ten countries. She next quotes a verse from the Qur'an that states, "For each [religious following] is a direction toward which it faces. So race to [all that is] good. Wherever you may be, Allah will bring you forth [for judgment] all together. Indeed, Allah is over all things competent."[8]

Striving toward all that is good sounds like a definite method toward peace. I send a message back to her, thanking her for including me, and promising to keep up with the daily posts. These friends of mine remind me of the real message of Islam. I can only hope that my mother can hear my examples and be reminded as well.

Patricia

My flowers for Mother's Day lasted two weeks and five days or thereabouts. To keep them fresh, I changed the vase every couple of days. Flushed dirty water down the drain. Washed the vase. Trimmed the stems. Refilled the vase with fresh water. Getting religious about it. Counting the days. So every forty-eight hours or so, I freshened the water. Each water change, I added a couple of teaspoons of sugar and vinegar. Sugar to feed the plants. Vinegar to kill the bacteria. Then for a final flourish, I set the trimmed flowers back in their clean vase.

Lots of work. Lots of time. But as Alana taught me, impoverished women in Colombia planted, grew, and harvested these flowers, working possibly under horrible conditions. The least I could do was take care of the bouquet. I was surprised how long the flowers lasted with faithful care. For all the time and attention they took, I enjoyed the bouquet all the more.

In that same way, love takes time. So does peace. When I was a working mother—for most of my daughters' childhood years—I must've cut corners with their care. I'm sure I did this. Too many wrong words said. Too many hugs overlooked. Not enough flushing away dirty debris out of our household and lives. Too much affection withheld in the rush of working, cooking, grocery shopping, going to Girl Scout meetings and church activities, and all the rest.

Now in my post-job life—no longer working at newspapers or teaching about newspapering—I have time to fuss over cut flowers. Just like I fussed over my students, fussed over every news story I ever wrote, fussed over every Girl Scout cookie box I helped my daughters sell. (And every cookie box I sold as a Girl Scout.) Yet for all of it, is the world any better? Is our peace any greater?

Do I display, as peacemaker Ken Sande would suggest, a way of peace "that honors God and offers benefits to those involved"?[9]

For an answer, I'm surprised to hear back from the CEO of Kroger. His e-mail arrived on the morning I threw out my finally faded Mother's Day bouquet. The e-mail was from his director of corporate sustainability—a woman named Suzanne, who wrote a nice letter:

Ms. Raybon,

Thank you for reaching out to Mr. McMullen. He asked that I respond to you.

And with that, the world grew smaller. I was a bit taken aback that anybody at Kroger would spend even five minutes to answer an e-mail from an ordinary customer. My own e-mail tried to be kind, however. Maybe that helped. Lord knows I tried to make my case kindly:

Dear Mr. McMullen,

I was disturbed to learn that Kroger, despite your leadership in providing Fair Trade–certified food, has no Fair Trade certification policy on cut flowers. Your oversight helps allow the cut-flower industry to exploit impoverished men, women, and children working under horrific conditions on cut-flower plantations primarily in Colombia and Ecuador, but also in Kenya and other countries in Africa.

I told him about the article Alana sent.

My daughter shared it with me on Mother's Day, and I decided to follow up by contacting you. Indeed, at both Whole Foods and Giant Food Stores, Fair Trade flowers are now available. So why not Kroger?

So that started it. A modest peace talk. Two people deciding to communicate. To détente. Thus, Suzanne said expected things, such as Kroger is "one of the nation's most trusted florists" and Kroger is "actively working" with "the best suppliers in the world" to provide to Kroger customers the "highest quality, most sustainable flowers available."

It sounded boilerplate. Then, at the end of the letter, something changed. Suzanne of Kroger said this:

We are proud of our progress so far, and understand there are always opportunities to improve.

So hang in there. Don't kick us to the curb. Her letter took that tone. We're working on it. Two steps up. Two steps back. But we're on the path. So I tried to hear that. In that way I could write back with my own right tone. Thanks for replying. Thanks for improving. Keep at it. You can change the world. I'm nobody important. Just an ordinary customer. But I will be watching.

Madeleine Albright, the former US secretary of state, said this about peacemaking: that it takes two. In her words: "No matter what message you are about to deliver somewhere, whether it is holding out a hand of friendship, or making clear that you disapprove of something, is the fact that the person sitting across the table is a human being."[10]

Sande, in his book *The Peacemaker: A Biblical Guide to Resolving Personal Conflict*, wrote that peacemakers are people "who breathe grace."[11]

Which brings me again to Jesus. At the Last Supper he arose from the table and wrapped a towel around his waist. Then he went to his knees and washed his disciples' feet—including those of his betrayer, Judas.

"Peace I leave with you," he told them that historic evening. "My peace I give you. I do not give to you as the world gives. Do not let your hearts be troubled and do not be afraid" (John 14:27).

The prophet Isaiah, many years before, delivered this stunning prophecy about this same Jesus: "For unto us a child is born, unto us a son is given: and the government shall be upon his shoulder: and his name shall be called Wonderful, Counsellor, The mighty God, The everlasting Father, The Prince of Peace" (Isa. 9:6 KJV).

Because peace is who Jesus is. All the heavy world on his shoulders. The Bible confirms it. "For he himself is our peace" (Eph. 2:14). Therefore, peace isn't some lack of trouble, wrote Scottish evangelist Oswald Chambers—or some following of rules or even living in a peaceful and good way. Peace, said Chambers, "is not dependent on your external circumstances at all, but on your relationship with God Himself."[12]

Then, added Chambers, in the storms of life,

In the midst of the awfulness, a touch comes, and you know it is the right hand of Jesus Christ. The right hand not of restraint nor of correction nor of chastisement, but the right hand of the Everlasting Father. Whenever His hand is laid upon you, it is ineffable peace and comfort, the sense that "underneath are the everlasting arms," full of sustaining and comfort and strength.[13]

So Jesus says love your enemies. That's why in South Africa, Archbishop Desmond Tutu told the hurting to forgive their oppressors, but first, "We must ourselves be reconciled."[14] If you want peace, he added, "create a new story."[15]

Charles Spurgeon, that rugged Baptist evangelist, understood the sweet result of harmony with all others: "The wheels revolve in happy order, and bear us blessings as often as they turn." The greatest peace, however, he wrote, is "peace *with God*, and peace *with our own conscience*." For God has "'reconciled us to himself by Jesus Christ'"—putting away the wall separating us from God the Father, "and now there is 'peace on earth' and 'goodwill toward men.'" Spurgeon offered this reminder to the divided: "God has no cause of warfare against his creature: Christ has put *our* sins away, and therefore there is a virtual substantial peace established between God and our souls." The result? Peace in the conscience. "Peace with God is the fountain," Spurgeon said, "and peace with conscience is the crystal stream which issues from it."

Such peace is divine—a "peace of friendship" with God plus "a peace at sweet enjoyment, of quiet rest of the understanding and the conscience." In his poetic way the evangelist concluded, "When there are no winds above, there will be no tempests below. When heaven is serene earth is quiet. Conscience reflects the complacency of God."[16]

So what's the therefore?

"Therefore," says the Bible, "being justified by faith, we have peace with God through our Lord Jesus Christ . . . by whom we have now received the atonement" (Rom. 5:1, 11 KJV).

I don't lie when I say I want Alana to know this peace. Peace without internal jihad. Peace without striving. Peace without wondering if you're okay with God. The peace of intimacy with the Creator. The peace with friendship. Friendship with God.

Our roofer, Tim, talked of the same yearning for his grown children.

"One of my boys has a new girlfriend, a young lady who has children. For the children, the two of them have returned to the Lord—going to church again. And I tell you, that is an answer to prayer."

Dan and I rejoiced with him. Another daughter of Tim's is already a follower of Christ and a regular churchgoer. His last daughter was a churchgoer but has stopped going.

"But I am praying," Tim said, looking confident. "That's what we do. We pray."

Then we have peace.

Meantime, we love.

Still, sometimes I wish I didn't despair so much. That I could be like a Presbyterian woman I met at a women's prayer event: "Both my kids are out of church," she told me, "but they're both moral people. I can live with that."

I can't. But in Christ, I can make peace with it. Otherwise, I fall into worry and religious despair. Aretha Franklin's father, Rev. C. L. Franklin, explained in a sermon why this happens: "When you've got too much religion that you can't mingle with people, that you're afraid of certain people, you've got too much religion."[17]

Too much religion. That's not peace.

Alana

I SILENCE THE ALARM FOR THE THIRD TIME ON A QUIET EARLY morning in June, and reach over to nudge my husband. "It's time to pray *Fajr*," I say sleepily. *Fajr*, the morning prayer before dawn, is the first of our five daily prayers. My husband, exhausted and recovering from the stomach flu, mumbles an okay and crawls out of bed. He goes first into the bathroom to make *wudu*, the ritual washing before prayer, by wiping water over his hands, face, ears, head, arms, and feet. We perform this literal and symbolic ritual to clean up before coming to pray to our Lord and to allow the cool water to wake us up a bit.

The living room is quiet, with only the sound of the ceiling fan breaking the thick silence. My baby's sweet sleeping noises trail into the room from our bedroom. Most of the lights are off, and the faint blue glow of the approaching morning sneaks through the blinds. It's a beautiful time to pray, right before the business of our lives takes over. Morning prayer is a form of jihad, a struggle to remain obedient to God despite lack of sleep. Despite this difficulty, it feels good making the sacrifice to leave sleep for prayer. We spread the prayer rugs on the floor, then put on our long and modest prayer garments. Mine covers my hair and body, my husband's long *thobe* reaches to his ankles. The prayer begins with my husband reciting the first chapter of the Qur'an in melodic Arabic:

In the name of Allah, the Entirely Merciful, the Especially Merciful.
[All] praise is [due] to Allah, Lord of the worlds—
The Entirely Merciful, the Especially Merciful
Sovereign of the Day of Recompense.
It is You we worship and You we ask for help.
Guide us to the straight path—
The path of those upon whom You have bestowed favor, not of those who have evoked [Your] anger or of those who are astray.[18]

We pray a little longer, each quietly in our own communication with God, then sleepily replace our prayer materials and rest for a bit more.

Muhammad was once asked, "What is *Ihsan* (perfection)?" He replied, "To worship Allah as if you see Him, and if you cannot achieve this state of devotion then you must consider that He is looking at you."[19]

This concept is the highest form of faith in Islam. It describes the believer as one who lives her life in the pursuit of pleasing God. Essentially, a Muslim tries to do the best she can to please God in every part of her life. It is through this path that a Muslim finds peace.

Praying with my husband every morning, seeing him sincerely seeking the pleasure of God, brings me peace. It brings us closer. Often our faith is a means of solving conflicts between us. We both want to please God through our relationship with each other. In my case, being married to someone who shares my faith enriches my faith experience.

Somehow I have to find a way to translate my peace into the relationship with my mother.

How do I achieve peace with a mother who claims that I don't know God? No one should have the right to pass such judgment. As a Muslim I am discouraged from claiming that someone doesn't have faith because only God knows what is in our hearts. Why is it okay for my mother to make that claim about me?

One of the last chapters in the Qur'an describes how a Muslim should behave when confronted with another person who disagrees with the message of Islam. "For you is your religion, and for me is my religion" is the sixth verse of chapter 109 of the Qur'an.[20] This verse encompasses much of the Muslim belief that Allah is the only one who controls our hearts. It is fruitless to devalue the beliefs of those who refuse to change their minds. In a way, this method robs them of their right to choose.

Free will. It's my God-given right as a human being—what separates me from the rest of creation. Verse 256 of chapter 2 in the Qur'an describes this concept in Islam:

> Let there be no compulsion in religion: Truth stands out clear from Error: whoever rejects evil and believes in Allah hath grasped the most trustworthy hand-hold, that never breaks. And Allah heareth and knoweth all things.[21]

When my mother relentlessly goes on about my lack of a relationship with Jesus, she seems to claim to know God's judgment, God's view of me. This is a bold step that I would never take. Of course, as my mother, she has the right to openly disagree with me and share her opinions, but at some point, it comes off as arrogance.

And with that I am reminded that many months before this project, I had already decided to stop challenging her. I thought it much better to be a good example of a practicing Muslim, than a jabbering talking head. So I stopped debating her, stopped bringing endless verses to the table for discussion, and just tried to live like a normal family.

I have not once claimed that she doesn't have a relationship with God. And here is where our differences in methodology lie, and where the conflict begins. The disrespect of personal boundaries bothers me the most.

I don't think we can live in peace until the respect of the other person's right to believe is upheld.

My mother is going to have to take this step if we are going to make any progress at all. I need her to meet me at a place of mutual respect. This is where empathy begins. Understanding the other is essential to peace, and appreciating one's right to experience one's connection to God is another. This was the methodology of the prophets, who never backed down about their claims, but who also recognized the need to be diplomatic in their approach.

I have tried to teach this idea to my children, by never attacking other faiths. When a holiday comes up that requires explanation from my extra-inquisitive daughter, I try my best to approach it diplomatically and to present the ideas to her as if a member of the other faith were listening. Like most parents, I don't want her to learn intolerance. My history-buff husband always chimes in, teaching the kids about America's being founded on the principle of freedom of religion.

On another early morning a few weeks later, my husband and I prepare to catch an early flight for a business trip to Tennessee. We rise much earlier than *Fajr*, doing laundry and cleaning the house so that's it's clean enough for my in-laws to babysit.

"We're going to hit Monday traffic," I warn my husband.

"It's Sunday," he reminds me. I'm relieved momentarily for the extra few minutes we'll have to drive to the airport.

"Don't drive like an idiot," my father-in-law jokes, warning my husband.

On the flight we rise quickly to fifteen thousand feet. The view is breathtaking, a small glimpse of God's magnificent creation. I glance over at my sleeping husband then back out the window, thankful I chose the window seat. The little houses dot the landscape of the expansive planet below. We continue to climb, and I spot what looks like a church. The members are probably worshipping since it's Sunday, lifting their prayers to the heavens. I'm thousands of feet above them, praying quietly by myself and glorifying the magnificence of the Creator. I know he hears each of our prayers, along with the billions of other prayers in the world. How can I judge them when I can't hear their prayers and I don't know their hearts?

I ask the advice of a friend of my husband during our visit. He's married to a Christian woman, and I am curious to learn how they find peace despite their differences. He grew up as a minority in a largely Christian community, yet he claims he never felt different from others. When speaking about his wife, he explains that they don't try to convert each other. Instead, the two community activists respect each other's faiths and simply love each other.

"It's the prophetic model," he says, explaining how these examples of patience and good manners are easy to follow.

He takes us to the only mosque in town as evening sets. The small group of faithful Muslims follows the imam as he leads the prayer. The believers end the prayer with the words *Peace be upon you and the mercy of Allah* as they turn their heads to the left and right, sending this wish to their neighbors sitting nearby.

We visit another mosque in Memphis that is working with the church next door to create a friendship park in the space between the two places of worship. My heart swells with pride at hearing of this wonderful idea.

"When we were building our mosque," our Muslim tour guide explains, "they let us use their prayer area for the entire month of Ramadan!"

I'm not surprised to hear about the church opening its center for the Muslims during their late-night Ramadan prayers. It's a Christian-like thing to do. I am, however, taken aback that it occurred in the Deep South. If two Christian and Muslim faith groups can unite in the middle of the South, surely my mother and I can make amends.

We make one last stop, a tiny BBQ restaurant owned by a Muslim. My mouth waters at the thought of beef ribs, a luxury I haven't had in years.

"Are you sure this place is owned by a Muslim?" I ask my husband skeptically. Tennessee is the last state I would expect to find such an anomaly. My husband laughs and reassures me that it is indeed the place.

The owner immediately recognizes us as the obvious visitors and comes over to greet us. "Don't worry," he says smiling, "we're going to take good care of you."

He isn't joking. He loads us up with piles of savory ribs and his unique Mediterranean brisket. The meat is so tender it falls right off the bone.

We stuff ourselves to the brim and then chat with our host as he describes his relationship with the community and his many non-Muslim customers and employees.

"We give the police and the firefighters half off," he says, describing the many ways he tries to give back to the community.

We head out to the car, load it up with boxes of leftovers—and an emotional high. That night I can't sleep. My mind is wrapped up in my peace dilemma. My husband sees the concern on my face and asks if he can help.

"Ultimately," he says, "peace comes from trusting God."

He nods off to sleep. I lift my hands and say a quiet prayer asking God to guide both my mother and me toward peace. I trust that he hears me, and I know he will answer.

nine

❧

WEARING THE HIJAB

———————————— *Patricia* ————————————

MY CLEMATIS VINE IS BLOOMING IN FULL GLORY. MASSIVE PURPLE flowers. Deep thick vines. A riot of purple. The blooms hug their trellis southside, petals rippling in dawn light, dancing shoulder to shoulder in a faint breeze. Their hard April prune is a memory. So for now, I lift my phone, waiting for full sun, finally snapping sunny photos of their splendor.

Then I stand back, shaking my head, reflecting on the obvious. Pruning works. This is the message God has sent me in the blossoms.

Even on old vines. Pruning works. I need to know that now. Looking for peace, I need to understand. To know God produces fruit by cutting away dead growth and old wood—giving air and space to give us light to find his path and see his way. I've been looking for peace, instead, by looking back.

In my sixth decade even a blooming flower pulls me into my past. I'm using a smartphone to take my photos of the beautiful vine. Yet in my mind I see Mama and Daddy—seeing *their* clematis vine—and what it took to plant it. Alana gets tired of these stories. My past is gone. Or that's what she seems to say.

But as I look at my daughter, still attached so tightly to Islam, still so full of knowledge against Christ, so full of wearing this other faith's garments, I try to understand what it means to cover up your physical body. Your *self*. Sincerely, I want to know what that means. But first I think about Daddy.

It is 1963.

So I'm going back.

Daddy is sitting in our front room talking to a white man. A lawyer. The white lawyer has come to tell Daddy no. No, he can't buy his dream. It's only a small three-bedroom brick ranch in the working-class subdivision north of Denver in a suburb called Northglenn. That's because the lot my daddy craves, on the neighborhood's prettiest, most showy street, would put our black family front and center in the brand-new subdivision.

Not acceptable, the lawyer is saying. But he says it with nice words. The lot my daddy craves, says the lawyer, is "not available."

Be invisible and go away, the white lawyer is saying to Daddy. And Daddy, a US Army veteran and a life fighter, is saying no. *I won't go away.* Or hide my physical self. Or hide my family. Or cover up my family. Or tell my children they can't play in the front yard. Nor will I accept, Mr. Lawyer, what you are offering—a lousy lot in the far reaches of the subdivision with a backyard adjoining the loud and fumy I-25 freeway.

This is a showdown. This is 1963. And Alana doesn't want to go back. Doesn't want to hear it. Doesn't want to know that Daddy hired his own white lawyer to stand his ground, to fight the race battle and the redlining and the race insults. And I idolize Daddy for taking a stand.

Ken Sande, the peace expert, says such idolizing is wrong. Peace is won, he says, by glorifying God, not our problems. My problem, he would say, is allowing my desire for Alana to know Christ to turn into a consuming demand—which I idolize instead of my God.

The Sande guy is right.

I have idolized my anger, feeling it righteous (when it's not). I have idolized my desire for a Christian-only family—more, perhaps, than I've desired Christ.

In that way I've idolized the end of my daddy's lawyer story—that at 8:06 a.m. on May 27, 1963, Daddy signed the mortgage on the small brick house that, by sweat and determination, he and Mama made into our home. Then they paid for it in full. Then my grass-growing, flower-loving daddy sealed the deal by planting deep, with his own beautiful hands, the clematis vine that on that house still blooms.

Our family doesn't even own that house anymore. Mama sold it years ago after Daddy died. Then she moved on, and then she died. But the vine planted by my daddy still stands tall. Yet alive.

Alana has my daddy's hands. When our publisher took photos of her for this book, and I looked at outtakes—some showing hands—I didn't see her hands. I saw Daddy's. Long fingers. Graceful shape. Clear resolve. Daddy's hands. I also see him in Alana's elegant face. Her determined chin: Daddy's. Her aristocratic nose: Daddy's. Her fighting, immovable spirit: Daddy's. Her skin is light. His skin was dark. But in both I see the same. I see Daddy.

He passed away when Alana was barely three. She doesn't remember him much. But in her, I see him. So I see family. And I idolize the connection.

But Sande says no.

Worship only God.

"When you find yourself in conflict," Sande says, "work backwards through the progression of an idol to identify the desires that are controlling your heart. Ask yourself these questions: How am I punishing others? What am I demanding to have? What is the root desire of that demand?"[1]

My answers?

I'm punishing Alana by questioning her. I'm demanding Alana by pushing at her to return to Christ. My root desire? To have my family back together again. To have Mama and Daddy still living just down the road in the house Daddy bought, fought for, and paid for in full. To have Alana love and respect me as much as I loved and respected my parents. To have us worshipping the same God the same way.

When I was a teen and searching, I still never questioned my parents. No talking back. No debates. No stomping. No eye rolling. No door slamming. Their rule was law. Did my sister and I fight that? We did not. Well, maybe we sometimes did—whispering a gripe to each other in our shared bedroom. Overwhelmingly, however, we simply obeyed. They were Mama and Daddy. What they dictated we followed. Because

we trusted Mama and Daddy. We didn't always understand their decisions. But we trusted them.

One summer I went to Girl Scout camp in the mountains, and the
other girls had fancy pink sleeping bags—but Daddy went to the army
surplus store and bought me a brown tarp bedroll, and said, trust me, this
will work—he was right. Those fancy pink sleeping bags were cute, but
not all were warm, rainproof, or sturdy. Daddy, an army vet who earned
stripes on the killing fields of the Philippines during the Second World
War, knew something of bedrolls. And he was right. I wanted pink frills.
But Daddy taught me thrift and how to say no to fluff, and thrift and
certain denial still bless me. So I trust my dad. To tell the truth, I trust
everything he ever taught me.

I worshipped him and whatever he said.

Now God is saying, *Patricia, worship me.*

That's the adventure.

When Alana turns from Christ and wraps her hair in a scarf, *worship
me, Patricia.*

When she doesn't believe that Jesus alone gave our family strength
to stand down Jim Crow and hate letters and name-calling and the white
boys who welcomed me to Northglenn Junior High School by ganging up
in the lunchroom that first day and throwing sliced, canned peaches all
over my freshly pressed hair—and the sticky juice ran down my neck and
the teacher monitor just shrugged when I told him what had happened—
and now she wants to cover her whole head with a scarf, *worship me.*

Worship me, Patricia Raybon. Then trust me.

But a head scarf?

Lord Jesus.

Could this be easier? Please?

No, it can't, Jesus answers.

So stop fussing about it. Instead, as I reflect on daughters and family and scarves and vines, the Lord sends me to help people with bigger,
harder problems. The husband of a church friend is dying. He needs a
loving visit. My childhood doctor is ninety-seven, confined to a nursing
home. He needs a loving visit. My neighbor is torn between caring for
an aging parent and a young adult daughter. She needs a loving lunch

break. My husband, Dan, is preparing notes for a men's workshop at our church on the "graduation crisis" facing young American blacks. I hear Dan's printer whirling out data. Heartbreaking statistics. Twice as many African Americans as whites drop out of high school. But the stats for white kids aren't that great either. Almost half of America's kids don't graduate from high school.

And I'm worried about Alana wearing a head scarf?

What if I stopped looking at her head? And focused instead on her heart? What if I invited her to work *with* me for suffering people—instead of fighting her on fashion and faith? *Oh, Jesus.* What if I understood that the days of my past—of wearing an Afro out to here, trying to be tough like Daddy, daring some college professor or some employer or anybody else to say anything about my hair or anything at all about my self—may mark my beloved past but not Alana's present. Let me, Jesus, understand that.

Let me appreciate that when I sat down last week at the beauty shop half a block from my childhood church—inviting the French-speaking shampoo woman from Senegal to coil flat twists all over my head, topping the whole thing off with fake hair braided on top—that the end result was not Alana's choice.

Let me get it into *my* head that my era is not hers. Neither are my traditions, my memories, my politics, my preferences, my hair, or my Jesus. Not now anyway. Therefore, Jesus, show me *your* to-do list.

A mother's prayer.

Because peace is not worrying about the outcome. Did somebody important write that? That peace is trusting God with the ends? The lovely Eugene Peterson wrote it better. In his words: "Any hurt is worth it that puts us on the path to peace."[2]

It's a long, winding, and rocky road. Not "one great spiritual experience" (Sande again). Yet if I let God steadily remove the gravel, "bit by bit from our hearts,"[3] will I live better? Walk taller? Love and respect my daughter? Serve the poor? Teach the needy? Feed the hungry? Love the old? Minister to the dying? Lay hands on the sick? Be Jesus in a broken world?

Reflecting on it all, I come to the end of this day, giving God my daughter in prayer—along with all my bits. I post my photos of my clematis vine on Facebook, updating my status: "Our lilacs didn't bloom this year. But the clematis vine outdid itself. Onward sweet vine!"

Then I lie down in bed, curl up next to my sleeping husband—my Senegal hair twists wrapped in a nighttime scarf—believing with Jesus for the peace of a brand-new day. Then I sleep.

Well.

Alana

"OOH, YOU GOT THAT GOOD HAIR!" AN OLDER BLACK WOMAN SMILED and squinted down at me, admiring my long braid.

I was about nine and at my regular two-week visit to Ethel's Hair Salon. I squirmed uncomfortably in the chair and smiled. It would be rude not to. I was used to hearing this expression from black people, especially in the salon. I grabbed the handles of the salon chair, dreading the five hours of torture that I was getting ready to endure. I took a deep breath and stared at the clock: ten a.m. I knew I would be spending the entire Saturday here. The smell of fried chicken, hair grease, and cigarette smoke coated the air.

"Lie back," coaxed Dora, an ample and kind black woman with a short golden crop.

Dora gently undid my braid and massaged the shampoo into my wet hair. I winced as her nails snagged some strands. I was "tender headed" the women would say as Dora combed through my tangled hair. I cried quietly through it all, staring at the clock and the posters on the wall of glamorous women with hair flowing down their backs.

The black hair experience. Every black girl I knew went through the same thing. By the time my generation came to be in the '80s, the "black and proud" iconic persona of African American women had been traded for black and proud—*as long as you have straight hair.* There were three categories often used to describe black hair: kinky, mixed, and good. I was on the far end of the second category, considering my hair was less curly than most other hair types.

That particular day I stared at the posters, convincing myself that looking like the women in those photos was worth all the pain—all the painful detangling, all the "pressing out" of my hair with a sizzling hot-iron comb, and all the burning of my scalp from chemical relaxers. It was all worth it to have "good hair" and, by default, look more white.

Dora and I didn't talk much during this particular visit although we never really did much talking anyway. She remained focused as her hands danced between grabbing my hair, her cigarette, and then a crispy piece of fried chicken. Each strand on my head sizzled as it touched the hot comb. I learned to ignore the initial burn if it touched my scalp. When the last piece was straightened and the ends curled, I climbed sorely out of the chair and politely said my thanks.

My mother filled out the usual amount in her checkbook. I sighed, relieved to be finally finished yet aware it would all happen again soon.

The whole experience fit into this false perception of beauty that revolved around having straight hair. I endured hours of brushing but, of course, never, never cutting. You don't cut "good hair"—even for a trim, I was told. I believed all of it for a large part of my adolescence, and for a while, I thought I was prettier than other people who didn't have hair flowing down their backs.

I watched *Roots*, the '80s slavery film that some black parents used to pound the issues of slavery into their child's head. I saw all of the sequels and the pictures of Jim Crow and segregation in books all over my parents' house. By my early twenties I started to play with the idea that maybe my hair wasn't so bad after all, and maybe it was okay to be nappy and curly and have short hair. Maybe I was okay, just the way God made me.

I cut off all my hair one day, in my best friend's bathroom, with her kitchen shears. As the long locks fell to the ground, I was liberated. I wrapped my bare head in an African kente cloth and went to meet my family downtown at a play. My mother was furious. *How dare I cut off my hair without consulting her?*

My grandma sat silently, not responding. My sister smiled.

Why does it even matter to her? I thought. *It's my hair, not hers.*

I started growing dreads, trying to look like Erykah Badu, the queen of natural, loving-yourself black women. My aunt was livid, claiming that I'd never get a job with hair like that. It only emboldened me to rebel more.

Many years later, when I started covering my hair with scarves, my reasons had very little to do with hair. Ironically, by then, I was totally comfortable with my natural self. No longer obsessed by my outer physical appearance, I was concentrated on looking inward and trying to "find myself."

I wasn't technically a Muslim yet. I was reading and searching, learning about different philosophies of religion. I agreed with the Muslim concept of monotheism, that there is only one God, without partners or intercessors of any kind. I was experimenting with dressing more modestly, wearing long skirts and three-quarter-sleeved shirts. I even wrapped my hair at times in an African style. The Qur'an sat on my bookshelf right along with the Bible and other books related to religion.

I came home one day upset that a man had made a nasty comment about my shape. I grimaced as he looked me up and down while we waited in line at the grocery store.

"You look *good*," he had remarked, elongating the word *good*, then smiled.

I stared at him, cold and hard, offended by his verbal violation.

"I just want to cover up," I told my Iranian but secular coworker after returning from my lunch break.

"It doesn't matter what you wear," she said, arguing that men will behave badly whether I am covered or not.

I didn't believe her and rushed home to look for guidance in the holy texts on my shelf. I picked up the Qur'an, randomly flipped open a page, and was surprised by what I found:

Say to the believing men that they should lower their gaze and guard their modesty: that will make for greater purity for them: And Allah is well acquainted with all that they do. And say to the believing women that they should lower their gaze and guard their modesty; that they should not display their beauty and ornaments except what (must ordinarily) appear thereof; that they should draw their veils over their bosoms.[4]

The verses were from the twenty-fourth chapter of the Qur'an called The Light. I had opened to the section describing the concept of modesty in Islam. I immediately took it as the answer to the inclination in my heart, and although I hadn't openly declared my conversion to Islam yet, I felt inspired to wear long, modest clothing and scarves from then on.

The word *hijab,* often used by laymen to mean "scarf," actually has a wider meaning. *Hijab* comes from the Arabic root word *hajaba,* meaning "to veil." The covering mentioned in the above verse refers to a modest way of behaving and dressing, not just wearing a scarf on your head. Men and women are encouraged to dress and behave modestly with others. It's a protection, for both sexes, and a way to focus on one's *inner* beauty. I was already dressing modestly, with the desire to attract less attention to my physical body. Essentially, hijab is about submission. It's a command from God, just like praying, fasting, and giving charity. I perceived this verse in that way, choosing to submit and follow the words of God.

I had no long scarves of my own, so I perused my mother's closet and found an old '70s-style checkered rectangular scarf. It was ugly and didn't match any of my clothes. I didn't care. I stepped out the next morning wearing a long skirt and shirt, with the clashing scarf wrapped loosely on top of my head and flowing over my chest. I stared at myself in the mirror and smiled. It felt like second nature to be dressed so modestly. I felt protected. My mother met me in the hallway and stopped dead in her tracks. She was speechless. We passed in silence as I descended the steps, and I tried to ignore her gaze as I left for work.

We continued like that for a long time, with her not asking why I was dressing this way and with my not seeing the need to explain. Years later, when my wedding day was only a few nights away, she surprised me.

"I found a scarf for you that matches your wedding dress," she said quietly.

I stared at her, amazed that she could put aside her misgivings to do such a kind thing. It was a perfect match, a long, silky cream-colored scarf with delicate lace around the edges. It matched my dress exactly, as if it had been designed by the same person.

A peace offering from her, I guess. She was willing to sacrifice her feelings about my hijab momentarily and allow me to have my moment.

It was touching, and it meant so much to me. But it's still just a scarf to her. She doesn't see that it is actually a form of worship for me. My hijab is a way for me to openly proclaim my belief in God. Why else would I cover? It's not for a man, a woman, for my husband or friends. It's not for that disgusting man in the grocery store. I cover because God told me to. I cover because I'm following God's direct commandment. Can't she respect that? Why can't she see through all her distaste and appreciate the piety involved in my expression of faith?

I want to hear her explain why it's so wrong. I wish she would tell me why a nun can cover, but I can't. She's been quiet for too long, hardly expressing her opinion about my new clothing choices. I'm ready to hear her now, and hopeful that she will hear me too.

Patricia

IT'S MY BIRTHDAY WEEK. AND MY PHONE IS RINGING.

"Hi, Grammy!"

Alana's three little ones light up the phone. With her help, they are calling Grammy and Grampa in Colorado. Their little voices are golden candy.

"Hi, Grammy! Hi, Grammy!" Even the baby tries to say it. "Hi! Gamma! Hi!"

I don't talk much about the children here. Alana asked me to leave them out of our story. But this week, I am soaking up their sweet sounds like a sponge. They are God's gifts. Gifts no grandparents can produce. The children of our children. Not ours. But ours to savor. I crave them beyond words. With every phone call—with every visit—I am beyond grateful.

So I'll tell a story. If Alana insists, I'll take it out.

And.

Alana insists.

Take it out.

Let it go.

She's on the phone. Calling with her objection. "I don't want this in the book."

Okay, I say, biting my tongue. Trying to listen.

"I know," Alana tells me, "that we agreed not to write about the kids—and I know I have written about them sometimes. But I'm their mother. And this is supposed to be about the two of us. I don't want them in the middle of this."

Okay. But take out this one story? After spending two days writing it? "It's one of my favorite stories. A story about hijabs," I say. "I was just telling Dad. I really like this story. It's so positive."

But Alana insists.

Take it out.

Let it go.

I'm disappointed, but I say no to conflict. To accept, reluctantly, what Jesus' brother James said about conflict in families: "What causes fights and quarrels among you? Don't they come from your desires that battle within you?" (James 4:1).

James is right, of course.

My battle *is* within me. Reading Alana's last story—and showing her disdain for her childhood hairdresser—broke my heart. Never look down on such people, I learned from my parents. Mama and Daddy taught this rule. Working people deserve respect. For sure, the woman who styled and pressed Alana's hair didn't have the best business manners. Her back-room booth in a hair "salon" on downscale East Colfax Avenue in Denver wasn't top-drawer chic. For her to smoke cigarettes, eat food, and talk on the phone while styling her customers' hair broke every rule of decency, sanitation, business protocol, and common sense.

Even more, for me to insist on straightening Alana's thick hair breaks every rule of my daughter's generation. Moreover, my attitude about hijabs—that wearing one doesn't make a person holy—is my problem, not hers. But what do we do about our different views?

In his work on relationship conflict, psychologist John Gottman—writing about marriage, for example—says relationships last when the two people show less defensive behavior and more validation. Such people say, "I hear you. Maybe I don't agree with you. But I hear you. Go on. Tell me more." Indeed, *I disagree with you.* But more importantly, *I still love you.*

In such relationships, despite conflicts, healthy people show positive validation over contempt and disapproval five times to one. A "magic ratio," Gottman says. "As long as there is five times as much positive feeling and interaction between husband and wife as there is negative, the marriage was likely to be stable over time."[5]

That magic ratio seems reasonable for any relationship—for mothers and daughters for sure. Diplomat Benjamin Franklin said it this way: There hardly ever "existed such a thing as a bad peace, or a good war."[6]

During my birthday week, I choose good peace. So I don't fight with Alana. I put aside my frustration, asking the Lord to replace it with something positive.

That same afternoon I learn from a pastor friend's affirming wife about a donation event at a nearby Arc. For every bag of donated items, her husband's ministry gets a cash donation for an upcoming mission trip to Ghana. So on Facebook the wife asks: "Have anything to donate?"

Me? I have piles of bags times ten to donate. A peacemaking, decluttering mother can donate ad infinitum. So I attack my piles of stuff, plus my closet, for giveaways. Shoes I never wear. Dresses I don't use. Suits from another era. Purses. Good grief. T-shirts from women's conferences, church fund-raisers, Denver Broncos seasons, you name it. All tossed into plastic bags.

Seeing the cleanup, Dan dives into his closet. A man of plaid, he soon builds a tower of unworn plaid shirts. He holds up another plaid button-down.

"This is a nice shirt."

I laugh. "Dan. It's plaid!"

"Yeah," he says, admiring it.

"But do you wear it?" I ask. Validating. Being diplomatic.

"Well," he says. "I could."

"Dan!" I groan, laughing. He laughs with me.

"Okay," he says.

I hold open the bag. In goes his plaid.

This moment counts for our five-to-one ratio. As a couple, we rack up more positive moments than negative. On purpose, we do this. That's important since decluttering in my birthday week takes us straight to a hard place. Dan says it like this: "What about your mother's room?"

My late mama lived with us the last year of her life. We remodeled for her. Our dining room became her bedroom—so she paid to add a mirrored closet on one wall. The closet is still jammed with her "final" things—items I couldn't give away or sell in this decade since she passed.

Her silky comforter is one of those things. Puffy and embroidered and '90s mauve, with matching puffy shams and puffy decorator pillows, the comforter consumes one complete side of the closet. Mama slept under it every single night she lived with us. I helped her pick it out. And she loved every silky, puffy, mauve, embroidered inch of it.

But today a pastor's wife needs donations so young people can go to Ghana.

"Grandma's bedspread?" Dan asks, meaning the comforter. "Can we donate that?"

I shut my eyes. Shake my head no. But, with my mouth, I tell him yes. Then at church the next day, I get a final push. The Sunday sermon is called "Holding On Can Hold You Back." Our pastor's son, a college sophomore, is preaching. I listen.

Let it go.

That's the essence of the sermon. Let it go. Bad habits. Regret. Conflict. Unforgiveness. Items you don't need. Deadbeat friends. Bad attitudes. Wrong choices. Puffy comforters. Let it go.

That's what Jesus told the young man seeking eternal life. Sell your possessions. Give it all to the poor. "And you will have treasure in heaven. Then come, follow me" (Matt. 19:21).

Poor young man. "He went away sad, because he had great wealth" (v. 22). But don't hoard like that, says our young preacher. Whatever holds you in its grip, let it go.

Do I want peace? Peace with my daughter?

Let conflict go.

Hijab disputes? Let it go. Book disagreements? Let it go. Doctrine debates. Let it go. Then hold to God.

As I turn sixty-five years young this week, I am compelled to seize on this way. To live and love like I believe it. Plus enjoy the process. Even if things aren't yet perfect, I will honor the commandment to love. Then to this love, and to God, I will answer yes. Just as I answered yes to Alana.

And that's how I will celebrate my birthday. My good friend Denise wants me to celebrate big. Plan something special. Acknowledge the day. After all, how many days does anybody turn sixty-five?

But perhaps I'll throw a party later. For now, instead, I'll enjoy the surprise of sixty-five. For one thing, gratefully, I feel great. When I pulled my back a few weeks ago, I determined to keep moving—going to physical therapy for a refresher on lower-back exercises. "Core strengthening," said the physical therapist. So I did the exercises. Strengthening the core.

And now, I feel great, and it's my birthday. And I will celebrate in peace. Dan makes me a Duncan Hines box cake—loaded with cholesterol, additives, and food coloring—but tops it with number 6 and 5 candles, so I receive it in peace. I give him a big hug, blow out the candles, and, for today, never mind the additives. He also gives me three Kroger bouquets, each sporting a packet of plant food saying, "Our Flowers Are USA Sustainably Grown."

And thank you, Mr. Kroger, too.

Alana mails me an Amazon gift card and also recommends an intriguing book on peacemaking. My little grandchildren, whom I'm not mentioning here, send my favorite birthday gift—a handmade bouquet of three tissue-paper flowers and a handmade card. "Happy Birthday, Grammy!" Arranging the tissue-paper flowers in a tiny vase on my neat kitchen counter, I thank God with Dan, both of us wiping away tears.

Then Dan takes me out for birthday dinner, telling me to wear a pretty dress because we're going to a nice place. So I don't complain when I walk into the restaurant—and longtime friends, including Denise and her husband, greet me with "surprise!"

I'm happy and smiling, but I'm tired—weary from cleaning out our closets and rewriting this chapter and struggling to walk in peace, but I let it all go, enjoying the yummy dinner start to finish.

Earlier that day Dan and I stopped by a nursing home to visit a longtime family friend—now widowed and ninety-two. He misses his wife and longs to live back in his home.

"But, you know, Patricia, I let that go," he tells me. "You do what you have to." He laughs his wonderful laugh. "That's life."

After church on Sunday Dan and I take our donations to the Arc.

Pulling up to the Donation Station, we help the volunteer unload our bags from our car's backseat. Then Dan opens the trunk, lifting out the last item—Mama's puffy comforter.

Mama loved it. And now I'm giving it away. Did that make for a perfect birthday week? No. But the week was great. And for a family making peace, great can be good. So this is the story I'm telling today. Making peace as I write it. Hoping Alana will receive it.

Praying God will bless it.

Alana

PEACE.

How do you know when you're there, when you've actually made it to *peace*?

My mother and I are on the phone, with me desperately trying to make her understand that I'd prefer she not tell stories about my kids and her torn feelings about our family's faith.

In essence, however, it's impossible to ignore the rest of the family, since everything we are dealing with trickles down to the other members. "At some point," I said to my mother one night, "we're going to have to bring Dad and Joi into this conversation, right?"

It seemed like the only logical thing to do if we truly want to achieve peace in our family. My father and sister have been left out of the dialogue. We haven't collectively talked about my conversion, ever.

Talk about an elephant in the room.

They've never once sat me down—all together—and asked me about my faith. To be fair, though, I haven't ever requested a discussion. It's avoidance on all sides, I guess. I'm reading as much as I can to get a hold on the situation and find a way through it all. I stumble across *The Anatomy of Peace* by the Arbinger Institute, and I become immediately engrossed in the narrative. Based on true events, it follows a group of parents attempting to intervene with their dysfunctional children. The book suggests that people often put themselves into boxes to "justify" certain behaviors. The must-be-seen graphic box struck me the most because it described a person avoiding confrontation so as to be seen as likable or agreeable. Inside, however, the person might be seething with anger and discontentment.[7]

This is our family most of the time, smiling and pretending that everything is okay. But when we get ready to leave, and I wrap my scarf around my head, I can see through it all. My mom's eyes darken, and her smile fades.

Self-realization is the first step, though, and I'm not trying to throw stones. Like her, I believe in Jesus' wise words, and I'm willing to look in the mirror in order to heal. Night after night I found myself up late reading this story of these desperate parents, partly because of my own children who will eventually be teenagers and also because of my mother.

The narrator shared this idea with the parents in this book: "The state of your heart toward your children—whether at peace or at war—is by far the most important factor in this intervention we are now undertaking." The parents discovered that this "way of being" determined how they interacted with everyone around them.[8]

I know this firsthand as a teacher. The environment of the room is determined by the emotional state of the teacher. If I have a bad morning, I have to mentally reset to a positive mode before my students arrive. I know my mood would directly affect the students' day.

Halfway through the book, I'm ready for the challenge presented to the parents by the author. "We are always seeing others either as objects—as obstacles, for example, or as vehicles or irrelevancies—or we are seeing them as people."[9] The author described this idea based on the works of philosopher Martin Buber. He challenged them to change how they "saw" people, and I decided to participate as well.[10]

How do I see my mother? Do I see her as an obstacle to the practicing of my faith? Do I view her objections as irrelevant? These questions poured through my mind as I tried to find clues to define my struggle with her.

Why do I feel so entitled to have her respect my faith? Is it my American upbringing that makes me believe so strongly in the idea of personal freedoms, even at the protest of my family?

And when I put on a hijab, why do I feel so hurt by her looks?

I claw through memories to try to answer these questions. The closest

I get to empathy is thinking about my children. I know how it feels to deeply want them to follow my faith and believe wholeheartedly in what I believe. As mothers we become entitled, as if it's our right for our children to follow us. Especially after all that we've invested in them, day after day, tirelessly and without asking for anything in return. But that's where many parents go wrong. The thought that we somehow deserve their blind obedience goes against the very fabric of faith. Our children are gifts, blessings bestowed on us from God. A trust, lent to us for temporary safekeeping and rearing. God is the only owner of our hearts, and for us to feel as though we can be slighted by our children's choice of belief robs God of what is eternally his—our hearts and our souls.

So when my mother looks at me with sadness as I don my hijab, I wish momentarily that she could walk in my shoes for a moment. She would experience my belief that my modesty is nothing to be ashamed of but is a virtue that many historical women of faith have upheld.

I wish she could feel how proud I am to look like Mary, the mother of Jesus, who, in manger scenes that decorate Christmas nativity displays all over the world, wears long, flowing clothing and a head scarf. I wish my mother could understand that when I go to the grocery store and see the magazine covers telling me that my body is an object for attracting the opposite sex, I think the opposite. My body is a vessel for the worship of God. This is why I cover—so that I am a model of purity and piety and a representation of obedient servitude to God. And last, as my mother walks with me in my shoes, I would hope that she would feel honored when a passerby doesn't stare at my rear end as he just stared at the woman who walked by before me.

That feels good, and that feels right to me.

We both said we would try to be empathetic. Jonathan Haidt in *The Righteous Mind* explains that using the words *I can* instead of *I must* has a profound effect on our brain's willingness to entertain an idea.[11] So I invite my mother to see if she "can" appreciate my experiences as sincere. I ask her if she "can" open her mind to understand my point of view.

I won't say that she "must," and I won't force her to comply. I'm trying my best to understand her, and it's hard. But our relationship is worth the effort. I'm ready for the challenge.

ten

⊗⟋⊗

PRAYER WORKS

————————— *Patricia* —————————

IT'S RAMADAN. THE TENTH NIGHT OF RAMADAN. I SAW IT ON
Facebook. But Alana and I haven't really talked about it. I know she and
her family have moved—relocating to a summer apartment close to a
mosque they like. They like the Muslim community there better. So they'll
celebrate Ramadan there. I think I'm telling this right. I am trying hard
at least to listen. So I know this: Alana is fasting sixteen hours a day. No
food or water. Sunup to sundown, that is. No food or water. In Texas. And
not feeling so good. She's having headaches. I try to find a way to think
about that. Her long, long fast. With no food during the day. Without any
water. Distressed about this ritual, on this night, I don't sleep well, trying
to reconcile her fast with something I can understand. And I can't.

Then around dawn I pray, asking the Lord to keep her. Bless her,
Lord. Keep her safe. *Jesus, be a fence.* Amen.

Then the phone rings. It's Dan's sister calling from New Jersey. She
wants Dan and me to try to meet her and her husband for a four-day getaway. Anywhere. *Thank you, Jesus.*

"I need a break," she says. "Pick a place."

Diana is an elementary school principal—an educator like Alana.
She works hard year-round. Her work schedule is full too. Her off-time is
usually packed, spent with her grown children and their families. Now,
however, she is calling Dan and me.

"Where we going?" she asks.

And suddenly, I am grinning. After a long, dry summer, I am grinning.

"What about Mackinac Island?" Diana asks.

"Mack-a-what?"

Dan likes to joke. So he interrupts his sister, kidding and being silly as she describes the place in Michigan. Upper Peninsula. Never heard of it. But I listen on the phone to Dan and his sister talk. Sibling talk. Joking. Understanding each other.

I smile. Close my eyes. Agree when Dan says Mackinac Island sounds "refreshing."

Later he also learns about a short cruise to Nova Scotia, leaving from Boston. Somebody mentions Mexico. Or a cheap flight to Nassau. Or maybe even Orlando, Florida. *Dolphins*. Or even Colorado.

Or just New Jersey in Diana's backyard?

I have no preference. I'm just happy. We're talking family here. People we're related to spending time together. No divisions. No arguments. No food rules. No clothing that people stare at. No stopping in the middle of Mackinac to lay a prayer rug down on the street while people gawk at your daughter down on the ground, in a long dress, facing east and praying.

This is hard for me. I should be cool and okay with it. God knows I tried when we were at the Houston Aquarium one summer night with Alana and her family and, as always, she and her husband had to stop and pray.

Here? That's what I wanted to ask. But I bit my tongue.

All around, families were together and enjoying the displays, joking and laughing and eating snacks, learning about the fish and outdoor attractions, and being together. Which God must love. Instead, while Alana and her husband found a place behind some bushes and knelt on the ground, invoking Allah, I grabbed the kids' little hands, trying to look matter-of-fact. And people stared.

Does God require this? Of Alana? Of me?

Surely, he requires my focus on him. That good apostle Paul nailed it, saying, listen, "Pray without ceasing" (1 Thess. 5:17 KJV). Keep a prayer on your lips all day.

During our family travel and outings over the years, Dan and I could have prayed like this. Just stopped. Cut the arguing about taking the wrong turn. Choosing the bad restaurant. Leaving too late. Starting too early. Whatever. Blah, blah, blah. Gripe, gripe, gripe. And, instead, just focused on God.

Now Dan and I have a word for it: HALT. We laugh just saying it. It's an acronym for what to do when you're Hungry, Angry, Lonely, or Tired. Yes, HALT. Take a minute.

Grab a snack. Take a breath. Share a hug. Close your eyes. Whisper *Jesus*. Then resume. Better than a prayer-kneeling in public on the ground? Maybe. Or maybe not. But on a family outing, when you need to hear from God, isn't a little HALT enough?

Or is this what I'm asking: Does everything in Islam have to be so showy? So difficult? So hard?

Or is the problem with me?

Alana says yes. The problem is me.

But I already wrote those words in a book. Already looked at myself in a hard mirror. Already dug under my skin to reflect—in that other book—on another hard problem: the "race problem" in America. That's the throwback term for racial tension. The "Negro problem." That's what mainstream experts called it anyway, regardless of their profession. Didn't matter. Sociologists. Psychologists. Economists. Theologians. You name it. All felt comfortable saying the race problem was that Negro problem.

And that problem, as experts saw it, started and ended with people like me.

I hear Alana saying the same thing. *You're the problem.* Fix you, and everything between us will be fine. It hurts to hear. But is she right, Jesus?

Am I the Satan you warn us from? The Satan you saw and heard in your disciple Peter?

Do you remember that story from church, Alana? Jesus was on his way to the cross. Of course, he was always on the way. So on this day, he was on the way and preparing his disciples—warning them what to expect. *I will suffer. I will die. On the third day, I will rise.*

Peter was undone. He actually rebuked Jesus.

"'Never, Lord!' he said. 'This shall never happen to you!'"

But Jesus responded: "'Get behind me, Satan!'" (Matt. 16:22–23).

Talking to Peter.

You're in my way. You're putting people over God. You're trumping God's plan with your own.

Reading the Bible story on a recent morning with my husband, I pause. Then I see: even Peter was labeled once by Jesus as a voice for Satan. Which can only mean this: if I don't watch out, I can speak for Satan too. By wrestling over Alana, I can become the very problem I'm struggling to avoid.

Is that what you're saying, Alana?

But even more: Is that what you're saying, Jesus? That I'm acting like Satan?

And so what if Alana wants to lay a prayer rug down at the Houston Aquarium or anywhere else? Get out of her way.

Because Alana is right. I see negatives in Islam—but not because I'm looking for negatives. God help me, I'm just trying to stay connected to my beautiful, younger daughter and her precious family. To still be a family. Yet even today, before I sit down to write these words, I get a negative.

It's an e-mail from a woman in the Republic of Guinea in a town called Kissidougou.

What? A place I've never heard of. Who? A woman I don't know. And what's she saying—this woman I've never met, in this place I don't know?

That she hates Islam. She is ranting. She is railing about being married off at thirteen by her parents to a man who already had three wives "as permitted in the Koran." (That's how she spells it.) I start reading her angry letter. Cringing at her story. Her heartbreaking life.

Then I stop. Who is this woman? Why write to me? Today? *Get behind me, Satan.*

Is she asking for money? Yes, in her last paragraph. And is her letter a hoax? A scam? Do I keep reading these raging words? Maybe even reply?

Or do I delete her e-mail and move on?

This is what Jesus instructed Peter: Don't look. Instead, look to God. Not to man. Heed God's way. Not the ways of people.

For the disciple Peter, that meant accepting that Jesus, the long-awaited Messiah, would sacrifice himself whether Peter liked it or not. Hang on a cross whether Peter approved or not. Reconcile the world to himself whether Peter approved or not. So Jesus would go to Golgotha. And hang there. And die. Nailed on a Roman criminal's cross—between two common thieves—even if a whole religion insists it didn't happen.

Peter couldn't bear it. Refused to see it. Too negative. But Jesus says the best way to rightly see anything, negative or not, even if it lands on your doorstep—or in your e-mail box—is to turn your eyes to God. One Bible scribe said it like this: "fixing our eyes on Jesus" (Heb. 12:2).

Then seeing him, everything turns right.

So today, looking to Christ, I delete the raging e-mail. Then what do I see in Christ? I see my blessed life. Born black and female in America in the poison of Jim Crow, I should be dead.

I am not.

From there the blessings trump the pain. So today I make a list. I sit down and write, not a gratitude list but a blessings list. But wait. I wrote a book about that too. An entire year of blessings.

Jesus.

Am I a slow learner? Or am I a mom?

Then Jesus answers. *No, you're not a mom. You're a woman with a grown daughter.*

Alana is grown. And how did that happen?

"The years," my husband says. "They flew."

At our age, sitting out back in the evening after our dinner—talking about where to meet his sister and her husband for a short getaway vacation—we look around ourselves, at our backyard, at the grass that needs a mow, at our home, at our graying heads, and we wonder, *What happened to the years? And where are the children?*

"They're gone," Dan says. "Grown and gone."

So where does that leave us? Our work is done.

Oh, God, what a journey.

I thought our girls would be like me. Bookish and quiet. Bible loving. Traditional and conforming. Church girls. Well, one is not. And even our daughter who follows Christ isn't traditional and conforming. Never was.

Alana? She is her own person. So, Patricia, can you celebrate her arrival? In spite of her faith? Can you let her pray wherever she likes? Let her fast as long as she likes? Then when Ramadan ends this year on July 28—and that's your daddy's birthday—can you honor his memory by honoring her? Honor your beautiful late father by honoring your fasting, praying daughter?

If I don't, I'm being Satan. And what are we saying to Satan?

Hell? No.

Eyes front instead on Christ. Now bless my precious daughter, Lord. Keep her in her life. Surround her in her choice.

Jesus, be a fence.

Amen.

Alana

IT'S FRIDAY, AND THE KIDS AND I HAVE JUST RETURNED FROM THE new mosque at the weekly congregational prayer called *Jummah*. The kids have conveniently fallen asleep for their naps, except for Laila, who reluctantly munches her tuna sandwich at the kitchen table. I take advantage of the quiet and pick up the phone to call my mom.

She messaged me about talking today, but I have been putting it off. I wasn't sure how to take her comments in her recent section and how this would affect our discussion. So I was surprised to hear the words she spoke over the phone.

"I finally get it," she says, explaining how she has now come to a place where she can accept my choice to be a Muslim but not necessarily accept Islam as a religion.

It's a huge step for her, when I was beginning to feel as if there was no light at the end of the tunnel. I'm not sure how to take the news, and I'm uncomfortable about showing my enthusiasm.

I bring up the child bride she mentioned from Africa and how

Muhammad forbade forced marriages. I continue to explain how unfair it is for me to have to explain every situation that she comes across like this, just like I wouldn't expect her to explain violence or immorality perpetrated by Christians or African Americans.

She understands, she says. It was unfair of her to ask that of me, and she won't do that anymore. I'm shocked, unsure how to respond. I take a deep breath and suddenly feel a release of stress.

"So where do we go from here?" I say, feeling like we are finally moving toward a resolution.

Many questions run through my head. How will this translate into our relationship when we are physically in the same location? Does this mean my mother will no longer appear bothered when she sees me practicing my faith? And when she says that she accepts my choice, does that mean she will just be putting up with me while remaining uncomfortable with my religious practices?

I think of that day she mentioned at the aquarium, when my husband and I prayed our evening prayer right there on the grass, and of another time at the science museum, where I prayed in the hallway despite her disapproving glances. "Why don't you think about *us* and how *we* feel?" she said after I had finished my prayer and folded up my prayer rug.

I almost laughed, thinking about how ironic it was for my mother to be embarrassed by me, when normally it's the offspring who claim to be embarrassed by their parents. She spoke of how Christians pray together and privately, and I remember feeling shocked that we were arguing about my praying at all.

That was a few years ago, yet now that my mother claims to be accepting of my choice to practice Islam, I wonder if she will react differently the next time we are out together and I pray.

Prayer is a part of every moment of my life, from before dawn when I rise groggily to pray *Fajr*, until the late night when I pray *Isha*. I actually schedule my day around prayer. But my mother is unaware that prayer for me is not only during those five scheduled times but also a constant part of my day.

Muhammad once spoke of one of the benefits of praying regularly five times a day. He said, "If there was a river at the door of any one of you and he took a bath in it five times a day would you notice any dirt on him?" His companion replied, "Not a trace of dirt would be left." Muhammad then continued by saying, "That is the example of the five prayers with which Allah blots out (annuls) evil deeds."[1] I always use this analogy when explaining to my stepson how praying five times a day makes it really hard for a person to do wrong in between these prayers. It hardly makes sense that a thief or a murderer could pray in the morning and then, with the intention of praying at noon, commence to committing a crime.

"Unquestionably, by the remembrance of Allah hearts are assured," the Quran states.[2] My mind was set on achieving this state as I noticed the time for prayer drawing nearer. So when I stopped to pray that day at the museum, the only thing on my mind was pleasing God and purifying my soul.

My prayer, regardless of its awkward location, was a moment of peace and reflection for me—a time to set the world aside, and for three minutes, focus only on God. I ignored the strange glances from onlookers, who couldn't understand how I could embarrass myself by worshipping God in such a location. I brushed off the feeling of being strange and weird because I knew that if they knew about Islam, they wouldn't find it odd at all.

After I pray, I continue to worship Allah in my words and deeds, as well as in silent and private nonritualistic prayer. The Qur'an instructs believers to constantly remain in the state of remembrance and praise of Allah as mentioned in chapter 3, verse 191: "Who remember Allah while standing or sitting or [lying] on their sides and give thought to the creation of the heavens and the earth."[3] There is a constant state of awareness, thankfulness, and glorification of God that a Muslim tries to achieve, and the five daily prayers are an essential part of reaching this goal.

At the museum that day I folded up my prayer rug and privately thanked Allah for the opportunity to pray. As we entered the dinosaur exhibit right next to my prayer location, I glorified Allah as I witnessed his remarkable creation in the display of the fossils. As we walked through the rest of the museum, however, I remained uneasy at my mother's objections, wishing she appreciated my desire to worship God this way.

Now, after our phone conversation, I remain worried about what the future holds. She sounded liberated and free, yet I could sense unease in her voice as well.

"Thank you for not giving up," she said to my surprise.

"I would never give up, Mom! You're my mother!" I replied, laughing.

I complimented her on her determined desire to sort through every gritty detail of her life. "Not everyone can do that, Mom," I said.

At the mosque that night I sat in the corner of the prayer room, reading Desmond Tutu's book *The Book of Forgiving*, lulled by the melodic sound of the Qur'an recitation. "Peace always comes to those who choose to forgive," Tutu says.[4] I stared at the quotation, believing the truth of this statement and knowing that forgiveness will have to occur in order to heal our relationship.

I will have to forgive myself—for the hurt I caused my mother, for all of the years I spent yelling and arguing my points. I know I've allowed my anger to overwhelm me and control my behavior, especially with my mother. But I also have to forgive myself for allowing my feelings of hurt, resentment, and frustration to affect our relationship. I have to forgive myself for avoiding this conversation with her and allowing my fear of confrontation to determine my relationship with her.

"We all have made mistakes and harmed others," Tutu says.[5] I know his words are true in my case, and I am willing to own up to this fact. Forgiveness is liberating, and my heart swells at the idea that I am not bound by my mistakes and shortcomings, that God, the Oft-Forgiving, wants us to come to him seeking his forgiveness.

The next step is to forgive my mother. Even as I write this, I am worried that she will think I am blaming her or casting stones her way. This is not at all the case. Her deep desire for self-reflection is admirable, and I have benefited from her model of introspection. I know I still have to forgive her, for my own liberation—so I can no longer feel bound by remnants of petty disputes or arguments lingering in my subconscious. She has to know that I'm not holding on to the negatives anymore, that instead, I'm clinging to the prospect of a new hope for our relationship.

Patricia

IT'S SUNDAY MORNING. DAN AND I ARE ON OUR WAY TO OUR CHURCH. Our beautiful church. Lord Jesus, bless that glorious place. We've remembered our Bibles—actually apps on our phones. We're also bearing stuffed deviled eggs and a yellow box cake with chocolate icing (Dan's favorite). This Sunday is the 146th anniversary of our Denver congregation, and a potluck picnic will follow the Sunday service. The 146 years brace our church family. All those years. Rich, good history. Founded in 1868, our long-standing congregation is older than the state of Colorado itself, which didn't gain statehood until 1876.

And look.

Two black women, both named Mary—the two Marys, as our church fondly calls them—founded the church in a log cabin when Denver was a dusty, bustling camp town on the banks of the Cherry Creek and South Platte River.

During the sermon today, our pastor will retell the story. Or maybe the Creative Arts Ministry will dramatize the tale: the two Marys boldly canvassing poker players in Denver saloons, going from door to door, asking for donations to open a church.

The story matters. Those few penniless pioneers "went through the gates of hell," as our pastor puts it, to stand up for right "and for righteousness." Bottom line: those two relentless Marys birthed a congregation that won't die. At Shorter Community African Methodist Episcopal Church, we don't faint. Saying that isn't prideful. It's gratitude for strong shoulders. At least three times the church was forced to move when white property owners protested a "colored church" moving next door.

Members sold the property each time, but for a profit.

Then in 1925, when a newer brick sanctuary burned to the ground— and arson was suspected of Denver's then burgeoning Ku Klux Klan—the Shorter Church members rallied and rebuilt. One determined year after the fire, on Easter 1926, they marched into their rebuilt building and never looked back.

And now? By God's grace, Shorter Church members keep praying.

Keep believing. Keep loving. Keep learning. Keep serving. A perfect church? Hardly. Yet, as we say, "We serve a perfect God."

And now here we are.

"You brought cake, Sister Pat?"

The ladies in the kitchen are bustling. We'll have our potluck.

Our bread and butter at Shorter Church, however, is social activism. Just this past week, our Social Justice Ministry staged a rally downtown at the Denver Sheriff's Office in memory of a jailed homeless street preacher killed in 2010. He was restrained in a brutal choke hold incident involving five sheriff's deputies who wrestled the man facedown to the jailhouse floor—one applying a nunchaku, one a Taser, and another pressing almost his full 240-pound weight onto the back of the fifty-six-year-old, 135-pound homeless preacher.

Murder. That was the Denver Coroner's Office ruling, although no officer had yet been charged. (A six-million-dollar settlement for the preacher's estate was approved later by the city of Denver.) That same sheriff's department is also under scrutiny, however, for a series of other jail incidents leading to injury or death of inmates.

"Justice may be slow," our pastor told our congregation. "But mark my word, justice will be served."

We are old enough, some of us, to remember lynchings, bombings of "Negro churches," murders of black children—Emmett Till in Mississippi and those four little girls whose Sunday school room in Alabama was bombed with a timed detonator by white supremacists, killing the four angels.

We grew up on these stories. So we drink from the social justice fountain. But our hope is built on nothing less than the sacrifice of Jesus and the righteousness of his love.

Is that right? And if it is, what does that mean? It means that every Sunday for the past ten years, I didn't have a clue how God would open my prison door. But on every one of those Sundays, I pressed through the church doors anyway with one goal: to worship while expecting.

Because here's the thing: It's odd to praise when you're stuck. To pray when you can't see. To worship when you don't understand. To stand clinging alone to the Lord's strong promise to an exiled prophet like Jeremiah: "'For I know the plans I have for you,' declares the LORD, 'plans to prosper you and not to harm you, plans to give you hope and a future'" (29:11).

I think hard on that today. That when we can't fathom what's happening, God knows. That's one thing I learn for sure at my church. Not me. God.

Alana can make Islam sound poetic. All the rituals.

But in the crucible and tumble and clinch and awe of life, give me Jesus.

And that's a song too.

Slaves with nothing to their stolen names sang it like this:

> *Give me Jesus.*
> *Give me Jesus.*
> *You may have all this world,*
> *But give me Jesus.*[6]

Strong God.

Tempering God.

What did Paul say about beautiful words: "If I speak in the tongues of men and of angels, but have not love" (1 Cor. 13:1 ESV)?

Then, speaking of words, here's what Jesus said about prayer—about folks praying

"on the street corners to be seen by others. Truly I tell you, they have received their reward in full. But when you pray, go into your room, close the door and pray to your Father, who is unseen. Then your Father, who sees what is done in secret, will reward you." (Matt. 6:5–6)

So I did that. I prayed in secret. Then, in secret, the Lord answered. *So love, Patricia. You did what you could. Let your daughter live her life.*

Our vacation plans with Dan's sister and her husband run into a snag. I don't blink. Our plans aren't working. I'd rather know the Lord's.

At my church on our anniversary Sunday, listening to a youth pastor recite our church history—describing the two Marys, the log cabin, the poker-playing donors, the arson fire, the rebuilding—that's what I ask. What now, Lord, are your plans? In this new world order with Alana, what can I do?

I could volunteer to help tutor kids at church during August, preparing them for school. I could rally Writing Ministry buddies to help with the tutoring. I could volunteer with the homeless women's program at my childhood Denver church.

Or I could call my daughter Alana.

She answers.

It's a Wednesday morning. Today is her sweet four-year-old boy's birthday. Typically, we'd be in Texas to help him celebrate. But Dan and I didn't travel this time. The road to peace has been rocky. Plus, Alana and her family are moving—getting their Houston house ready to sell, so they can move to Tennessee, after living in Clear Lake in temporary housing.

Alana puts our grandson on the phone. He's down a bit with a cough. But we all sing "Happy Birthday" and hear about his gifts, including a new toy robot. Then he's off the phone to go and play.

"How's everything else going?" Dan asks.

Alana fills us in. We listen. We laugh. We talk. We sing with the baby when she wants to hold the phone. "The itsy-bitsy spider crawled up the water spout. Down came the rain and washed the spider out."

We talk some more.

This is family.

This is what I've been asking God to deliver.

My family.

No fireworks.

So we don't talk with Alana about fighting in the Middle East. On this same morning Hamas in the Gaza Strip has broken a cease-fire agreement with Israel, letting loose with rockets. In turn, Israel retaliates. In the cross fire civilians on both side die. Talking about it later with Dan, I mention the now obvious about religious war: there is no peace in attack.

This is what God wants me to know. For peace, hold your fire. To be sure, during my peacemaking season with Alana, I have found enough ammunition to make my case *against* Islam. But what do I gain by letting it fly?

So I didn't mention to Alana something else that happened this week. When I went to my longtime dentist for a regular checkup, I met the new dentist who's replacing him at retirement. And she's a Muslim.

"Hi, I'm Neda!"

We shook hands.

Then she put on her gloves and did her work. Afterward, we chatted. I asked her about her name, embroidered in pretty letters on her white doctor's coat. She told me how to pronounce it.

"It's 'Neh-dah' in my language, but Americans want to say it in English like 'Nah-da,' but in Spanish *nada* means 'nothing.' So I just say 'Nee-da.' Like that."

I listened. Admiring her rich accent. Her beautiful smile. Her graceful hands. Her glistening dark hair. So I asked.

"What's your native language?" I hoped this was okay. I didn't want to quiz her with the typical question of immigrants, "Where you from?" You know how we say it—asking about nationality but meaning "you're from someplace else." As if that's a wrong thing. So I didn't want to say all that. Or imply that. But even more, I didn't want to ask what I was longing to know of this kind dentist: Are you a Muslim?

God, I wanted to ask this. Ever since my dentist sent his retirement letter, explaining that a talented young couple was taking over his practice—and mentioned their names—I wanted to ask. Are they Muslims? Not that it mattered, dentist wise. Or teeth-care wise. I was just curious.

Instead, I asked the pretty dentist about her native language.

"It's Farsi," she said. Still smiling her lovely smile.

So I pressed for more. "You're from Iran?" I smiled.

She nodded, still smiling back. She said *Farsi* with pride and warmth.

So since we were both smiling and being open and warm, and since these things seem to matter so doggone much now, I went ahead.

"Can I ask?" I said. "Are you a Muslim?"

She didn't blink. Didn't stop smiling.

"Yes," she said.

I explained why I asked. I clicked off reasons: I write books. I'm cowriting a book with my daughter. The focus is interfaith peace. Because I'm a Christian—but my daughter converted to Islam.

Then Dr. Neda said the oddest thing: "Why?" Her smile disappeared.

I looked confused. But she asked again.

"Why did she become a Muslim?"

I breathed deeply. Thinking about her question. Thinking about our world. Thinking about faith and how it defines how we all live. And we all have to talk about it. Without going to battle.

"It's a long story," I said. Then I smiled. "Maybe you'll read the book."

Dr. Neda nodded. Smiling back. "I really do want to read it." Then she told me her story.

"I'm a Muslim. But in name only."

"In Iran," she said, "the government dictates that you're a Muslim. But a lot of people, we don't follow the government. We don't do the fasting. We don't pray. We don't memorize the Qur'an. The Arabs there try to force this on us. But we are not Arab. My family, here in the United States, we celebrate the Zoroastrian festival every spring. But we also celebrate Christmas. We buy a Christmas tree. We give each other gifts. I mean, why wouldn't you celebrate Christmas? It's the most joyous season of the year."

Yes. Well.

I could remind her that Jesus is the reason for the season. But she's my new dentist. And we've already perhaps said enough.

But she's not finished. I've opened a door.

"I believe in God," she says. "And God doesn't want all this fighting. All this killing." She went on. "I'm not religious, but I teach my kids to be good—to do what is right. No lying. No stealing. No cheating. I don't teach them to be religious because back in Iran some of the people in power, who promote religion so much, are the ones who lie, who steal, who cheat."

Yes. Well.

Once I arrived back home, I looked up Iran in my global prayer guide. The dentist is right. The government there runs the show. Religionwise, especially. However, in this atmosphere, ironically, Christianity is growing. "Never since the seventh century has the Church in Persia grown so fast,"[7] the prayer guide declared. So despite threats of death for apostasy against Islam, Jesus speaks to hearts. People are listening.

But I didn't mention this to Alana. We can talk about it another time. For now, not every talk we have has to land us on faith.

Instead, I brought home 120 toothbrushes the dentist's staff shared for the homeless women's program at my childhood church. I'd asked for a donation. "They already have toothpaste on them," the receptionist told me, "so for the first time they can be used as is."

Outstanding.

That evening, I went to the volunteer-training meeting for the tutoring program at my church—mentioning Alana and her passion for character education to accompany academics, and the group adopted the idea. So at the first tutoring session, the leader will invite the kids to write classroom rules for mutual respect and sharing.

Dan, meantime, asked Diana to put our vacation on hold.

The next day I went to my internist for my regular physical checkup.

"Your blood pressure is really down," he said. "Great job. What are you doing?"

I answered: Eating less. Exercising more. Cutting back on salt. "And praying more," I could have added, and my doctor—who is of Chinese descent and not Christian but knows my faith choice—would have typed that on his computer. "And praying."

Driving home, I remembered one other thing.

I'm not fighting.

Not with Alana. Not with my husband. Not with my church. Not with God. Because God knows my plans.

Plans for peace? Plans to forgive? Plans to love? Yes to all.

But plans for hell?

No.

———————————— *Alana* ————————————

A TURNING POINT? MY MOM'S STORY ABOUT HER DENTIST FEELS LIKE the same old thing—another example of a disgruntled Muslim that's supposed to illustrate the deficiency of Islam. Of course I can't expect her to ignore the bombardment of Islam in the news or pretend as though the state of Muslims in the world isn't in disarray. I don't expect her to turn a blind eye. I just wish she would recognize that much of what she comes across about Islam is so different from my experience, that she would see the obvious contrast in my life.

Added to all of this stress is our family's move. My husband is never at our temporary apartment home where we moved before the start of Ramadan. He spends his days and nights painting and fixing our house back in our old neighborhood, trying to ready it for sale. We're ready to move, to leave our quickly deteriorating neighborhood. But to leave Texas? I'm not sure. My husband has a new job waiting in another state—in Tennessee. As for me, meanwhile, I'm starting to feel detached, stuck here, with my sick son.

We haven't attended the mosque in at least four days, despite its being the last few days of Ramadan. I miss the camaraderie, the lectures, and the prayers. A new friend texts me, asking about us. She hasn't seen us in a while. She knows my son was sick. I reply that we're going today, but inside I'm not really feeling up to it. My mom's recent comments drag me back down again. I'm exhausted from this fight, ready to move out of this rut that we seem to be in.

I look at the wall of our interactive Ramadan decorations—thirty balloons filled with candy that we pop for each day of Ramadan, an idea I stole from a friend on Facebook. The empty balloons lie sagging on the wall. I look at the remaining eleven balloons and feel anxiety about the lack of time left before moving to a new state, settling down, and somehow getting it all together to begin teaching in the second week of August.

The kids pop the nineteenth balloon on the day that we are rushing to an interfaith dinner my husband helped plan. A wave of Jewish-Muslim fasting dinners is being held around the nation, a symbolic demonstration of solidarity and peace. My husband's employer decided to cash in on this opportunity and host one in our city. I am excited to go, especially because of the new wave of violence between the Gaza Strip and Israel. This is my nonviolent struggle for peace.

Iesa calls me right before the event, asking me to pick up the vegetarian food and hors d'oeuvres. The Jewish participants are fasting today as well, and he wants to make sure there is nothing they can't eat. I rush to the Green Seed Grill and then to the nearest Kroger to get hummus, fruit, and dates—foods we hope both the Muslims and the Jews will appreciate.

We enter the community hall next to historic St. Paul's Methodist Church, which offered to host the event. The program has already begun, and the Jews are reciting a series of prayers and performing rituals. A woman stands in front of the group with her prayer cloth draped over her shoulders, carefully reciting Hebrew prayers. Everyone smiles at us as we come in, despite our lateness.

I sit down and spot some people I know—Rabbi Dan, whom I met at the Race Against Violence; my husband's former Jewish boss; a few Muslim friends I always run into at these types of things; and our family's favorite sheikh. He drove at least an hour to join in the event, and I'm thankful an Islamic scholar is present.

The kids can't sit long among the quiet worship, so we sneak out to the car to get the baby's lost shoe.

"Is that a castle?" my daughter asks, pointing at the massive Victorian-style church right next door.

"It's a church," I reply, remembering that my kids still haven't gone into one. "Let's go inside," I say, after grabbing the baby's shoe.

The kids pretend to be knights and princesses while we walk through the huge double doors. They gasp as we enter the main chapel and gaze up at the huge arches in the ceiling. We sit down in the second pew while I point out the intricate stained-glass windows and the giant organ in the front. The kids are impressed, oohing and aahing, in awe of the sights. They laugh as the baby says "book, book" and grabs for a hymnal.

"Let's go," I call out, worried that I've missed so much of the interfaith event to be considered rude but glad that my children have officially been in a church.

By the time we get back, everyone is breaking their fasts. I hang out in the back of the line, chatting with Rabbi Dan, then grab my food and find my family at a table near the back. A Jewish man I haven't yet met asks to sit next to us. Somehow he and I get into the topic of politics, a subject I was hoping to avoid.

"If everyone would just follow their religion," he comments, "everything would be better."

Would it? I wonder, but nod so as not to be controversial at this dinner. I try to change the subject, bringing up Desmond Tutu's forgiveness book I'm currently reading and remarking on how South Africa overcame so much hate.

"Mandela used to be a *terrorist*," he remarks, explaining how he did so many "terrible" things before his jailing. I gulp, taking a huge bite out of my veggie lasagna. I really do not want to get started on the topic of terrorism here, especially about Nelson Mandela.

Thankfully, my son interrupts at the right moment. He stole the remains of the fruit tray and brought the whole thing over to munch on. The ice breaks, and we all laugh at his innocence.

"I feel bad," I say to my new Jewish friend, "that I didn't learn about the fast you were observing today before I came here."

He explains how it's not commonly practiced among all Jews, admitting that he didn't observe it as kid.

"It's a day of sorrow," he says, "a day for us to remember the things that have happened to our people."

A solemn day, indeed, I say to myself.

He continues to explain about other Jewish holidays, including Yom Kippur, a holiday his family has always celebrated, and how they all come together from all over the world on that day. He laughs, describing how his wife is trying to get everyone back at their house this year instead of his daughter's.

I smile, but inside I'm suddenly sad, thinking of how my family doesn't share such experiences anymore.

By then the crowd has dwindled, and some of the Muslim men have rushed out to get to the mosque for evening prayers. We stick around to help clean up and figure out what to do with the remaining food, and then we load up the car for the long ride back home. I high-five the rabbi's wife, who helped me clean up so quickly.

"It takes a woman," she jokes, and for a moment I feel like this night was worth it, like it achieved something. I'm not sure exactly what that something is yet, but I'm glad I smiled at a good share of people who may never have met a covered Muslim woman.

"Do you need this tablecloth?" the rabbi asks me. He's holding it to his chest, having already neatly folded it into a rectangle.

We used it as a prayer surface, placing it on the floor of the hall in order to have a clean space for the evening prayer.

"Oh, I don't think anyone will eat off it," I reply, "since it's been on the floor."

"No," he states. "I mean, does it have any intrinsic holiness since you prayed on it?" he asks with a serious face.

I am taken aback at his concern for our holy things but impressed that he cares. My mind flashes back to my visit to Rabbi Gross's synagogue, when he explained the reverence Jews have for certain holy artifacts.

"Oh, I'm sorry," I stutter. "I understand what you mean. No, it doesn't."

I'm touched that he cared enough not to destroy something that might be holy for Muslims. That certainly feels like an example of inter-faith mutual respect.

"I made a Christian friend!" my daughter exclaims after spending the last ten minutes sharing favorite things with a twenty-something Jewish woman.

"Actually, she's Jewish," I say kindly to her.

"Oh," she replies, momentarily bewildered, not sure exactly what that means.

An explanation of Judaism will have to come later. For now, we head back home and to the late night prayers at the mosque. I ask my husband what he thinks about these types of events. Do they actually help to achieve interfaith peace?

"It helps to get things started," my husband explains. "It's a place to begin working together and help people get to know one another."

He believes in this process as a worthwhile investment that will make a difference in our community. I know he's right. I look up at him and smile, inspired by his hope, and encouraged by his optimistic spirit.

eleven

❧

ROCK THE BOAT

———————— *Patricia* ————————

SO I HAD A DREAM. AT LEAST IT SEEMED LIKE A DREAM—EVEN
though I spent most of the night awake. Not sleeping at all. That's how
I felt. But I dreamed. And like most dreams, mine was odd. Not even
exciting odd. Instead, I dreamed my life as a news reporter was over. Odd
because, technically, I haven't been a reporter for years. Not for decades,
in fact. But I can still act like a pup reporter. Sniffing out details. Like Lois
Lane. Tail wagging. Asking tail-wagging questions. "Are you a Muslim?"

Alana loathes that.

So the dream said to stop it. Stop the sniffing, tail-wagging, digging
up news on Islam. I recognized this message because, in the dream, a
reporter friend I haven't seen in forever showed up to visit me. She was
mourning me. I can't remember her words. But, in the dream, she was
saying good-bye. Good-bye to me as a news reporter.

I didn't wake myself up. When I have a disturbing dream, I wake
myself up so I won't have to "watch" it. But this time, I kept watching. Eyes
closed. Looking. I kept letting my friend mourn me, telling me—as a news
reporter—her good-byes.

The reporter in me is gone? Dead and gone?

Right away, I suspected what the dream meant. That for peace, Alana
and I won't succeed if I act all NewsChannel 9 reporter-of-all-things-Islam.

"That's just the journalist in you," my sister always tells me.

But Alana is asking for a mom.

My beautiful friend Denise would understand this. In her work life she's a global consultant, analyzing organizational management. In her married life, however, global consultant doesn't fly. Time-out, says her husband. No analyzing here. *I don't need a workshop. I need a wife.* She has confided these moments in me as her friend, explaining how her professional role can't lap over into her home life. Doesn't work. Not if she wants peace.

And this matters to me, Lord?

Oh, the journey.

Getting up from my bed and praying about it today, I thank God for teaching.

Just this week, while finishing a Rodney Stark book, I was drawn to his explanation of how Jews and Christians work effectively together. He calls it "religious civility." It's common, he said, "for Christian and Jewish clergy to participate together in public ceremonies during which all religious utterances are limited to those acceptable to both."[1]

No "thank you, Jesus" when Jews are around? No "praise the Lord"?

Is it concession? It is. And concession is what Alana is asking of me as her mother; she asks: Concede the news hound. Stop reporting back to me on Muslims and Islam. That doesn't work. Not for me. Not for us.

How did Benjamin Franklin put it? "He that would live in peace and at ease must not speak all he knows nor judge all he sees."[2]

Jesus?

This rocks my boat.

Just today, the heartbreaking Hamas-Israeli fight in the Gaza Strip is in full swing. It's Ramadan 2014, but neither side will stand down. Neither will rock the boat with something new, brave, good—something such as laying down arms.

Tit for tat. Back and forth. I follow it all on the Internet. Four little Palestinian boys, cousins, were killed while playing on a Gaza beach. Israeli Prime Minister Benjamin Netanyahu, sounding gritty and irritated, growls that "Hamas chose to continue fighting and will pay the price for that decision. When there is no cease-fire, our answer is fire."[3]

Jesus.

In our family, however, we've run the limit on fire. So I call Alana.

"Can you talk?" I ask over the phone.

"Hi, Mom," Alana says.

In her voice I hear the same yearning that I have. To take a new direction. Stop the fighting. Cease the tit for tat.

Instead, we talk about her visit to St. Paul's Methodist Church in Houston.

"I love what you wrote," I tell Alana, starting there. She thanks me.

We talk then about the Hamas-Israeli battle. I determine not to be a reporter. Instead, we share our sorrow over the everlasting fighting on the Gaza Strip. Alana tells me about something an imam said about Muslim extremists and why they believe they alone know God's desires.

"Hmmm," I say. I don't understand exactly what the imam meant, but I listen to Alana's take on it—hearing her frustration with extremists.

Then, taking a risk, I inquire of Alana about our own peacemaking. I ask her not to react every time to what I say but to reflect on why it matters.

"Your dad and I learned that in couple's therapy," I tell her. "You look at your own triggers, not just what the other person is saying. Or what they did. Or didn't do."

Alana agrees this is important. "I do need to do that," she says.

I thank her for considering. Then I take a risk and ask a second thing.

"I'd like to feel safe to mention something about Islam that I saw on the news—without feeling I'll be attacked for saying the wrong thing. To feel like I can ask a question or share what somebody told me, if it's about Islam or about a Muslim, and have that be okay."

So we are talking. No fireworks.

Unlike Hamas and the Israelis, we are talking. Praise God. On this summer day we are talking. I think of John Kerry, shuttling between two hard-liners, trying to get them to at least sit down. To rock the boat. To not do what they've always done.

Peace requires it. As Desmond Tutu said, if you want peace, destroy your enemies "by turning them into friends."[4] Status quo won't fly. Mahatma Gandhi affirmed it like this: we promote peace "through peaceful means."[5]

Instead open your arms. Ask a question. A plain question. "How are you feeling today?"

When I talk to Alana like a daughter and also a friend, the stormy waves sit still.

"Oh, I'm stressed," she says, laughing. Her move to Tennessee with her husband is imminent. Moving three young children, an aging cat, a minivan, and their whole household to another state in time to start new jobs is punishing. So we talk about that.

In the talking, I don't mention Jesus.

But he is sitting there beside us. I can feel his presence. Feel his love. See him on the water.

"'Lord, if it's you,' Peter replied, 'tell me to come to you on the water.'

"'Come,' he said" (Matt. 14:28–29).

This is his invitation. A few Christian friends want me to keep pounding on Alana. Even more want me to keep pounding on Satan. To take authority and pray Satan back to hell and Alana back to Christ. Jesus, instead, asks me to step out of the boat.

When Peter did that, he walked on stormy water. Unsunk.

"But when he saw the wind, he was afraid and, beginning to sink, cried out, 'Lord, save me!'" (v. 30).

That sinking feeling is a killer for sure. When I took the toothbrushes to the downtown church for the homeless women, the secretary opened the office door with a smile—but in her eyes I saw sinking. So we talked.

I was in a hurry. At least, I thought so. But Jesus said take a minute. Rock the stupid boat.

So I stood on the porch and listened. Oddest thing. Hearing her. She's struggling to write a book.

"A book," I said. "No kidding?"

No kidding. But her elderly dad is sick. And she's uncertain of her next steps. And money is tight. And she's losing hope. Sinking.

So I said to the secretary what Jesus told Peter. *Don't give up.*

Come on, friend.

Walk the water.

That's what we told the kids at the summer tutoring program at our church. After opening prayer, the leader announced an assessment quiz would be next. Immediately the kids' spirits sank.

"A quiz?" asked one boy. He frowned. Lip poked out. "I hate those things. I hate the questions." He looked dejected. "I can't do it." Sinking.

So the leader said to the boy what Jesus told Peter. *You can do it.*

Come on, son.

Walk the water.

That's what I offered a young lady planting a campus ministry on a Colorado college campus. Feeling inspired but unsure, she questioned for a moment her vision. And her sanity.

So I told the young church planter what Jesus told Peter. *Keep believing.*

Come on, servant.

Walk the water.

I hear Jesus saying that to Alana and me. Peace seems impossible. Laying down arms looks weak. But rock that boat. Come on, soldiers.

So here we are. Alana and Mom on the water. Hold my hand, Jesus. We're walking this stormy sea by faith.

Alana

I STARE UP AT THE CEILING FAN IN MY APARTMENT AND SIGH. THE house is finally quiet. It's a bit lonely without my husband here. He called earlier, proudly explaining that he fixed the oven in our house that's pending a sale.

"I still need to paint the closets, so I'm going to sleep here again," he added, sounding tired.

I placed the phone on the counter, accepting the reality of another night without him.

The urgency of his finishing draws near as we reach the end of our stay at our temporary apartment. I keep trying to repress my deepest worries about the move. "There are hardly any Muslims in Tennessee," I protested to my husband when he was first considering this job.

"We'll see them at the masjid," he reassured me, putting his arm around my shoulder.

I knew I would miss seeing Muslims everywhere—at the stores, the restaurants, even at the gym. Each time I encounter an example of my city's multiculturalism, I dread the lack of diversity awaiting me in Tennessee.

"Nice henna," the cashier at the grocery store remarked as she admired the intricate ink-stained design on my daughter's hand. She had kind, accepting, and nonjudgmental eyes. My daughter swirled her hand around to show it off. She had begged me to get her henna done as a yearly tradition during the end of Ramadan.

"I'm going to get mine done this weekend," she continued, sure of the possibility of finding a henna place around town.

I listened to her, loving that she knows about henna, then looked over at the bagger in the next aisle, a teenage girl wearing a white hijab. My heart cringed at the thought of leaving a place like this, where henna and hijabs are commonplace.

I am clinging to the hope that the people in Tennessee are open-minded, but then I remember the main reason why we are moving: Tennessee had become ground zero for anti-Muslim hate. My husband had informed me of opposition to the mosque in Murfreesboro, Tennessee; hate crimes at other mosques in the state; and the very public battle to pass anti-Shariah legislation in an attempt to make it illegal for Muslims to practice their faith in Tennessee. *Shariah*, an often-misunderstood term, is a word referring to the overall body of Islamic jurisprudence. The anti-Shariah bill that became so famous in the news a few years back galvanized a movement in Tennessee against Shariah, and some of the Muslim communities continue to be plagued with bigotry and opposition.

"It's the perfect place for me to influence the way Islam is viewed in America," my husband explained.

He's just the right guy for the job, but I can't help feeling scared. Tumultuous current events add to my anxiety as I worry about how Tennesseans will treat our family. Astronaut Alexander Gerst tweeted from the space station, "My saddest photo yet," showing a photo of Gaza and Israel illuminated by the light flashes of bombs dropping. He had a true bird's-eye view. He didn't take sides in his tweet or mention any of the common political talking points people use to indicate their opinions about who is wrong or right in this conflict.

Maybe being hundreds of miles above the earth helps put it all in perspective. His statement was quite the departure from what people actually *on* the planet are saying. Angry pundits and politicians spout who's to blame, and protesters take to the streets. A worried Israeli mother blogs about "not being okay" and being tired of fretting about the safety of her young children. A fifteen-year-old Gazan girl tweets pictures of bombs dropping on the home next door.

My conflict with my mom seems so trivial compared to these huge issues plaguing the world. Our small interfamilial problem that seemed so huge at first is now reducing to a manageable size. We've stuck with it, not allowing our disagreement to tear us apart, and now I'm beginning to see signs of peace.

"Do you think these extremists have sabotaged Islam?" my mother asks over the phone.

That's an insightful way to put it, I think.

"Yes," I reply, surprised that she would ask a question that demonstrates such empathy. "They have hijacked and defamed the religion. They don't care about how much they have hurt the image of Islam."

My mom listens with what seems like an open mind. It feels good to be heard and to think she is starting to understand how I feel.

She carefully asks about the "triggers" that set me off. I admit that I need to examine myself and figure out how I can talk with her about controversial issues without feeling so slighted. I definitely don't want her to think that she can't ask me about what is on her mind—or mine.

I can talk with my husband and friends about political and social issues without incident. Perhaps that's because I know they understand me and sympathize with my opinions.

On the contrary, my mother's questions feel like they come from a skeptic or someone who is openly against Islam and trying to prove it wrong. This puts me on edge; this is my trigger. When she brings something up, I'm wary about where she is going with her questions. I've got my guard up immediately, ready to defend myself and my faith against her interrogations.

I want us to be able to talk, and I know I have to calm my reactions to her questions. The world's conflicts lie at the whim of these triggers, with either side blaming the other for "starting it." But once it has begun, it matters less who started it and more how to stop it. Now I'm beginning to understand my mother's need to understand and demystify Islam. My patience is tested with every question she poses at me, and the boat inside me rocks with each emotional jolt.

We have fewer of these jarring events now, and our conversations are relatively positive.

She texts me while on her way to meet my sister in Chicago, then again on a beach next to Lake Michigan. The picture she attaches is beautiful, and for a moment I wish I was there with them. She calls later, too, leaving a message. I text back, wanting to avoid a phone call and that awkward moment when I explain that today is the Muslim holiday marking the end of Ramadan.

Hey, Mom, got your message. I'll call back tomorrow, I text back.

It's *Eid al-Fitr*, and I'm not sure if my mother knows. I look at her text and think about whether I'm bothered that she didn't mention the celebration today. My heart stirs slightly, wishing that she would care, but then I realize that's not fair. She has the right not to acknowledge my holiday, for her personal reasons. I can't fault her for that.

She reveals her feelings in her own way, in a comment about a picture I posted on Facebook. "Fun, fun, fun!" she wrote in response to a post I wrote about ending Ramadan in the pool with my kids. I think I get what she's saying. I know she can't yet wish me a happy Eid, but that won't change her love for me and my family. I stare at her comment and wonder if both of us will ever be at a place where we can acknowledge each other's holidays positively.

We talk the next day, after she's back in Colorado. Again there's no mention of the holiday from either of my parents, but I find myself not offended.

"Justin called," I say, mentioning how my cousin reached out to me after almost eight years of no communication between us. I was touched by his call and his attempt at preserving our family ties.

"You have no excuse not to visit now that you're moving to Tennessee," he'd said, since I'll be only three hours from him.

He doesn't ask about my faith choice or way of life. He just wants our family to stick together. We agree to plan a reunion of some sort soon, before our kids are all too grown-up.

"Thanks for your writing," my mother says before getting off the phone.

I'm not giving up on us, I think in response. I'm committed to healing our relationship, and I'm hopeful that we will find our way.

Patricia

IT'S DADDY'S BIRTHDAY. HE'D BE NINETY-NINE YEARS OLD IF HE HAD lived. Yet his spirit persists. I can still hear his teaching and vision, his values and voice. *Live right. Work hard. Don't give up. Trust God. Make your bed.*

Yes, Daddy. Every morning I still get up and do that. Wash my face. Brush my teeth. Talk to God. Put on clothes. Make my bed. The bed thing isn't to decorate. It's to start right. Nothing sloppy about Daddy. He lived by one mantra. Do the right thing.

So I will call Alana. To ask about Eid.

I've never Googled it. Never given Eid a single thought. Never heard of it. Well, not before Alana became a Muslim. So I didn't know I was supposed to say "Happy Eid." Or that she expected me to say that. We never talked about it. Looking it up, however, I read the information—learning that there are actually two Eids. Greater and Lesser. The Eid just celebrated marks the end of Ramadan. The other Eid commemorates the willingness of Abraham to sacrifice his firstborn son, Ishmael, as an act of submission to God's command. At the last second, however, God stepped in with grace—providing Abraham with a lamb to sacrifice instead.

That's what Wikipedia said anyway. To confirm, I call Alana—already knowing the risk because the Bible tells the Abraham story differently.

Not with Ishmael but with the covenant son—Isaac. Alana's Muslim narrative takes the Bible story and drops in a different son.

So here we go.

We start to get into it, throwing opinions back and forth. I start to say one more thing, but instead, I step back. Alana does too. We've been wrestling on the phone too many times anyway. On this day her children are getting restless. Lunchtime has come and gone. Alana and her family are packing for their move. And what did we gain? We argued a little. Debated the Gaza War. Managed to offend each other. Finally took the high road and said enough.

Then we hung up.

Sitting quietly in my office, I reflect on our struggle. On the tension of it. On the resistance to it. On the lip service paid to it. On the failures in it. As I write, on the other side of the world, the Gaza battle rages too. Casualties climb daily. Real people are dying, getting maimed, falling injured.

This never-ending fighting, at home and abroad, brings to mind the Camp David Accords. Jimmy Carter as president brokered that 1978 deal.

When the dust settled, the brawling leaders of Egypt and Israel were awarded a shared Nobel Peace Prize. But their road to peace was rugged.

The two hard-liners barely spoke. At one point Carter took the two to Gettysburg National Military Park, in hopes of using the American Civil War as a sobering metaphor. Back at Camp David, Carter hand carried documents from one leader's cabin to the other, back and forth, across thirteen grueling days—finally gaining approval for the hard-won pact.

But was this peace? Two old soldiers refusing to talk? In news photos at the signing, both Anwar Sadat of Egypt and Menachem Begin of Israel are smiling wide—through their teeth—hands clasped tightly by Carter, his grip seeming to hold the two adversaries together by will and force.

Then after all of that, Sadat went home and was assassinated.

The reluctant peacemaker, betrayed by turncoats in his army, was gunned down during a military parade by members of the Egyptian Islamic Jihad. Bitter over Sadat's peace with Israel—which still occupied Palestine—they launched hand grenades at Sadat in his review stand, then followed with gun blasts. Killed were ten state officials, including the Cuban ambassador, a general from Oman, and a Coptic Orthodox bishop.

All dead.

The road to peace *is* ugly. Or else Mahatma Gandhi was correct to know: "There is no royal road."[6] Certainly not to peace—except to walk it in peace.

Jesus said it like this: *I am the road.*

The Way. The Truth. The Life (John 14:6). Our Peace. God himself. The ram in the bush. The Lamb of God. Sacrificing his Self. As he said, "I and the Father are one" (John 10:30).

When Alana finally sees that one day, she will fall on her face, astounded. Then like the grateful woman at the Samaritan well, she will tell everybody: "Come, see a man . . . !" (John 4:29 ISV). God right here. Right with us. A friend. All that time.

When you think about it, that really is something. C. S. Lewis, a one-time atheist, described his surrender to Christ in three words: *surprised by joy.*

But winning Alana to Jesus is not my work now. As the king Jehoshaphat was reminded: "The battle is not yours, but God's" (2 Chron. 20:15).

So I sit myself down. Study history some more. I also find a great series of video teachings on negotiation skills by the Kellogg School of Management in Chicago. The workshop leader, a woman named Professor Leigh Thompson, advised participants to remember two things in a back-and-forth battle:

- Don't ask any questions you're not willing to answer yourself.
- Don't use any tactic you wouldn't want someone to use on you.[7]

Alana said the same to me today. I made some final flip comment that maybe Muslims just don't "get" Jesus. Flip. Dumb. Not helpful. I set up my beautiful daughter, in turn, to come back at me. So with her, we pulled back from that flare-up.

Two days later it's Dan's birthday. He is seventy-four years young, indeed. I slip out of bed and head to my office, finding the birthday card

I bought for him at Hallmark, signing it with a wife's words: *I love you, sweetheart.*

When I tiptoe back in the bedroom, Dan is already awake, kneeling by our bed. He looks up at me, explaining, "I'm just thanking the Lord for one more year." He smiles, getting weepy too.

I understand. I kneel down beside him, giving him a wife hug. We're introspective today. Two longtime friends passed away over the past two weeks, one while we were away in Chicago with Joi. I learned of both deaths on Facebook.

Jesus.

Dan quietly starts to sing:

> *Amazing grace, how sweet the sound*
> *That saved a wretch like me.*[8]

Then he tells me, "I woke up singing that song."

I sing with him for a minute. Then I tell him, "I woke up singing 'Oh to Be Kept.'" Oh, to be kept by Jesus. An old-fashioned song. I don't know if churches sing it anymore. But Dan knows it, and I grew up on it. So we sing a little of that too.

The next day at church, on Sunday morning, our pastor preaches about Jehoshaphat—from the battle passage in the second book of Chronicles—pointing out that Jehoshaphat's problem, besides a horde of enemies planning to attack, was that Jehoshaphat was afraid.

As Pastor spoke, I pulled my phone from my purse, looking up the scripture on my Bible app—the King James Version, because it's a free app. So the wording is King James fancy. The names hard to pronounce. Even so, I read along silently, listening to the Bible words: "There cometh a great multitude against thee from beyond the sea on this side Syria; and, behold, they be in Hazazontamar, which is Engedi. And Jehoshaphat *feared*" (2 Chron. 20:2–3 KJV, emphasis mine).

I marked the word because I've shared the problem. Fear. I'm afraid of the end. That Alana never will journey to Christ. Not all the time do I fear this. But enough times. Then while I was sitting on my pew, holding my phone, the word of the Lord spoke to Jehoshaphat and even to me: *fear not.*

"Be not afraid nor dismayed by reason of this great multitude; for the battle is not yours, but God's" (v. 15).

My pastor's sermon title: "It Ain't Your Fight."

"Amen!"

I love church.

When Pastor told the title of his sermon, standing under the skylight in our soaring sanctuary, the giant wooden cross suspended behind him, our congregation had already started clapping and shouting. *It ain't your fight.*

"Preach, Pastor!"

"I'm trying!" he joked back. Everybody laughed, settling in for another great sermon. Another great promise.

Not your fight.

Professor Thompson at Kellogg didn't exactly say that. But in negotiation, she said, stop fighting that lose-lose battle. That fight says if you win, I lose. And if I win, you lose. But both my pastor and the Kellogg lady invited me to upend that boat. Throw overboard the idea that Alana and I are in a contest—a battle royal.

I could try instead just to win the battle of love. Now that's a good fight to win.

Alana

I SIT IN THE DINING ROOM, EATING A FEW HALF-FROZEN CHICKEN nuggets and not caring about the taste. The kitchen table is shoved into the corner of my partly put-away apartment. My bed's headboard leans on a mattress that's blocking some of the doorway. It's the first time I've sat down in a chair in my new apartment since we moved in. I spent the day unpacking and cleaning, then finally got around to attaching the legs to the kitchen table, only to find out that just two chairs barely fit into the packed dining room.

I'm not complaining, though. I'm grateful to have a place to sit. The sound of the air-conditioning unit and ceiling fan lull me as I soak in the much-needed silence. It's late, and the kids are finally asleep. I forget where I am for a moment then hear the pounding of feet in the upstairs apartment. It's been eight years since I lived in an apartment, and I realize that I'm going to have to get reacquainted with the noise from the people above me.

My husband shuffles into the room with his sandaled feet scratching the floor.

"You scared me," he says, looking over the bed frame.

He gives me a yogurt drink to help ward off sickness. I've been complaining of a headache all day. We've been living out of bags and suitcases for the past two weeks. He circles around looking for the shower curtains we just bought today.

"Hope we didn't leave them at Ross," he says.

He goes outside to look for them, leaving me alone to my thoughts.

I'm grateful that the move is over. I drove, by myself, 760 miles to Tennessee, with our kids. My husband was delayed with the house, painting and doing odd jobs that the buyer requested.

"I'm probably going to leave tonight," he would say again and again as I drove through Baton Rouge then Alabama. I was beginning to think he would never arrive. When I finally reached Tennessee, he still hadn't left.

"I'm just going to drive the whole way," he proclaimed to my disapproval.

I begged him to stop if he got too tired. He did stop, pausing for three hours in Alabama before finishing his journey four hours later.

I'm in Tennessee! he texted me at six that morning. I was already one day late to report to work and staying at a hotel with the kids. It seemed surreal that we moved our entire family here, in the middle of the South. I tried to downplay my fears about encountering biased southerners, feeling nervous whenever the kids and I left the hotel room for something.

My dad was angry when he found out I drove by myself. I purposely didn't tell my parents about Iesa's delay initially, knowing they would worry.

"You're an identifiable Muslim woman driving though the heart of the South," Dad reprimanded me after discovering the truth.

I apologized, not intending to worry them, but emphasized the necessity of my leaving when I did.

Later I was able to describe to my parents how courteous the people are in Tennessee. My previous conceptions of them were slowly melting away as I traversed our new area. Tons of people smiled at me, and almost consistently passersby said, "Hello." A random stranger in line at the grocery store struck up a conversation with me about school uniforms.

"These people are even friendlier than Texans," I told my husband in disbelief. I had expected the opposite. I had thought I would be stared at, pointed at, even yelled at because of my hijab. I had thought I would hardly see any diversity or Muslims anywhere. I was wrong.

The first person I met at my new apartment was a Muslim woman from Palestine. She saw us walking to the leasing office and offered to give us a ride. We spotted a few scarf-wearing women walking later that day, and at the grocery store we even saw a clerk at Walmart wearing a white hijab with the store's telltale navy-blue uniform.

I felt guilty for being so ignorant about Tennessee and believing Wikipedia's claim that it was so monoethnic. I was even more surprised to meet three non-Muslims working at my Islamic school. One of them had already been teaching there a few years.

"I love this school," she said, smiling during the teacher orientation meeting.

The principal promised to give the newest teacher a list of common Islamic phrases to help her become more familiar with frequent lingo used during the school day.

"Muslims are very God-conscious," she began. "Many of the comments we make during the day are in reference to God."

The new teacher nodded her head slowly, taking it all in. I tried to imagine what it was like for her, then listened to her describe her husband's wariness about her teaching here. I told her about my initial fears about Tennessee, wanting her to know that she wasn't the only one who was poorly informed.

She offered to help me move the next day.

"My family helps people," she said.

I sighed and quietly said a prayer of thanks on her behalf, amazed at her kindness. I had already told her about our initial apartment, the one we found online while still in Texas.

"But we found mouse poop in the kitchen drawers!" I explained to her, describing how we had to stay in another hotel that night and then search for a new apartment. "My teaching stuff is still in the moving truck!" I lamented. She told me not to worry.

"My husband will come over right after work," she insisted. "We've been there. We know how hard it is to move."

I smiled, not even knowing how to respond to her generosity. By this time the illusion of a scary, bigoted Tennessee had completely dissolved.

Maybe it's the landscape that calms people. The rolling hills, the winding roads, and the trees are welcome sights to me after living among so much concrete for a decade. I feel myself slipping away into meditative thought as I drive though the scenic route to my school.

Nature always makes me feel connected to God, and here I am surrounded by it. I sigh as I look up at the green tree-filled hills behind my school. It feels ideal, as if I've been transplanted to a remote sanctuary. I'm not surrounded by politics and controversy, just good people trying to make a difference.

I haven't talked to my mom in days, mainly because of the stress of the move, but the break has given me time to think. It's been nice going a full week without having a controversial phone call with her. We finally talk Sunday morning as she and my dad drive to Sunday school. They're going to pick up their elderly friend.

She wants to move forward, move beyond the negativity in the world and work together for change. She understands my stress, and she wants to listen to me.

"I don't want to make you late for Sunday school," I say.

She insists that I continue, allowing me to unload about the move.

"Whenever you get ready to finish something good," she says, "the world tries to stop you somehow."

I know what she means. It's Satan trying to get in the way of our progress, trying to stop God's work from proceeding. Our move and this project with my mom are stressful, but they're worth it. I understand her point. She and I are so close to a breakthrough, and I'm not going to let the trials of life get in my way.

twelve

PEACE IS THE ROAD

———————————— *Patricia* ————————————

THE TUTORING AT CHURCH IS PICKING UP. AFTER A BUMPY START, with just seven or eight kids dragging in for the Wednesday night sessions, a turnout of fifteen kids clamor in for the final night of the summer, all excited to be here. The children are days away from starting another school year. For some, deferred maintenance means they're not ready. For others, despite summer intervention by determined parents, the problem is fear. Lack of confidence.

"I don't like to read," says a soon-to-be high school sophomore.

His sister, who will be a freshman, agrees. "He don't like to read. Not out loud."

I sigh. I understand. "So, look," I tell them. "I understand. But it's just us." I point to our small circle. Just us three. "You can read with me. It's okay."

It's okay to read *The House on Mango Street* by Latina author Sandra Cisneros. Her language is raw, beautiful, and experimental. Like life. So these children in our circle understand it perfectly. The high school boy starts to read out loud. Lovely voice. He's a good reader. Not just calling out words. He reads the part where Esperanza, the girl in the story, calls herself "a red balloon" tied to "an anchor," describing her younger sister.[1]

"It's an analogy," I say to the students, and we talk about that.

"I got three little sisters," the high school student says, accepting the word play. "So that's me. A red balloon. Tied to an anchor."

We discuss that a bit.

The standardized test awaiting these students won't allow them this freedom. To just talk. Ask questions. Laugh. Cry a little. The test is too removed from real life. Only when you're living it can you ask raw, beautiful, experimental questions. A nun in Cisneros's story asks her narrator about her family's run-down, third-floor flat over a boarded-up Laundromat—the place where they lived before Mango Street. "You live *there*?" said the nun. Pointing to it.[2]

Hard, raw questions. Somebody has to ask them.

So I'm asking my own.

Especially now. Especially tonight. Alana is driving across the South alone with her three little children. Traveling from Texas to Tennessee. Through Louisiana. Through Mississippi. Through Alabama.

I don't have a clue where she is exactly. But I do know this: she is wearing a hijab. And acts like she isn't concerned. Isn't worried. Isn't losing sleep.

Yet my husband is a wreck. "Why would she do something like that?"

Raw question. He is up, pacing his little home office. He is angry and worried. A red balloon. When I walk in to assure him, he's wiping away tears. Or sweat. He's fretted himself sick.

We are tied to our grown children. Tied by love. Anchored by hope.

Dan and I thought Alana was driving with her husband, following him in a U-Haul truck with their furniture and boxes. But Iesa was delayed a day or two with their house sale in Texas. So as the sun went down on a summer, Tuesday evening, Alana packed their kids in their Honda minivan by herself, locked up their Ramadan apartment, and hit the road. Hijab and all.

So it is my turn to pace, keeping up with my husband.

"Did she think?" I am angry at her judgment or lack of it. Dismayed at her husband for letting her make the drive solo.

But halfway from our bedroom to our bathroom for the umpteenth time, I stop. Do I trust Jesus more? More than my worry? More than my daughter? And, of course, the answer is yes. Trusting him means I am free just to love. If I don't know that by now, I'll never know it. So I stop my pacing. I get undressed, stand in a hot shower, and sing "How Great Thou Art." Sing it loud. Then get ready for bed. Not because I've figured everything out. But because I've let it go.

Richard Foster the Quaker calls this "relinquishment." When we pray it, he says, this "moves us from the struggling to the releasing."[3] When our grown kids do their own thing, relinquishment is the prayer to pray. *Here she is, Lord.* We do it, or we go crazy.

So on this night I choose the Nazarene, singing all the way. Then in fresh pajamas I kneel beside the bed and pray a release. Dan paces into the room. Then he sighs and kneels down beside me. *Dear heavenly Father.* One of us says the words, and I feel my husband relax beside me.

So we pray to relinquish. To cut the cord. Like this: "thank you, God, for sitting high and looking low."

I pray it in words. "You know every mile from Texas to Tennessee. Every bend in the road, O God. Every turn of the freeway. Every hill and dale, every valley and peak, every twist and turn.

"*We* can't see what's up ahead, O God," I pray, holding my husband's hand. "But *you* know, Lord. And we know you. So put a hedge of protection all around her, heavenly Father."

Old Christian words: *hedge of protection.* That's how we prayed—like the old black saints of my childhood church.

On Facebook, somebody asked, "What exactly is a hedge of protection? I mean, what does that mean anyway?"

It means this: *Dispatch your angels, O God.* Be a fence. Part the waters. Guide her feet. And steady that Honda minivan.

Listening to the Holy Spirit, we pray, indeed, for random kindness. "In stores and gas stations and hotels, let her see Jesus. Let a kind person offer a warm word."

It is way past midnight. But as parents everywhere know, late in the midnight hour is the sweet hour of prayer. God knows, we paced many midnights, worrying over our independent daughter, Alana, and spent wee hours of the morning, sitting on the side of the bed, our night-light still on, and wondering where Alana was. I can't count the nights we did this. But this time, something in my spirit says no. Cut the cord. Let go of the red balloon. Trust God.

"I'm going to bed," I say to Dan. *For the battle isn't mine; it's God's.*

I stretch and yawn then pull our clean, worn quilt up to my chin. I don't bother to pray again or even whisper that David psalm. How does it go? *In peace I will lie down and sleep.* I could look it up. My old Bible sits on my nightstand. With a flip of a few pages, I could find Psalm 4:8. But I let myself remember it, as best I can: "In peace I will lie down and sleep, for you alone, O LORD, will keep me safe" (NLT). Safe in your arms. My daughter and the grandbabies. Driving through the night.

In peace, indeed, I turn out the light, close my eyes, and sleep until morning.

When we pray well, according to prayer warriors, we lift our prayers to heaven, then leave them at Jesus' feet. That's how the four men with the paralyzed friend prayed in the Gospels. Desperate for Jesus to heal their disabled friend, they pressed their way through the crowds to the house where Jesus was staying. Folks blocked every door, every window. The four could've turned back, but their friend needed God. So the friends did what any good praying folks would do: they broke through the roof.

Now *that* is praying. Breaking through. Then "they lowered the man on his mat, right down in front of Jesus." Not saying a word. Just lowered their friend down to the feet of Christ. Then Jesus Christ healed him (Mark 2:2–12 NLT). Some situations apparently don't require as much praying as they do action. Words are words. But action shows trust.

So I got in the bed and went to sleep.

Would my daughter make it safely to Tennessee with three little children in a not-so-new Honda minivan? I could've wrestled all night with that question, worrying myself sleepless, turning the quilt into a frayed, twisted mess. Instead, daring to trust God, I turned out the light and went to sleep.

While I slept, I was aware somehow of how peacefully I rested. Because I trust God more? More than my daughter? In truth, the answer is yes. He is the way. I keep repeating Gandhi here, but his words are true: "There is no royal road."⁴ Peace is the road. Peace is the way.

To make this peace with Alana, she is indeed the destination. But the road is God.

Next morning I woke up. To bright sunshine. To a rested soul. Dan looked a little worse for wear. As soon as he awoke, he wanted to call to see how far Alana had traveled, but first we started our morning. By the time we called an hour or so later, God had worked his miracle.

Whatever annoyance I had about Alana's solo drive across the South had evaporated into the night along with the worry. In its place God gave a fresh kind of understanding—that Alana drove alone trying to get to her new job. She was already a day late—a mix-up in dates. She wasn't indifferent to our concerns, and she wasn't being irresponsible. Well, maybe she was a little. However, her aim was to get herself to work.

So we listened to her tell us about it. About the Holiday Inn where she and the kids bunked in Baton Rouge. She told us about the kindness of strangers. Our answered prayer? I believe so. Bottom line: she and the children encountered no problems. No incidents. No funny looks. No flat tires. No busted transmission. No radiator leaks. No empty gas tank.

"How much longer is your drive?" I asked.

A mother's sincere question with neither judgment nor anger attached to it. It was peace. And God was the road.

Dan said something about his worry. So Alana apologized, sounding almost surprised.

"Oh, I didn't mean to worry you!"

I laughed a parent's laugh. But I kept quiet. *This is a new day.*

Then it was time for her to go. To hit the road again.

Finally late that night, she and the babies pulled into their Tennessee town. Trip all over. Without incident. *Thank you, Jesus.*

With the kids, Alana stayed this next night in an Embassy Suites—upgrading a little, she said, after the long, long drive. Then a few days later Iesa drove into town too—bringing up the rear with the U-Haul, joining his wife. Our Muslim daughter.

On our knees again, Dan and I thanked God they'd all arrived safely. Not yet in Christ, but by grace, they'd landed in a kind town.

In the next few days they would work out the details of their housing. Did I need to know all the details? In fact, I did not. I let that go. A grown daughter can figure out with her husband where they will live. So I didn't bother her with phone calls and questions. What I didn't know, God could take care of.

Then is this peace?

Not totally. I'm still desperate for Alana to know Christ in the way that I do. To know him well and for her husband and babies to know him too. We used to sing of this in my childhood Denver church—how everybody *ought* to know Jesus.

Until then, get a good night's sleep. Charles Spurgeon put it like this: "Do not sit down to sigh and lament; while the beloved Physician lives, there is hope."[5]

Is hope what I feel in my heart? Is hope what I see in my dreams? Is hope what I follow in my prayers? Is hope what I believe Alana will encounter in beautiful Tennessee? Yes. It is.

Folks sing day and night there. "Meanwhile Back at Mama's." Songs like that one. (Thank you, Tim McGraw.) Alana might like that tune. I like it myself. Back at Mama's, the red balloon is rising.

Peace is a song.

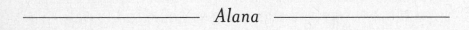

Alana

THE ROLLING HILLS OF TENNESSEE PASS BY MY WINDOW AS MY FAMily heads to a small town called Clarksville. We drive over a bridge covering the Cumberland River. It seems to stretch for miles toward the city and then abruptly cuts off right before it reaches the high-rises of downtown.

We head into the hills, driving through the cliffs carved out from the rock.

"This is beautiful," my husband remarks, smiling. He's right. A majestic carpet of trees envelops the landscape and stretches to touch the clear blue sky. My husband tries to play a song on his phone. I chuckle as the song starts and I hear the harmonica interlude of "Mountain Music."

The kids sleep silently in the back, their bellies full of popcorn and Chinese food after an afternoon at the movies. We're on our way to see a car we found on Craigslist, and despite the fast-approaching deadlines in my calendar, I willingly agree to the road trip. We wait in the van as my husband test-drives the car, watching the shoppers come and go in a small grocery store parking lot.

I sit and reflect on the words my mother said earlier that day over the phone.

"Do you feel like you've achieved peace?" I asked her that morning.

It's a funny question to ask, as if anyone can answer it objectively. We're nearing the end of our project, and she keeps making concluding statements.

"At the beginning of all this," I said, "you mentioned you felt hurt and painfully sad. Are you not feeling this way anymore?"

"No, not anymore," my mother began, explaining how she feels at peace now but never would have achieved that peace without going through this process.

"I understand so much more," she continued, describing how much she had learned from our dialogue.

We get off the phone, and I reread her last selection. I have to admit that it still stings when I read how she openly wishes that I become a Christian. I read her words again and again and realize that I struggle to feel at peace when she says that she hopes that I can someday know Christ, assuming I don't know him already.

I don't want to start hashing it out again, debating our differing claims to Jesus. We've passed the stage of needing to prove each other wrong, and I'm so grateful for that.

I sigh, looking out the window. At least twenty minutes have passed, and my husband hasn't returned with the car.

"Why isn't Daddy back yet?" Noah whines. He's the only child awake and can't stand the wait.

I rub my forehead, thinking about my unfinished lesson plans, our messy unpacked house, and tomorrow's lunch box preparations. I stare at the clock, count the remaining daylight hours. Then I calculate the amount of sleep I'll probably get tonight. It won't be much.

My husband finally returns and motions for me to sit in the car we're considering. When I turn around in the driver's seat to check out the incredibly small backseat, I realize there's no way three kids are fitting back there.

"I don't want it," I say.

His smile fades. He's slightly disappointed, but it didn't fit his standards either. We'll have to put up with another few days of carpooling until we find something we like.

We drive back mostly in silence. I try to write on my phone, but I soon nod off. My thoughts drift in and out as I sleep, thinking of my mother's declaration of peace. It all seems too good to be true. We haven't seen each other in months, and I wonder if my mother's sudden peace will continue when in my presence.

I call her the next day and summon the courage to ask her the question that's been occupying my mind. "Don't you want to know how I am feeling about all of this?" I ask.

She pauses and listens, ready to hear my side of the story.

"I feel nervous that you are going to continue to wish that I convert," I say.

She claims that she won't, that although she longs for conversion in her heart, she won't openly push the issue anymore. She's "leaving that to God."

I'm slightly satisfied with that answer but uncertain how it will play out in real time.

"I do want my grandbabies to know Christ," she says.

My stomach cringes at this statement. It strikes at my core, stirring up feelings of possessiveness. I realize that I worry about feeling uncomfortable around her when doing anything Islamic for fear of receiving a disapproving glance. I don't believe she can just turn off the emotions she once had and not act bothered by everything we do. But it's impossible to tell until we are together again.

We might reunite sooner than I had expected. My dad calls a few days later. He wants to visit soon and check out the new place. He's nervous about the spiders, though. They're everywhere. We laugh as I describe the spider I saw floating in my coffee one morning. He can tell something's up.

"You sound tired," he says knowingly.

I can't hide it from him. I sit slumped on the couch, staring at the books I just finished unloading from their boxes and wishing that I was finished with unpacking.

"Wish we could be there to help with the kids," he says sympathetically. He always says that, but the distance stands in their way.

I confide in him, telling him that I'm tired from the journey to Tennessee and the stress of setbacks at my job.

"Iesa is out of town this weekend too," I add, trying to make light of the situation.

Dad instantly feels bad for me. I shouldn't have mentioned it. I know he worries so much. I conceal the rest from him, not mentioning how this emotional roller coaster with my mom has worn me out and how her newfound declaration of peace makes me insecure.

My uneasiness unsettles me, but I try to withstand it, remembering the verse from the Qur'an that states, "Verily, with every difficulty, there is relief."[6] I know that Allah won't test me with more than I can handle.

Mom calls the next day. It must have been her motherly senses warning her of my insecure feelings. I confide in her about my worries.

"Trust," she says. "You have to have faith that it all is going to work out."

Her words encourage me. We talk for a while, completely on the same page for once. I marvel that I'm willingly receiving spiritual advice from her, a first in a long time.

Her words strike me to the core and cause me to reflect on my inner state. I realize that the stress of the move and a new job and the pressure of this project have affected my trust in God. I search in the Qur'an and read a portion of a familiar verse. "And upon Allah rely, if you should be believers."[7] I find more verses echoing the same idea. With my trust weakened by the stress of the journey, I've forgotten that everything is ordained by God and true believers put their complete trust in God. Shame fills my heart momentarily at my lack of gratefulness, but then I realize that my mother's reminder was a blessing.

So I hunker down, quit complaining, and put on a smile for my kids. The stress of the move has been enough for them to handle, and the last thing they need is a fretting mother. I begin to hope for more moments like this with Mom, when we can spiritually align in some mutual understanding about God.

We rise early the next morning to pick up Iesa from the airport. The kids and I have come down with colds. Noah is coughing the worst; it takes all I've got to get him in the car. He falls asleep on the road, and we drive in silence. He wakes up when we arrive, and the kids scream in delight as they see their dad walking to the car. Another father nearby receives a similar welcome home from his toddler. My husband glances over and smiles, then notices how tired I look.

"When we get home, we'll all rest," he assures me.

His face shows surprise when we get to the apartment.

"Thanks for making the house a home," he says, knowing that I needed that compliment.

It feels good to hear that, and we sit back to relax for the first time in a long while. The relief that was promised is here at last, and I soak in every moment of this repose, trusting in God to guide me through the next turn in the road.

Patricia

SUMMER IS OVER. TRYING TO BE ANYWAY. IT'S BARELY SEPTEMBER. Days are shorter. Nights are cooler. Dan's sister and her husband are back home from their vacation. They cruised the Caribbean, sailing south from San Juan on a trip they both needed. We needed it too. But after a scheduling glitch, we backed out.

"Too much going on now," Dan said. I agreed.

As if on cue, our aging air conditioner hit the dust and had to be replaced. Groaning, into our dwindling emergency fund, we're grateful we canceled the vacation after all. This year, we replaced my late mama's broken roof (with the insurance payout) plus repaired half a dozen other major and minor home maintenance problems (on our dime) at our place too.

But that wasn't my only reason for feeling grateful. Something small, but huge, topped my gratitude list. In short, *Alana heard me.*

Agreed. Understood. Affirmed me. And I almost missed it. How'd she put it—writing about her embattled mother?

I understand her point.

Reading the words, I stare at the good feeling—letting it sink in, allowing it to baste my soul. *Alana understands.* Not everything about me. Not all about us. But she understands one small point. I close my eyes, smiling at this, thankful to God. I've been waiting since Alana was a teenager to hear those words. *I understand you, Mom.* That's what I longed for, to know some small iota of wisdom I shared was heard.

Even better, when it happened, we weren't arguing about religion.

We'd been talking about our peace story—this story—and the deadline for our manuscript. At that point we were way behind. I dread the thought of being late for a deadline, especially when we'd struggled to reach détente. But obstacles fly at us left and right. There's Alana's move from Texas. Our costly house repairs. A modern, first-world family's mountains.

To the rest of the world, these setbacks are nothing.

To help me remember, out of nowhere, a young black man is killed by a white policeman in Ferguson, Missouri—shot six times, twice in the head, despite being unarmed. In response the St. Louis suburb rages. Night after night, protesters defy police—angry about this common occurrence in African American life. White cops killing black men.

Jesus, can I say that?

Joseph Campbell says our hard places, emotionally, are gold mines. So dig. Like this: "It is by going down into the abyss that we recover the treasures of life. Where you stumble, there lies your treasure." At the darkest moment, says Campbell, comes the light.[8]

So stumbling, watching the news and weighing in on the news and being horrified to see the world unraveling again, I lay everything at the cross. Without words. This old world, as Paul said to the Romans, can leave you so lost that you're lost, indeed, for words. When that happens, Paul wrote, let the Spirit pray it for you. Allow the Spirit, indeed, to help "us in our weakness" (Rom. 8:26).

Now feeling weak, weary, and careful, I kneel by my prayer-worn bed—burying my face into the quilt. *Pray, Holy Spirit.* Pray for the world. Pray for Alana. Pray for Ferguson. Pray for our family. Pray for the families of the world.

Then this hard moment determines to teach Alana and me both its hard lesson: Peace *is* process.

Process is love.

And when it breaks down?

Keep walking the road.

Bump in the road? Keep stepping.

Twist in the bend? Keep climbing.

Potholes in the pavement? Stop and fix.

Road maintenance. That is peace. One step, one repair at a time.

Knowing that, Alana and I—as daughter and mother—can determine to rest in this knowing. Then we can trust each other more. We can see the other, not as an adversary but as a fellow traveler on this unlikely road called life. Most of all, we can trust God along the way.

In the meantime, here's one more thing Alana and I might do: turn off the daily news. Good-bye, Don Lemon and CNN. Good night, Anderson Cooper. See you later, Brian, Scott, David, Katie, Kyra, Nancy, and all the others. At least for now. Is this a surrender? Not if you're walking upright. Or trying.

In that way I turn off the news. Close my Twitter feed. Click off my Facebook. Shut down my Yahoo! and Google. Then I can hear my husband, Dan: "Oh, look! Some pictures of Noah!"

Alana's husband has e-mailed photos of our little grandson, Noah. At four years old, he's grinning for all he's worth. All dressed for school, he's sporting a new white shirt, plaid school tie, dark pants, and spiffy new school shoes. One shirttail is loose, and his shirt's a bit wrinkled. His new backpack is dragging the ground a bit. Long day at school. But he's beaming.

"Look at our little guy!" Dan says. "Good job, little Noah!"

Pulling up the pictures on my computer, I grin at the photograph. Seeing Noah's hope. Seeing his love. Seeing his joy. The vantage point in Noah's bright eyes? Looking closer at the photo, I see it right away.

Wearing his new school clothes and gazing into the lens of his future, little Noah sees his family like this: he sees us with trust.

And why not? The road of peace counts on it.

The next day a little bird gets trapped in our garage.

"Look at it!" I point to the bird, showing my husband.

Dan frowns and looks up. "Always something," he says, but he's chuckling and shaking his head, trying to shoo out the bird.

"Want a broom?" I grab one off a hook.

Dan takes the broom, waving bristles at the bird. But the bird flutters past him, deeper into the garage. Past the cars. Past the paint cans. Past the mop bucket. Past the Christmas wreath, landing on some boxes.

I clap my hands at it. "C'mon, little bird."

The bird is tiny. A baby. Beautiful. Blue wings and tail.

"Pretty little bird," Dan says.

"Look at her," I say, smiling, watching her dive off the boxes and fly around the rafters. "We want her to fly *out*. But she's flying *up*."

I clap my hands again. "This way, little birdie," I coo. "Come on out. Out this way."

Maybe she'll get the idea. So Dan and I walk outside, heading toward the light. Standing in the sunshine. Enjoying the day. Giving the bird room. Soon enough, she figures it out: go to the light. Then with a flip of her tail, she sees her path free.

Then what does she do?

She follows.

Alana

I DRIVE ALONG THE WINDING ROADS OF TENNESSEE WITH THE WINdows open. The cool autumn breeze fills the car with fresh country air. We float in and out of hilly, single-lane detours trailed with trees, and then arrive at Red Caboose Park. My kids hop out excitedly and run over to the playground. The baby immediately heads toward the swings, directing me to begin pushing her by shouting, "Ready, set, go!" She beams and lays her head back, allowing the cool breeze to swish her hair around on her face.

I watch her happily and think about my experience with my mother. For so long I was waiting for us to reach a defining moment, when we would both proclaim and declare our newfound peace. As I watch my daughter, I realize that peace doesn't spring up suddenly and announce itself. Peace is a journey, an experience that continues to develop as one passes through life and encounters challenges.

The baby swings for a while. My son bounces over, tired from his game of tag, and starts to push the swing.

"Let's walk over to the caboose," I say. My request gains immediate approval, and we round up Laila for the walk up the hill to the red caboose.

The day is beginning to wane, and I think of the grocery trip we need to make before nightfall. I glance at the baby, who stops every now and then to point out something amazing and babble about it in her baby language. I normally would walk behind her and usher her forward to speed up the process, but today we take our time and don't rush. Let's just walk—and enjoy it.

We approach the caboose, which looks much larger than it did at the bottom of the hill. The kids ask if they can board, and I check for warning signs. There are none, so they climb up, peering into the windows of the cabin.

"Up!" the baby demands, and I hoist her to the second step.

"No, no!" she protests immediately, trying to get down. The caboose is less attractive now that we can physically experience it, and she is wary of such an imposing object. I help the baby down, thinking of when my mother first began to share with me the changes she was experiencing during this, our faith journey. I was cautious when my mother reached a breakthrough—seeing peace, not as a place or destination but as the way. Still, I was nervous about jumping onto her peace bandwagon, but now I see that it was only the beginning.

"Oh, look! The library is right there," I say, excited to finally step inside one since our move.

"Can we buy some new books?" my son asks eagerly.

"Borrow," I correct him, "and yes, we can borrow some books." I smile at his naive misinterpretation of library privileges and steer the baby toward the brick building next door.

A stone pathway leads us to the front walk, where a group of kids is hanging out. One of them pours water on another boy's head. The boy, obviously the object of their recent torment, is close to tears and attempts to jump his tormentors.

I look around for adults, debating whether to intervene, then decide to focus on keeping the baby from being knocked over as the scapegoat chases his attackers around the front lawn.

"This isn't the library," my daughter remarks, reading the sign that says "Community Hall."

"It's down there," I say, making a silent wish that the fighting kids would follow us to the library and read, instead of brawl, as we head down the hill to our destination.

"I don't see any books I like," my son whines after perusing the aisles for a few minutes.

A librarian overhears him and inquires about his tastes in books.

"What about Magic Tree House books?" I suggest. "I bet the librarian knows where they are."

His eyes widen as he remembers this summer when we read four of those books. He comes back with five books, dropping half of them on the way.

"I want to read all of them," he insists with a serious face.

I think back on the feeling these books gave him this past summer as we journeyed to other worlds with the characters. We would snuggle together on the floor of the apartment and spend hours immersed in the reading. He didn't want the ending to come. That would mean the end of the adventure.

Like him, I don't want my peace adventure to end. I had been expecting to reach a final destination, not knowing that the journey was my destination. Walking the peace path is what matters most.

In the library I happen accidently across a youth biography collection called *Peace Warriors*. "One movement. Six bios," the cover states, listing the names of some famous nonviolent activists in the subheading.[9] I pick it up, marveling at the irony of having the words *peace* and *warriors* in the same phrase but thinking about using it in my classroom somehow.

At home I skim the introduction. "Through the life stories of six extraordinary people," the book begins, "we can discover why peace has been a guiding presence in an often violent world."[10] I think about the truth of this statement, agreeing with the author that the entirety of the lives of these people provides examples of peace. They understood that peace is a journey, and along the way they experienced moments of affirmation of this truth.

I also read the short section covering Mahatma Gandhi, and having already read his autobiography many years before, I recall many of the events mentioned in this anthology. I glance over the chapter on Dorothy Day, then read a few pages of Desmond Tutu's section, noticing how each figure regarded every moment as an opportunity for peace.

My thoughts are interrupted by my son, who runs over with one of his new books, ready to jump into the story with the characters. We sit on the couch and read three chapters, with him completely in a state of bliss as we enjoy the experience of listening to the author's words.

Bedtime comes too soon, and he sighs, staring dreamily at the wall, cherishing the fading mental imagery created from the book.

He looks forward to tomorrow, when we will continue to read it. I am looking ahead as well to the many moments I intend to have with my mother as we walk on our peace journey.

"Peace is not for sissies," she writes in an e-mail to a mutual friend, expressing how tough our experience has been.

I laugh and agree, knowing that with each step, we have become stronger and more able to tackle life's trials. With a sigh, I thank God I've made it this far. We've overcome a huge obstacle, but our journey doesn't end here, nor will it ever truly end. Peace is a journey, and we've got a ticket for the ride.

EPILOGUE

Patricia

Morning, Alana.

It's six thirty a.m., and your dad and I are already up and dressed. We're in the car, driving. To the airport? To see you? To see your family? I wish we were. But that's next week. I wrote a big star on my calendar. *Get up early. Going to Tennessee.*

By God's sweet grace, there you'll be. Waiting by faith. That's what it took to get to this point—or to get anywhere. So, by faith, Dad and I have gotten up early to drive in the dark to a downtown hotel for a fund-raising breakfast for Muslim Bedouin women. The event starts at seven thirty, but your aunt Denise—who is on the board of the group—asked us to come early to get our seats.

So Dad and I got going to be obedient. Your aunt Denise, who, as you know, isn't your aunt by blood, is my faithful friend. So for her, and for decades of friendship, I have arisen early and put on a dress and Sunday shoes to arrive at her event and be on time.

It takes extra work, doesn't it? To arrive at an important place and look okay, feet shod and ready with the gospel of peace, and not be late.

So first, in this letter, I will get up early to put on my peace and say thank you. For saying yes. For believing we should try to write our way to healing. For not calling me desperate and crazy to wrestle over religious hurt, to try to shine a light on it, and then to struggle to turn the whole endeavor into peace. Thank you—because I *was* desperate and crazy.

Yet what a beautiful trip.

We started this journey holding our breath. Not sure at all. Feeling doubtful, looking raggedy, acting angry, sounding unsure. At least I was. You sounded cool, looked calm, and acted assured. But I was a downright mess. Angry. Hurting. Mad at myself. Mad at God probably. Mad at you for sure.

Then when I sat with that anger, I knew things must change. Mothers can't be angry at daughters. That math doesn't work. Angry at your own child? Nothing in that lines up with God. So I couldn't be angry at God either.

So thank you for not turning your back and walking away. I heard recently about a family whose daughter cut ties. Won't speak. Won't answer e-mails. Won't answer phone calls. Well, is anybody's family member that far gone? That much beyond redemption that you can't at least try to mend an old hurt? Try just one more time?

I can't judge. But that could've been us. And I'm not even sure how we got off track. When I was pregnant with you, looking forward to your birth, I would stare at my swelling belly in my dresser mirror, imagining a lifetime of happy, perfect years ahead of us.

But children have other plans. Certainly you did. You wanted life on your terms. To go your own way. And I struggled with that. I had to learn the truth of all parents. Our children aren't our own. We're entrusted by God with training you up in the way you should go (Prov. 22:6).

What a surprise that your way would be so different from mine. So now comes the next parent stage: trusting God to take our offspring the rest of the journey. For now, indeed, I am confident in this: that God is still doing his good work, both in you and in me. In his own time.

So thank you, Lana, in his time, for not kicking me to the curb.

We didn't tackle every matter on our journey. Like salvation. Or heaven. Who gets to go. Who doesn't. With you, instead, I learned to hold the reins. To wait on the Holy Spirit. In his time—in the fullness of his time–we can move along and talk of such things along the way. On the road together.

So I'm thinking of you this morning as your dad and I sit in a beautiful downtown hotel with your aunt Denise and other faithful friends and break bread at a fund-raising breakfast for Muslim women in Israel.

And here's a surprise. The women raising the funds are Jesus people like me. Red-letter Christians. Housewives and businesswomen and teachers and girlfriends in Colorado, reaching out to women living in tents and tiny villages halfway around the world.

Why do they help? Because for peace, the world needs love.

For proof, the keynote speaker steps to the stage. A young Bedouin man, he was born in a little tent, where he lived the first eight years of his life. "I had to walk three kilometers each day from the hills of Galilee to my Christian-Arab school in Haifa."

The third of eleven brothers and sisters, whose parents promised "to do everything possible to send me on to college," he is speaking to us, that is, of love.

To build it, this young man, whose name is Ishmael Khaldi–and who is Israel's first Bedouin Muslim diplomat–has been booed off stages, called a sellout and traitor (and worse), and shouted down on college campuses from California to New York and beyond. Why does he do it?

"Because Israel is my home. My family. My family's family. My grandmother and her generation reached out to Jewish pioneers from Europe in the 1920s, 1930s, and 1940s. Now people ask me how I can work for Israel. But Israel *is* me. They criticize Israel, and I hear that. Israel isn't perfect. But no family is."

Listening to Khaldi, now age forty-three, I could empathize and relate.

Family isn't neat, simple, or politically right. At college campuses around the world, students barring his speaking events want easy answers. As a college student, back in the day, I would've agitated for easy answers too.

Now as your mother, I can step back to listen. Listen especially to you. And I am proud of our listening. But more than proud, I am grateful.

When folks worldwide are murdering each other, we are talking. When families from pillar to post are dogging and cursing and dissing each other, we are granting grace. I am grateful to God for that and grateful, indeed, for you.

You stayed with me until I could offer what you demanded of me. Respect.

That's the key. I thought wrongly for years that respect worked best outside family. You know, respect your elders–those older people on the front pew at church. Respect your teachers–those sacrificing educators in classrooms. Respect your neighbors–those unrelated people in the house next door.

But here's what Mother Teresa said about respect: start in your own house.

It's there, she said, where it's needed most. "Find the poor here," she said, "right in your own home first."⁴ That's the saint of Calcutta, pleading with the world, to first go home. Go with respect. Go to love.

That kind of honor is the gold standard in relationships, including marriage. Dad and I have worked thirty-eight years and counting, learning that lesson for sure.

But you taught me it starts at the cradle. With your own kids. I love watching you with your children, giving them time and tenderness, discipline and diversion, fairness and fun. (Oh, to be the fun mom! I'm sorry that wasn't my destiny.)

For now, my husband–your dad–says I should make this closing letter a contract. *I promise to do this. I promise to do that.* Or I promise *not* to do this and that.

He is right. So I promise this: to walk with you day by day. Hour by hour. Morning by morning. New mercies? We'll see them for sure.

Will we make mistakes? Of course. But now we know what to do. Get back on the road. Following after God. Thank you, sweetheart, for traveling along with me.

Peace and love,

Mom

Alana

Dear Mom,

Once again I'm up late. You know me, trying to cram a million things into one day. Then finally settling down to reflect at night. Its 11:10 p.m., and the kids went to sleep only an hour ago. The baby is still up and, I'm embarrassed to admit, is watching TV with her dad on his phone. I'm not going to hassle him, though, because he's had a tough day all by himself, watching the kids while I had to work on Columbus Day.

We got home super late last night after driving more than four and a half hours to a little town in the Smoky Mountains. I thought of you and Dad and how we used to spend our summers cruising in and out of the winding Rockies. I loved gazing out the window at the shimmering golden aspens in the fall or, in the summers, the sparkling waterfalls as we headed to see hot air balloons in Steamboat Springs. When we traversed the twisted hills, I stared at the evergreen trees carpeting the mountains towering above me, stretching into the clear blue Colorado sky.

The cloudy, rainy weather in Tennessee threatened our plans yesterday, and we spent most of the drive deciding what to do once we arrived. I squinted out the window into the gray sky and sighed. Not a patch of blue in sight. Since the weather wasn't constant, we found ourselves unsure about whether the trip was worth the money we had already spent.

Doubt was creeping in. We were already forgetting that this was a road trip and we were supposed to be enjoying the journey. Iesa tried his best to remind us of that fact, asking us every now and then to look out the window and marvel at the magnificent landscape.

"Put away your technology!" he begged everyone, grabbing my stepson's Android phone before he could start playing on it again.

I was too stressed about my deadlines and preoccupied with my computer to notice the sights. The kids, meantime, were too busy squabbling over the iPad.

"Uh-huh," I mumbled, then thinking, as I considered the scenery: *They're trees, and I've seen those before. Right now I have to concentrate!*

Right then and there my computer battery died. A blessing in disguise. I packed it away and gazed out the window, sorry for missing so much beauty with my head stuck in my computer.

The kids were still complaining about being "so bored" and "having nothing to do" despite the many types of technology and backpacks full of toys that we brought along. But as our ascent began to steepen, their interest in our surroundings increased.

"Are we there yet?" they began to ask as we ascended a particularly winding road to Ober Gatlinburg.

Iesa slowed down as the slick path began to close in. All around us was a sea of fall leaves.

"Yes," my husband said sarcastically. "We are *here*. Now."

They didn't get that joke and kept asking until I eventually told them that we would arrive when they counted to sixty, five times. They began counting until they got confused and then became more anxious.

"Are we *here*?" they said desperately as we continued to climb.

"You are supposed to be enjoying the *journey*," I said again and again.

"Oh," Noah said, calming down a little, and looked out his window.

He stared at some quaint wood cabins and chalets that dotted the mountainside, but the effect lasted only a minute.

I get it now, Mom. Peace is about the journey, not the destination.

I was also like an impatient little kid at the beginning of our journey, wondering when and where we were going to "arrive" at our destination of peace. It took me half the journey to realize that the experience brought us closer and mended the division between us. I was anxious and impatient, just like my kids, when we began this project together. I just wanted to "get there."

When tensions arose between us, I was unsure about continuing and if it was even worth it. I asked for guidance along the way from God, family friends, and even you, during the many times when my insecurities led me to doubt this process.

I've made it to the top of the mountain now, Mom—my metaphorical hurdle—and I can see clearly ahead.

As my family and I soared high above the Smokies in a cable car, I looked down at the tiny cars and houses below and realized how small our troubles are in the eyes of God. I held the baby in my lap, staring at her face as she marveled over the sights, then pointed and shouted "house!" at each one she saw.

"The car is going to rock up ahead," the conductor warned us as we approached one of the towers connecting the cables.

The passengers held on to the ropes hanging from the ceiling and braced for the turbulence.

"Notice how your body reacts to the rocking at first so you can prepare for the next bump," he advised.

Good advice for life too, I thought.

Your upcoming visit will be a test for me, Mom, to see if I can hang on and balance on this journey in new situations. Unlike before, I will be introspective this time–making sure that I'm holding on to the rope of Allah that keeps me centered and aware of my actions, my words, and my inner state.

I'm glad you asked me to travel with you on this turbulent road. All it took was one step out the door. It was worth every moment and every tear, and I don't regret any of it.

I have faith now that we can help others move past their hurt and dig themselves out of the pit of the chasms in their lives. It takes courage, dedication, and, most important, faith, but it can be done. You and I are a testimony to that.

So as we move forward, hand in hand, I want to thank you for your pledge of respect. I needed that from you. You listened and cared. I also want to commend you for your willingness to learn so much about me and my faith, a task that many would refuse.

Last, I know that deep down it is your hope that I see God as you do, just as many mothers–even I–hope for my children. I thank you for your honesty, and I hope that as we continue to be mother and daughter, we can grow in our understanding of how to allow each other to embrace our faiths without facing scrutiny and criticism from each other.

My family and I rode the cable car back up the mountain after we visited Ober Gatlinburg. The kids were quiet this time as if they knew that our day was coming to a close. Sure enough, when we reached the top, Laila said, "What are we going to do *now*?"

I felt this way, too, when we finished this book–as if I wasn't ready for it to end. I know now that there is plenty for us to do. As mother and daughter, we will have to continue to work on our relationship because relationships take work. As peace advocates, we can continue to be lights of inspiration to those who see no hope in their struggle. And as servants of God, we can both strive to live up to what our faith teaches us–and extend this peace to others.

So pack your bags, Mom. We've got work to do, and the peace train never stops.

Love always,

Alana

NOTES

CHAPTER 1: CAN WE TALK?

1. Stephen R. Covey, *The 7 Habits of Highly Effective People*, Anniversary Edition (New York: Simon and Schuster, 2013), 251.
2. *Hadith Reader*, Sahih Al-Bukhari, 8.73.160, copyright TriosLabs Limited.
3. *The Qur'an: Arabic Text with Corresponding English Meaning*, ed. Saheeh International (Saudi Arabia: Abul Qasim Publishing, 1997), 17.23, 31.15.

CHAPTER 2: CAN WE LISTEN?

1. *The Qur'an: Arabic Text with Corresponding English Meaning*, ed. Saheeh International (Saudi Arabia: Abul Qasim Publishing House, 1997).
2. All quotations from the Qur'an in this chapter are taken from *The Qur'an: Arabic Text*, ed. Saheeh International (1997).
3. *Qur'an*, 112.1–4.
4. *Qur'an*.
5. Ibid.
6. Scott Jaschik, "I Was Doing My Job," Inside Higher Ed.com, April 1, 2013, https://www.insidehighered.com/news/2013/04/01/interview-professor-center-jesus-debate-florida-atlantic.
7. "Death Threats for 'Stomp on Jesus' Professor," Moral Compass blog post by Terry Firma, April 2, 2013, http://moralcompassblog.com/2013/04/02/step-on-jesus-prof-on-leave-after-death-threats.
8. A. W. Tozer, *The Knowledge of the Holy–The Attributes of God: Their Meaning in the Christian Life* (New York: Harper One, 2009), 9.
9. Frederick Faber quoted in Tozer, *The Knowledge of the Holy*, 10.
10. Stephen R. Covey, *The 7 Habits of Highly Effective People* (New York: Simon and Schuster, 1989, 2004), 267.
11. "Inside Islam: What a Billion Muslims Really Think," Unity Productions Foundation, July 3, 2009, www.upf.tv/films/inside-islam/watch/.

CHAPTER 3: FAMILY MATTERS. WELL, DOESN'T IT?

1. "Didn't It Rain," *Negro Spirituals Arranged by H.T. Burleigh* (New York: G. Ricordi & Co. Inc., 1919).

2. Dr. Barbara Fiese quoted in Katie Gilbert, "Holiday Ritual or Rerun?" PsychologyToday.com, November 8, 2006, http://www.psychologytoday.com /articles/200611/holiday-ritual-or-rerun.

3. *The Qur'an: Arabic Text with Corresponding English Meaning*, ed. Saheeh International (Saudi Arabia: Abul Qasim Publishing House, 1997), 71.26.

4. Ibid., 11.40–42.

5. All quotations from the Qur'an in this chapter are taken from *The Qur'an: Arabic Text*, ed. Saheeh International (1997).

6. *Qur'an.*

7. *Qur'an.*

8. Eugene H. Peterson, *Run with the Horses: The Quest for Life at Its Best* (Downers Grove, IL: InterVarsity Press; 2009), 41.

9. Ibid., 42, 41.

10. Mahatma Gandhi, *An Autobiography: The Story of My Experiments with Truth* (Boston: Beacon Press, 1957), 260.

CHAPTER 4: NOW, WHY ISLAM?

1. C. S. Lewis, *The Weight of Glory* (New York: HarperOne, 2009), 140.

2. Latif Ahmed Sherwani, comp. and ed., *Speeches, Writings, and Statements of Iqbal*, 2nd ed. (Lahore: Iqbal Academy, 1977), 3–26. Quoted from "Sir Muhammad Iqbal's 1930 Presidential Address to the 25th Session of the All-India Muslim League Allahabad, 29 December 1930." See http://www.columbia.edu/itc/mealac /pritchett/00islamlinks/txt_iqbal_1930.html.

3. Mara Rose Williams, "MU Researcher Dispels Notion of a Single 'God Spot' in Brain," *Kansas City Star*, April 19, 2012, http://www.kansascity.com/news/local /article302418/MU-researcher-dispels-notion-of-a-single-'God-spot'-in-brain. html. See also Brick Johnstone, Angela Bodling, Dan Cohen, Shawn E. Christ, and Andrew Wegrzyn, "Right Parietal Lobe-Related 'Selflessness' as the Neuropsychological Basis of Spiritual Transcendence," *International Journal for the Psychology of Religion* 22, no. 4 (October 2012): 267–84.

4. C. S. Lewis, *Mere Christianity*, rev. ed. (HarperSan Francisco, 2009), 126.

5. Alister McGrath quoted in "Thinking About the Trinity, Part Two," *In Touch* magazine, March 2014, © 2014 In Touch Ministries, Inc., All rights reserved. Used with permission. http://www.intouch.org/magazine/content.aspx?topic=Thinking _About_the_Trinity_Part_Two#.VEfOUvldU84.

6. Ibid.

7. Dr. Charles Stanley, "The Holy Spirit, Our Teacher," *In Touch* magazine, February 2014, © 2014 In Touch Ministries, Inc. All rights reserved. Used with permission. http://www.intouch.org/magazine/content.aspx?topic=The_Holy_Spirit_Our _Teacher_devotional#.VEfQTvldU84.

8. Blaise Pascal, *Pensées*, ed. A. J. Krailsheimer (New York: Penguin Classics, 1995), 50.

9. A. W. Tozer, *God's Pursuit of Man* (Camp Hill, PA: WingSpread Publishers, 2007), 77.

Chapter 5: And Why the Christ?

1. Kira S. Birditt, Laura M. Miller, Karen L. Fingerman, and Eva A. Lefkowitz, "Tensions in the Parent and Adult Child Relationship: Links to Solidarity and Ambivalence," *Psychology and Aging* 24, no. 2 (June 2009): 287–95.

2. Nabeel Qureshi, *Seeking Allah, Finding Jesus: A Devout Muslim Encounters Christianity* (Grand Rapids: Zondervan, 2014), 121.

3. *The Qur'an: Arabic Text with Corresponding English Meaning*, ed. Saheeh International (Saudi Arabia: Abul Qasim Publishing House, 1997), 112.1.

4. Ibid., 112.4.

5. Qureshi, *Seeking Allah, Finding Jesus*, 87–88.

6. Max Lucado, *A Love Worth Giving: Living in the Overflow of God's Love* (Nashville: W Publishing Group, 2006), 163.

7. DWillard.org, "New Age of Ancient Christian Spirituality," transcribed by Scott Sevier, July 18, 2002, www.dwillard.org/articles/artview.asp?artID=95.

8. *The Qur'an: Arabic Text*, ed. Saheeh International (1997).

Chapter 6: Letting Go

1. Thomas Aquinas, "We Are Fields Before Each Other," quoted in *Love Poems from God: Twelve Sacred Voices from the East and West*, ed. Daniel Ladinsky (New York: Penguin Books, 2002), 129.

2. Rodney Stark, *The Triumph of Christianity: How the Jesus Movement Became the World's Largest Religion* (New York: HarperCollins, 2013), 36.

3. Emmanuel Katongole and Chris Rice, *Reconciling All Things: A Christian Vision for Justice, Peace and Healing* (Downers Grove, IL: InterVarsity Press, 2008), 43–45.

4. Ibid., 43–44.

5. Brenda Salter McNeil, *A Credible Witness: Reflections on Power, Evangelism and Race* (Downers Grove, IL: InterVarsity Press, 2008), 16.

6. Gabe Lyons, *The Next Christians: Seven Ways You Can Live the Gospel and Restore the World* (New York: Doubleday Religion, 2010), 20.

7. Ted Falcon, Don Mackenzie, and Jamal Rahman, *Getting to the Heart of Interfaith: The Eye-Opening, Hope-Filled Friendship of a Pastor, a Rabbi & an Imam* (Woodstock, VT: SkyLight Paths, 2009), 12.

Chapter 7: Walking in Light

1. Ted Falcon, Don Mackenzie, and Jamal Rahman, *Getting to the Heart of Interfaith: The Eye-Opening, Hope-Filled Friendship of a Pastor, a Rabbi & an Imam* (Woodstock, VT: SkyLight Paths, 2009), 13.

2. Dallas Willard, *The Divine Conspiracy: Rediscovering Our Hidden Life in God* (New York: HarperCollins, 1997), 386.

3. Richard Foster, *Prayer: Finding the Heart's True Home* (New York: HarperCollins, 1992), 249.

4. Michael Zelenko, "The Human Cost of Your Mother's Day Flowers," Vice.Com, May 8, 2014, http://www.vice.com/en_ca/read/the-human-cost-of-your-mothers-day-flowers.

5. Phillis Wheatley, "An Hymn to the Evening," quoted in *Unchained Voices: An Anthology of Black Authors in the English-Speaking World of the Eighteenth Century*, ed. Vincent Carretta (Lexington, KY: The University Press of Kentucky, 1996), 63.

6. *The Qur'an: Arabic Text with Corresponding English Meaning*, ed. Saheeh International (Saudi Arabia: Abul Qasim Publishing House, 1997), 5.15.

7. Leonardo da Vinci quoted in Mario Salvadori, *Why Buildings Stand Up: The Strength of Architecture* (New York: W. W. Norton, 2002), 9.

8. Salvadori, *Why Buildings Stand Up*, 313.

9. Ibid., 49.

10. C. H. Spurgeon, "The Holy Spirit Compared to the Wind," no. 630: A Sermon Preached by C. H. Spurgeon at the Metropolitan Tabernacle, Newington, Metropolitan Tabernacle Pulpit, http://www.spurgeongems.org/vols10–12/chs630.pdf.

11. *The Qur'an: Arabic Text*, ed. Saheeh International (1997), 17.23.

12. *Hadith Reader*, Sahih Al-Bukhari, 7.73.2, copyright TriosLabs Limited.

13. Sunan an Nasai, free version, 1.25.20, copyright 2014 e-Deen.

CHAPTER 8: PEACE. MAKING.

1. Anna Jarvis, quoted in Brian Handwerk, "Why Mother's Day Horrified, Ruined Its Own Mother," *National Geographic News*, May 8, 2011, http://news.nationalgeographic.com/news/2011/05/110508-mothers-day-google-doodle-history-jarvis-nation-gifts-facts.

2. Davide Demichelis, "Central African Republic, Archbishop of Bangui: No More Law of the Jungle," *Vatican Insider*, February 15, 2014, http://vaticaninsider.lastampa.it/en/world-news/detail/articolo/repubblica-centrafricana-republica-centroafricana-central-african-republic-nzapalainga-32097.

3. Louay M. Safi, *Peace and the Limits of War* (Herndon, VA: International Institute of Islamic Thought, 2001), 1.

4. Ibid., 6.

5. *The Qur'an: Arabic Text with Corresponding English Meaning*, ed. Saheeh International (Saudi Arabia: Abul Qasim Publishing House, 1997), 49.13.

6. Islamic-Dictionary.com, http://www.islamic-dictionary.com.

7. Jami al Tirmidhi, free version, 1.27.2083, copyright 2014 e-Deen.

8. *The Qur'an: Arabic Text*, ed. Saheeh International (1997), 2.148.

9. Ken Sande, *The Peacemaker: A Biblical Guide to Resolving Personal Conflict* (Grand Rapids: Baker Books, 2004), 22.

10. Madeleine Albright quoted in Marianne Schnall, "Madeleine Albright: An Exclusive Interview," *Huffington Post*/The Blog, June 15, 2010, http://www.huffingtonpost.com/marianne-schnall/madeleine-albright-an-exc_b_604418.html.

11. Sande, *The Peacemaker*, 11.
12. Oswald Chambers, *My Utmost for His Highest*, ed. James Reimann, rev. ed. (Grand Rapids: Discovery House, 2012), July 4 devotion.
13. Ibid., May 24 devotion.
14. Desmond Tutu, *The Rainbow People of God: The Making of a Peaceful Revolution*, reprint ed. (New York: Image Books, 1996), 222.
15. Desmond Tutu, *The Book of Forgiving: The Fourfold Path for Healing Ourselves and Our World* (New York: HarperOne, 2014), 54.
16. C. H. Spurgeon, "Spiritual Peace," no. 300: A Sermon Delivered by C. H. Spurgeon at Exeter Hall, Strand, The New Park Street Pulpit, The Spurgeon Archive, http://www.spurgeon.org/sermons/0300.htm.
17. C. L. Franklin quoted in Preston Ni, "Inspirational and Humorous Diversity Quotes," Communication Success column, PsychologyToday.com, January 21, 2013, http://www.psychologytoday.com/blog/communication-success/201301/inspirational-and-humorous-diversity-quotes.
18. *The Qur'an: Arabic Text*, ed. Saheeh International (1997), 1.1–7.
19. *Hadith Reader*, Sahih Al-Bukhari, 1.2.47, copyright TriosLabs Limited.
20. *The Qur'an: Arabic Text*, ed. Saheeh International (1997).
21. *The Meaning of the Holy Qur'an* (English and Arabic Edition), 10th ed., transl. Abdullah Yusuf Ali (Beltsville, MD: Amana Publications, 1997).

CHAPTER 9: WEARING THE HIJAB

1. Ken Sande, *The Peacemaker: A Biblical Guide to Resolving Personal Conflict* (Grand Rapids: Baker Books, 2004), 111.
2. Eugene Peterson, *A Long Obedience in the Same Direction: Discipleship in an Instant Society*, 2nd ed. (Downers Grove, IL: InterVarsity Press, 2000), 30.
3. Sande, *The Peacemaker*, 110.
4. *The Meaning of the Holy Qur'an* (English and Arabic Edition), 10th ed., transl. Abdullah Yusuf Ali (Beltsville, MD: Amana Publications, 1997), 24.30–31.
5. John Gottman and Nan Silver, "What Makes Marriage Work?" PsychologyToday.com, March 1, 1994, http://www.psychologytoday.com/articles/200910/what-makes-marriage-work.
6. Benjamin Franklin, *Letters from France: The Private Diplomatic Correspondence of Benjamin Franklin 1776–1785*, ed. Brett Woods (New York: Algora Publishing, 2006), 42.
7. The Arbinger Institute, Arbinger Properties, Inc., *The Anatomy of Peace: Resolving the Heart of Conflict* (San Francisco: Berrett Koehler, 2006), 115.
8. Ibid., 27.
9. Ibid., 80.
10. Ibid., 30–31.
11. Jonathan Haidt, *The Righteous Mind: Why Good People Are Divided by Politics and Religion* (New York: Pantheon Books, 2012), 83–85.

CHAPTER 10: PRAYER WORKS

1. *Hadith Reader*, Sahih Al-Bukhari, 1.10.506, copyright TriosLabs Limited.
2. *The Qur'an: Arabic Text with Corresponding English Meaning*, ed. Saheeh International (Saudi Arabia: Abul Qasim Publishing House, 1997), 13.28.
3. *The Qur'an: Arabic Text*, ed. Saheeh International (1997).
4. Desmond Tutu, *The Book of Forgiving: The Fourfold Path for Healing Ourselves and Our World* (New York: HarperOne, 2014), 7.
5. Ibid., 22.
6. "Give Me Jesus," adapted and arranged by Charles Lange (St. Louis: Balmer & Weber, 1883).
7. Jason Mandryk, *Operation World: The Definitive Prayer Guide to Every Nation* (Downers Grove, IL: InterVarsity Press, 2010), 465.

CHAPTER 11: ROCK THE BOAT

1. Rodney Stark, *The Triumph of Christianity: How the Jesus Movement Became the World's Largest Religion* (New York: HarperCollins, 2013), 367.
2. Benjamin Franklin, *Poor Richard's Almanac* (Seattle: CreateSpace Independent Publishing Platform, 2013), no. 243, 18.
3. Benjamin Netanyahu quoted in Cheryl K. Chumley, "Benjamin Netanyahu on Hamas: 'Our answer is fire,'" *The Washington Times*, July 16, 2014, http://www.washingtontimes.com/news/2014/jul/16/benjamin-netanyahu-hamas-our-answer-fire.
4. Desmond Tutu, *No Future Without Forgiveness* (Colorado Springs, CO: Image, 2000), 178.
5. Mahatma Gandhi, *India of My Dreams* (New Delhi: Rajpal and Sons, 2009), 80.
6. Mahatma Gandhi, *The Gandhi Reader: A Sourcebook of His Life and Writings*, ed. Homer A. Jack (Bloomington: Indiana University Press, 1956), 315.
7. Leigh Thompson, "Negotiation Tactics 101," Kellogg School of Management Video, Northwestern University, 2014, http://www.kellogg.northwestern.edu/news_articles/2014/08012014-negotiation-tactics-101.aspx.
8. John Newton (1725–1807), "Amazing Grace," Olney Hymns (London: W. Oliver, 1779).

CHAPTER 12: PEACE IS THE ROAD

1. Sandra Cisneros, *The House on Mango Street* (New York: Knopf, 1994), 9.
2. Ibid., 12.
3. Richard Foster, *Prayer: Finding the Heart's True Home* (New York: HarperOne, 2002), 47.
4. Mahatma Gandhi, *The Gandhi Reader: A Sourcebook of His Life and Writings*, ed. Homer A. Jack (Bloomington: Indiana University Press, 1956), 315.
5. Charles Spurgeon, *Morning and Evening: Daily Readings*, rev. ed. (New Kensington, PA: Whitaker House, 2001), 460.
6. *The Meaning of the Holy Qur'an* (English and Arabic Edition), 10th ed., transl. Abdullah Yusuf Ali (Beltsville, MD: Amana Publications, 1997), 94.6.

7. *The Qur'an: Arabic Text with Corresponding English Meaning*, ed. Saheeh International (Saudi Arabia: Abul Qasim Publishing House, 1997), 5.23.
8. Joseph Campbell, *Reflections on the Art of Living: A Joseph Campbell Companion*, reprint ed. (New York: Harper Perennial, 1995), 24.
9. Andrea Davis Pinkney, *Profiles #6: Peace Warriors* (New York: Scholastic, Inc., 2013), back cover.
10. Ibid., 4.

EPILOGUE

1. Mother Teresa, *The Joy in Loving: A Guide to Daily Living*, comps. Jaya Chaliha and Edward LeJoly (New York: Penguin Books, 2000), 242.

ABOUT THE AUTHORS

PATRICIA RAYBON IS THE AWARD-WINNING AUTHOR OF *I TOLD THE Mountain to Move*, a 2006 Book of the Year finalist in *Christianity Today* magazine's annual book awards competition; and *My First White Friend*, her racial forgiveness memoir and winner of the Christopher Award. She is also author of the One Year® devotional *God's Great Blessings*. A journalist by training, Patricia has written essays on family and faith, which have been published in the *New York Times Sunday Magazine*, *Newsweek*, the *Chicago Tribune*, *USA Today*, *USA Weekend*, and *In Touch* of In Touch Ministries; and have aired on National Public Radio. She is also a regular contributor to *Today's Christian Woman* online magazine.

With degrees in journalism from Ohio State University and the University of Colorado at Boulder, Patricia worked a dozen years as a newspaper journalist for the *Denver Post* and the *Rocky Mountain News*. She later joined the journalism faculty at the University of Colorado at Boulder, where for fifteen years she taught print journalism. Patricia now writes full-time on "mountain-moving faith."

Patricia and her husband, Dan, are longtime residents of Colorado and have two grown daughters and five grandchildren. Founder of the Writing Ministry at her Denver church, Patricia coaches and encourages aspiring authors around the country and is a member of the Colorado Authors League and the Authors Guild.

ALANA RAYBON IS A SEASONED ELEMENTARY- AND MIDDLE-SCHOOL educator. During the past ten years, she has served as a third- through seventh-grade lead teacher to a diverse population in Texas and, more recently, in Tennessee. She has been a mentor to both new and student teachers and was nominated by her peers for Teacher of the Year. Alana has also been an adviser to a school's accreditation process, a tutor, and a member of various school-related committees.

Alana found her calling to education while working with troubled youth in a youth home and later as a paraprofessional in a second-grade classroom. Alana entered the elementary education program at the University of Northern Colorado and converted to Islam during her sophomore year. After graduating with a BA in education, she married and moved to Texas, where she began teaching fifth grade.

Four years later Alana became a mother, and now she and her husband parent three young children and a teenager. As a recent Tennessee resident she now teaches middle-school language arts, social studies, and science. She was featured with her mother in a 2011 Mother's Day reflection in *Glamour* magazine on unique mother-daughter relationships.